MAURO CIVAI • ENRICO TOTI

SIENA
THE GOTHIC DREAM
A NEW GUIDE TO THE CITY

Edizioni
ALSABA

Siena, The Gothic Dream
A new guide to the city

Authors
Mauro Civai • Enrico Toti

Design and cover
Maruska Pradelli Rossi

Photography
Fabio Lensini

Mauro Agnesoni, pag. 15, 23, 60, 159, 225, 235
Mario Appiani, pag. 10, 44, 55, 85, 88, 94, 95, 97, 101, 110, 113
Bruno Bruchi, pag. 22, 36, 38, 52, 82, 92, 102, 106, 117, 122, 130, 131, 132, 138, 153, 154, 155, 160, 165, 168, 170, 177, 178, 185, 195, 204, 214, 215, 216, 220, 226, 227, 236, 254
Pietro Cinotti, pag. 65
Foto Gielle, pag. 62, 64
Mauro Guerrini, pag. 8, 21, 80, 83, 84, 116, 119, 122, 139
Federigo Sani, pag. 6
Scala Firenze, pag. 127

Video editing
Graphicomp/Siena

Colour selections
Studio Leonardo/Firenze

Printed by
ALSABA Grafiche/Siena

English translation
Christopher McConnell
c/o Eurostudio, Colle Val d'Elsa

Editor
Leo Salvietti

Technical Director
Aliberto Barabuffi

Special thanks to:
Roberta Baldini, Curzio Bastianoni, Roberto Barzanti, Luigina Benci, Gian Piero Bonelli, Luciano Cateni, Marco Ciampolini, Alberto Cornice, Rosanna De Benedictis, Mario De Gregorio, Alessandro Falassi, Roberto Ferri, Sonia Fineschi, Carlo Fini, Alessandro Leoncini, Italo Moretti, Cesare Olmastroni, Niki Pappadakis, Gabriella Piccinni, Coralia Pignatelli della Leonessa, Giovanni Pratesi, Francesca Rossi, Federigo Sani, Bruno Santi, Marco Torriti, Piero Torriti.

This volume has been published under the patronage of the *City of Siena* and with the authorization of the *Consortium for the Protection of the Palio of Siena.* Our heartfelt thanks go to both.

2nd edition, May 1997

ISBN 88-85331-08-4

CONTENTS

DEDICATED TO SIENA

Writing a guide to Siena is certainly not an easy task as, at a certain point, it becomes inevitable to make comparisons with famous men of learning and scholars who over the centuries have produced works of great value, from the fantastic medieval chronicles to recently published volumes, compiled with scientific criteria and saturated with information.

Our guide has, however, some pretext of originality. Even though, in fact, it is largely dedicated to an exact, if rather synthetic, description of the tourist routes of the city, it also presents, by means of special documents, a deeper and more original version of a whole series of particularly evocative subjects. The reader will be faced with points of view that he may not agree with but that are certainly not haphazard as they are motivated by precise choices and pondered convictions.

This method and the interpretations derived from it, is certainly born from experience, study and work, but not only from these. It comes above all from the love of this city and the full awareness that being Sienese represents, as Ranuccio Bianchi Bandinelli sustained, "a privilege".

A privilege that must be merited and maintained. We aim not only to supply the reader with a list of prestigious monuments and wonderful works of art, but also to give him the opportunity of actively participating in the emotions that can be experienced if the city is observed from a "partisan" point of view.

This book, therefore, is principally dedicated to Siena. We also wish to dedicate it to Armanda, Monica, Elisa and Guido who have, once again, put up with the tortuous evolution of its creation.

Finally, our thoughts turn to Aldo Cairola who was to us both a friend and teacher and – we are certain – would have wished to write this book together with us.

Mauro Civai, Enrico Toti

A 'GUIDE' FOR SIENA

Bruno Santi
*Superintendent of the Artistic and Historical
Heritage of Siena and Grosseto*

My friends Mauro Civai and Enrico Toti are perfectly right when they say (perhaps with a touch of *captatio benevolentiae*) that compiling a guide to Siena "is certainly not an easy task".

But not because so many illustrious historians and so-called art critics have dedicated themselves to describing one of the most attractive and fascinating cities, not only in Italy, but in the whole world. In this case, of course, one must face the inevitable comparisons.

It is rather for the objective difficulty of penetrating the spirit, the ideal background that has given birth to this unique pattern that, while making bricks and stones and streets and towers and churches and palaces and bell towers and paintings and sculptures, also formed the character of its inhabitants and of those who have had the "privilege" (supreme but justified impudence of the Sienese) of living and working in this city, so circumscribed but so tying. (But let me pass over the regret of not having being the spectator of a magical scene, a mirage, that of the panorama of the city right at the beginning of this century, emerging from the wooded and cultivated hills of Chianti and the bare clay cliffs of the "crete", without suburbs, just with small groups of houses bunched around their little church on scattered hillocks, "humble amongst so much splendour"!).

But – to return to the work of Civai and Toti – breaking with the by now obsolete though canonical descriptive habits, tied to historical or artistic itineraries that are described with abused but unobjectionable terminology, seemed to the two authors the best way of presenting the various aspects of Siena to the curious visitor.

Thematic treatment, then, where the descriptions of the various zones of the city with their major historical, urban and artistic monuments, synthetic but rigorous, corresponding even with the most recent periegetic sources, live together with – a lively counterweight to the traditional descriptions – the close attention paid to the individual curiosities, even of convention and gastronomy, that joyfully enliven the impeccable descriptions of the monumental side of Siena and its artistic heritage, so large, so important, that it seems almost to lacerate and spring out like a sparkling firework unwilling to remain closed in its casing any longer.

(Not to mention the Palio that here is described with particular joy and fervour, as are its protagonists, the contradas, which is just another way of saying Siena).

It is indeed thanks to this intelligent and acute change of perspective, and in letting other matters in the analysis of Siena and its characteristics emerge that I believe that the true "spirit" of Siena has been identified in this book.

In other words, that fascinating mixture of simplicity and *grandeur*, of nostalgia for the past and inexhaustible curiosity for the future that leaves the common but contemplative visitor to Siena most perplexed and fascinated.

(I can cite two extremely relevant examples – Simone Martini who owes his origins to the Byzantine strain of Duccio; the Archbishop's Palace rebuilt in Gothic style at the beginning of the eighteenth century).

Civai and Toti have perfectly identified
the real root of the extraordinariness of
Siena, and they illustrate it with
that ironic, discrete and perfectly
genuine affection towards their city,
without which I think it would
be impossible to give such a fascinating
and authentic representation of it
as this guide has done.   ●

THE MYSTERIES OF SIENA

di Emilio Ravel

In the heart of Tuscany, with that enigmatic landscape known as the "crete" – a wasteland suitable for conversations with the devil – as a backdrop, rises a "magical" city with an intense silhouette of towers and pinnacles. No, not magical in the sense of "fabulous" or "extraordinary", expressions that an unthinking tourist might use, but magical in the sense of "inexplicable", and capable of authentic prodigies. There are many cities in the world that have attained a certain notoriety in the sphere of the occult. We know that, for this reason, Prague attracts hoards of visitors; we know all about the overcrowded community of ghosts that dwells at Turin, at a stone's throw from the production lines and the robots of the Fiat car factory; to mention but two. According to the scenario, magical places

● Siena by night: a magical atmosphere pervades the old streets and great squares.

carry with them a certain reek of sulphur or of cemeteries. Instead, Siena has different aromas: because it is both "magical" and "alive". It is for this reason, I believe, that it has become an exception to the rule. Here, unworldly things happen that have, however, firm roots in the most commonplace matters of life. For example, witches are summoned, not for the usual, rather debasing conjectures regarding jealousy or money, but to bring victory to the contrada (city ward) in that great and lively horse race, the winner of which takes possession of the prize, the Palio. It is impossible to enumerate the invocations and spells cast to protect the horse and colours of each contrada from the enchanted arrows of its adversaries. The often derisive tone does not rule out a profound sincerity of feeling.

There are, though, other more touching facts that reveal a bond with mystery that is much stronger than those customs commonly defined as superstitious.

Here – among a hundred – is an episode to which I was an eye witness on the occasion of a victory of the Palio by the Contrada of the Chiocciola. The city quarter was, of course, transformed into a kind of simple, popular, earthly paradise where all came to drink wine from the fountains and eat at tables put out in the streets closed to the traffic. The members of the Chiocciola gave an incredible significance to the celebrations: they even invited the dead to the banquet. Entering the Oratory of the Contrada, in fact, one could see all the altars covered with portraits of the deceased relations of the members of the Contrada. Hundreds of photographs, both recent and yellow with age. In other words, the vital miracle of the triumph of the Palio had also to be shared with those who were no longer of this world, but lived on in the memory of the living: grandparents, old uncles and aunts, prematurely dead cousins and friends of once upon a time were asked to leave their heavenly paradise and relive a few hours in the collective joy. "Because in Siena nobody is alone – they told me – not even when they are dead!"

In every contrada they will tell you stories similar to this. Sometimes a colour is enough to start up emotive mechanisms that would be unthinkable elsewhere. And so, during the 1990 football world cup, half the Contrada of the Selva supported Italy while the other half cheered on Ireland that had the extraordinary honour of wearing the same colours as the Contrada: green, orange and white.

● The cathedral embraces the city and hides secrets that have never been revealed.
Facing page: the mysterious writing on the side of the Cathedral.

Who really wishes to "see" the Palio must do so through the eyes of paradox and mystery. Otherwise he will miss the very essence and the profound vibration of it all. Mario Bussagli – in his latest book, "Art and Magic in Siena", published by Il Mulino – explains how the whole "historical" pageant that precedes the race

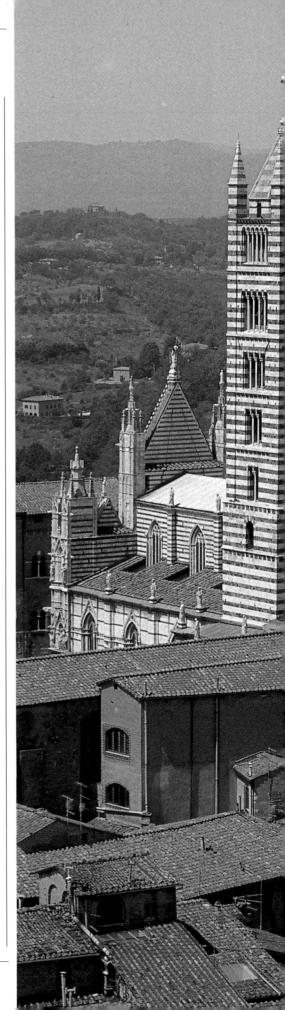

is none other than a strange time machine going backwards. It leaves from the banner of Montalcino – the last light of liberty that was extinguished in the middle of the sixteenth century – and going back in time, we witness the appearance of the Carroccio, the war cart on which the Palio is unfurled: we have returned to the Battle of Montaperti at the height of the ancient Republic in the middle of the thirteenth century when Guelf Florence bit the dust. In the moment in which the Palio leaves the Carroccio to be displayed in the square, at the starting and finishing point of the horse race, the great bell of the Mangia tower – that has set the pace of this tournament for almost two hours - stops. Time stops, too, together with the hearts of the Sienese, and induces a moment of anguish.

Logic and routine are sometimes forgotten in Siena. And the Palio is not the only moment of magic. A thousand signs are scattered along the sides of the streets, over the heads of passers by, or under their feet. The bollards – ancient symbols of fecundity and possession – mark out special areas like the Piazza del Campo. A real and proper forest of allusive symbols awaits you in the Cathedral. Allegoric figures look up from the inlays of the floor and on the left-hand side wall, opposite the Archbishop's Palace, is inscribed the famous formula that also emerged from the thousand year silence of Pompeii.

As many as a thousand scholars have tormented themselves over this formula that here, using the centre word "tenet" as the key, seems to mean: the Cathedral "resists" against the forces of evil.

Let us refer once more to Mario Bussagli's valuable book in which he informs us on how old the Sienese propensity to believe in wonders is: "specialised" witches and

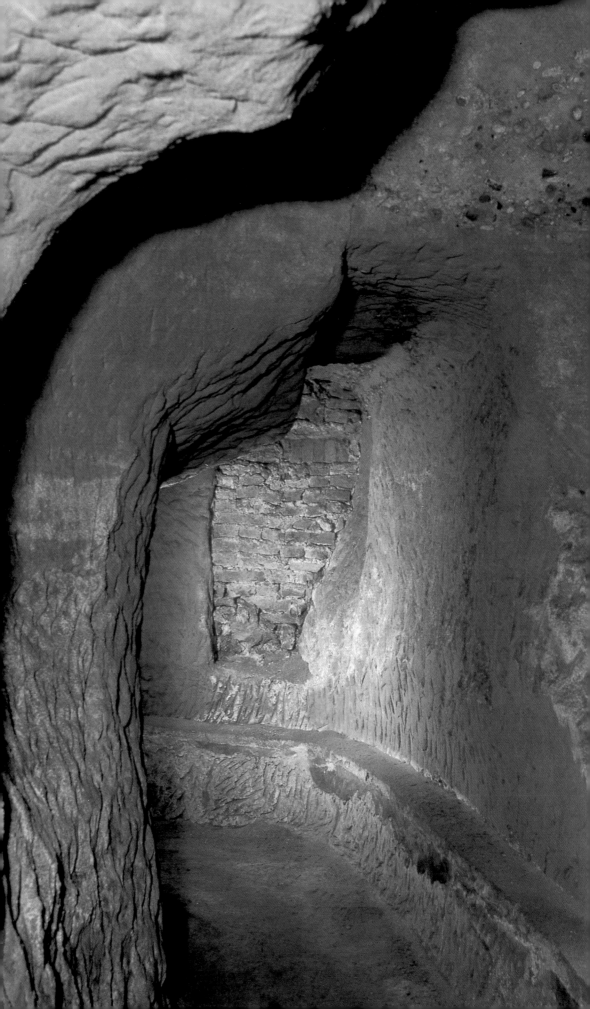

archers were paid to spread and shoot deadly and inauspicious powders on the enemy hosts (we are not talking of trifles: each time sums equivalent to hundreds of thousands of dollars were spent). For centuries, a magical underground river had been sought after that would bring wealth and happiness to the city. A name had even been given to it, though it was never found: Diana. Mysterious stories and the most audacious fancies, together with pranks and songs, while away the evenings in the contradas.

But if we try to leave these pagan beliefs behind us, we will come across unusual goings on also in the field of the Christian religion. Here, on the contrary, one can feel the Sienese soul even more closely, for

● The remains of the automaton used to ring the great bell called the "Mangia".
Facing page: The subsoil also hides a complex and intriguing reality that is cared for in every detail: the old aqueduct that until a few years ago supplied water to the city is now forgotten. Nowadays visits to the "Bottini" are real and proper excursions that must be made with the precautions of a spelologist.

"enemy", the domineer that – long ago – deprived the Sienese of their liberty, but not their spirit of independence and joy in going against the tide. We have already said that the usual classifications here are different. Siena takes pride in inverting ways of thinking and acting that are accepted in the rest of the world. It is a city that loves the sensation of doing the opposite of what the others do. This doesn't mean to say that it is right; however nothing that hasn't sunk into its deepest veins is accepted. This irreducible and clear-cut nature is reflected in the most famous symbol of the city, the stem that bears two opposite and irreconcilable colours: black and white. And this emblem, in which the spirit of the ancient Republic, which has never been erased from

example, in the display of affectionate love for the Virgin Mary, quite surprising in a city that had always so proudly flaunted its lay and Ghibelline roots. How many times have the Sienese seen the protective mantle of Mary unfold over their roofs and their streets! These maternal visions originate from the medieval sieges and continue, uninterruptedly, to the most difficult days of the last war... and beyond. And how intense and even irreverent is the dialogue with the saints chosen to safeguard the contradas and the whole city. The typically Tuscan malicious confidence is certainly not lacking! The four patron saints of the city, poised in their niches in the Loggia della Mercanzia, all look just in one direction: Florence, the

the common memory, lives on and has a name that is a story all by itself. It is called the Balzana. After all, what else can one expect from a population that descends from the grandchildren of Remus who escaped from Rome after a difference of opinion with Uncle Romulus.

They have been at the opposition, going against the tide, right from the very beginning. Even today, it's no wonder they refuse to become "just like all the others", ferociously defend traditions, sentiments, memories, and spurn habits and customs that, elsewhere, are accepted as inevitable. Here, time, logic, even deadly common sense and everything that makes the world more and more alike, go backwards. There is something in this paradox that can be understood more with the beating of the heart than with the mechanical activity of the brain. And so, from the spectacular top of the tower of the Mangia it is easier than elsewhere to catch sight of the secret signals that struck down, long ago and in a far away place, Prince Hamlet: "There are more things in heaven and earth, Horatio, than are dreamt of in your philosophy". ●

SIENA, A PASSIONATE STORY

Siena was rather an unimportant centre, first in Etruscan and then Roman times, compared with much more relevant urban nuclei such as Chiusi, Volterra or Arezzo. Ancient historians documented very few Sienese events and what little has come down to us is was aimed at highlighting that sprinkling of folly that was to mark the Sienese character for many centuries to come. In medieval times Siena possessed fairly modest territories even though it was a diocese. The Longobards annexed much more land under Sienese jurisdiction, including borderlands that were to be disputed between the bishoprics of Siena and Arezzo up until the thirteenth century.

An ancient coin of the Republic. The Mint of Siena was housed for a long time in Palazzo Pubblico.

The Gastaldo, the Longobard leader who ruled Siena, controlled a territory united and protected by walls enclosing little more than the hill where the Cathedral and hospital stand and, further up, the hillock of Castelvecchio.
Later the city was ruled by the Conti Franchi, the most famous of whom was certainly Guinigi towards the end of the ninth century. At this time trading networks began to develop that were to ascribe to the city a role of primary importance on an international scale. Two phenomena occurred, in fact, that laid the foundations for the future development of Siena: firstly, the progressive amalgamation of many villages and castles in the land surrounding the city, and secondly, the increasing importance of the main road from Rome to France that passed through the Elsa and Arbia Valleys. Siena adapted herself perfectly to this itinerary, and rapidly became one of the principal stop over points. As a result, a number of settlements sprang up along the road, Camollia to the North and Valdimontone to the South, that were then embodied into the city together with the fortified houses built by noble families near the walls.

At the beginning of the eleventh century, Siena already had a well-defined urban consistency and an administrative code, albeit rudimental, principally aimed at imposing tributes on the land owners, as well as trying to enlist their support to withstand the claims of the bishop of Arezzo regarding the usual contested borderlands. From this moment on the growing ambition of Siena gave rise to the open hostility of Florence, a strong and deeply rooted hatred that was to conclude only with the destruction of one of the two rivals. This antagonism with Florence was not a secondary factor in the decision that Siena made in favour of the Emperor and that led it to side itself against Pope Alexander III, of the Sienese family of the Bandinelli Paparoni, and to expel the bishop from the city for his obvious loyalty towards the Pope.

At the end of the twelfth century the City obtained the privilege of minting its own money by means of the Bulgano (the mint) and it is clear that this reflected the sharp rise in financial and commercial activity and stimulated further growth. Not by chance was this the time in which many powerful families, more or less recently arrived in the city, had sumptuous palaces and austere fortified houses built. It was also the era in which the City began to build fountains and aqueducts. In these years the habit of forcing the owners of land and castles to bring gifts in sign of homage to the Madonna, protector of Siena, on the day of the Assumption, began. This ceremony later became extremely important and it is from this, in fact, that the Palio horse race draws its origins.

The city, therefore, took on a precise configuration and the public offices, up till then the exclusive privilege of the nobility, became accessible also to the so called "commoners", most of whom, however, were devoted to commercial and financial activities. Nearly all the Sienese adhered to the Ghibelline cause, while the small number of Guelfs were, as all political adversaries are, persecuted and exiled.

The unconditional adherence of Siena to the Ghibelline cause was one of the main factors that, after tens of years of small and large battles, led to what could have represented the final conflict with Florence: the brilliant and fortunate battle of Montaperti, transformed into a clamorous and unexpected victory (see page 22), a glorious day inscribed in glowing letters in the history of Siena. The extraordinary outcome of Montaperti did not, however, stimulate the growth that one may have expected for Siena. The economic disadvantage compared with Florence was enormous. But, more than anything else, the general collapse of the Imperial cause that also overthrew the Sienese government, took its toll, even if what happened after 1276 in Siena was above all a conflict between the aristocracy and the middle classes for the control of the financial markets and the management of administrative power.

The result was decidedly in favour of the middle classes that gave life to the famous government of the Nine, the longest lasting and most enterprising magistracy, that from 1287 to 1355 was to decide the outcome of Siena. During this period vast portions of territory were acquired and the most important monuments of the city such as the Palazzo Pubblico and Piazza del Campo were built.

This age of political stability and consequent economic health was brusquely interrupted by the plague of 1348, a terrifying event that reduced the population of Siena from about 50.000 inhabitants to little more than 10.000 and suspended a number of important projects such as the building of the new Cathedral that, according to the aspirations of the Sienese, would have been the most majestic church in all Christendom.

● The myth of "Good Government" has always accompanied, with varying fortune but with unwavering insistence, the history of the city.

These catastrophic events, together with an impending economic crisis brought about by the disinterest of the regime in the productive classes to the advantage of the middle classes, that not by chance, were totally in the hands of the Nine and their families, provoked an abrupt change of government.

This also sparked off a period of intense social conflict that reached its peak with the revolt of the wool workers of the Contrada of the Bruco that in 1371, headed by a commoner called Barbicone, even managed to overthrow the government, if only for a few days. The decision was then made to give life to a government of coalition in which were represented the interests of the various social classes, that by then had organised themselves into groups called "Monti", rather like political parties, and to which the Sienese were more or less obliged to adhere, as the membership of a certain "Monte" was one of the fundamental elements of citizenship.

The need to reach a beneficial social peace also led to a greater confidence being placed in the nobility to whom were granted greater powers, especially in the management of the castles in the territory.

In general, the fifteenth century was marked by the determination of numerous important families to assert themselves and by a distinct state of

conflict between them which, as a result, provoked hatred between the various Monti to which these families inevitably belonged.

All of this evidently caused great political instability which didn't cease, even when Siena was faced both with the growing menace of the Florentine Republic in full expansion and an economic recession constantly around the corner.

It was thus easy for a statesman of the calibre of Pandolfo Petrucci (see page 150) to arrogantly take advantage of this disgregate situation and hold the reins of power alone for over ten years, until 1512.

Pandolfo was both competent and ruthless and merited the appreciation of Machiavelli who considered him an ideal "prince".

The descendants of Pandolfo instead paid the price of the fortune of their father and were immediately challenged and removed from power. This period was very complicated, due not only to the incessant argumentativity of the Sienese but also to international events. In the delicate balance between the great powers, Siena was just a pawn to be moved, independently of her wishes.

The first, violent coup de main was staged in 1526 by the Florentines, supported by the army of Pope Clement VII, but the siege that should have compelled the city to surrender restored to the Sienese that force and unity, so long lost in internal quarrels, that transformed the sortie of Camollia into one of the most luminous episodes of heroic valour in the whole history of the city.

In those years Siena was allied with the Spain of King Charles V, a sincere friend of hers. But the protection of the Spaniards became increasingly suffocating and menacing and culminated with the arrival in 1547 of the new, ruthless governor Don Diego Hurtado de Mendoza and the construction of a threatening fortress which together took total control of Sienese political life.

The coarse cruelty of the occupiers that inspired a vast number of popular anecdotes, was certainly the cause of the rebellion of 1552, during which the Sienese expelled the Spaniards and destroyed the fortress, doleful symbol of their detestable despotism.

At this point Cosimo I, duke of Florence, came back on the scene (if ever he had left it). He had taken possession of a large part of Tuscany and the ancient Sienese state, rich and civilised, was evidently of great interest to him.

Moreover, Siena had become the only secure hiding place for the Florentine outcasts, all of whom were fierce enemies of the Medici family and therefore potential threats. Florence therefore declared war on Siena and thereby put an end to a Republic that, even though it was able to draw from its awareness of its past importance the force to conduct for a long time an unequal, desperate but exalted defence, surrendered not so much for what happened on the battlefields and under the besieged walls, but for the modified European political situation and for what was being decided at an international diplomatic level.

The war of Siena was, in all probability, a useless sacrifice for the Sienese. But, in the event, they were able to write a page of history that, even taken on its own, can illuminate with glory the whole reality of a community.

Once the "War of Siena" had been victoriously concluded, the Medici were intelligent enough to govern it with a certain flexibility. The grandukes left, at least in name, power in the hands of the government of the Sienese Monti, flanking it with a governor for whom they built a new palace: Palazzo Reale in the Cathedral square, not considering it suitable to occupy the Palazzo della Signoria in Piazza del Campo, ancient and cherished symbol of the liberty and history of the city.

The disastrous outcome of the last Sienese war coincided with the beginning of the end of a historical parabola that had already reached its apex.

While maintaining its dignified aspect,

there was little else to be done in Siena than cultivate the memories of a glorious past, mainly with the development of the Palio of the contradas that is the most significant and popular celebration of the intricate history of Siena.

Nothing survived of the ancient mercantile traditions and the albeit significant banking institute of Monte dei Paschi, important heir to the medieval bankers, operated only locally.

In the seventeenth and eighteenth centuries, Siena was similar to a "Sleeping Beauty". To the ever increasing number of visitors attracted by her suggestive history and by the fame and grandeur of her monuments, the city seemed empty and detached from her medieval splendour, even though this state of affairs was partly offset by the activity of the ancient university and the academies of sixteenth century origins, a peculiar cultural life.

We have to wait for the Unity of Italy to witness the substantial rebirth of Siena, the first city in Tuscany to adhere to the Kingdom of Savoy, and which actively participated in the new national reality, strong, not only in her unparalleled past, but also in a fairly efficient manufacturing sector and an artistic school, faithful to the somewhat "retrò" canons of Purism, but much appreciated at the time.

In the present century and particularly after the war, Siena has not been helped much by national politics that have isolated her from the principal infrastructures of communications and development.

Notwithstanding this, Siena has maintained her historical identity and her rare community spirit, qualifying herself for these reasons as a major tourist attraction. ●

● **A detail of the battlements of the Tower of the Mangia.**

MONTAPERTI

The hill of Montaperti, the theatre of the famous battle.
Facing page: The church of St Cristoforo, where the meetings during which the Sienese population decided to hold out against the Florentines were held.

In the eyes of the Sienese, the little hill called Montaperti, on the banks of the River Arbia, is not just the site of an important battle fought on 4th September, 1260, between the Guelfs and the Ghibellines. Montaperti can also be considered the greatest expression of the independence, pride and liberty of the population of Siena. It is a story that has been handed down over the centuries and still today evokes, like a precious reliquary, the dignity of a glorious republic that refused to surrender, not even to history.

Dante, when narrating the event, writes of "the torture and great slaughter that turned the River Arbia red", and emphasises the anguish that his fellow citizens suffered for the tremendous defeat and for the treachery of the Ghibelline exiles, Farinata degli Uberti, above all, on whose head the Florentines placed the responsibility of the defeat. What really happened at Montaperti?

From the beginning of the thirteenth century, the competition between the Sienese and Florentine bankers and merchants for the conquest of the important markets of France and England became increasingly fiercer.

Moreover, the Florentine border to the North of Siena arrived almost at the gates of the city, thus keeping the tension high.

Therefore, Florence pursued the policy of obstructing the trading routes of Siena that pointed more and more towards Rome. With this in mind, two strongholds were built at the strategically vital towns of Montepulciano and Montalcino, located on the heights to the East and to the West of the Via Francigena from which the Florentines were easily able to control the traffic.

In 1260, Montepulciano was soon neutralised and Montalcino remained the only castle left to guard the Francigena.

So as not to let it fall into the hands of the Sienese, too, it became essential to supply and fortify it.

In the manoeuvre of approach to Montalcino, the Guelf army chose to pass nearby Siena and halted at Montaperti. Two ambassadors left the Florentine camp for Siena with an ultimatum.

They were received by the Government of the Twenty-four, assembled in the Church of San Cristoforo (St Christopher), and pronounced words of fire as a precious document of the time narrates:

"It was their intention to take Siena, and as they were not willing to pass through the gates, they required that all the walls be thrown down so that Siena could be entered at any point; and in every quarter of Siena a governor was to be appointed, as is their custom, and they wanted to build a strong and grand castle on the hill of Camporegio and keep it as a stronghold, well garrisoned and full of victuals, for the safety of Florence".

The ambassadors returned to their camp convinced that they had terrified the Sienese.

The government played for time and assembled on the same day in San Cristoforo. After the intervention of a few counsellors inclined to come to terms with the Florentines, Provenzan Salvani rose to his feet and exhorted the assembly to resist, reminding it of how the presence in Siena of a number of German horsemen, faithful to King Manfred, would allow them to defend the city with honour.

The Twenty-four immediately deliberated to grant the German horsemen *"double pay"* for a total expense of 118.000 golden florins. As the government did not possess such a sum, *"the wise and noble Salimbeno de' Salimbeni, rich and powerful, seeing the great need of his birthplace and city"*, decided to put the sum at its disposal. Immediately he returned to his palace and brought the money to San Cristoforo in a cart covered with scarlet cloth and decorated with olive leaves, followed by a cheering crowd. The Germans *"danced for joy...and sang many songs in their language"* With this money they bought the leather for the armour and the harnesses for the horses and all the craftsmen of Siena, *"master leather workers and harness makers"*, goldsmiths, painters, tailors and master wood workers put themselves to work to fulfil the requests of the cavalry of Manfred. In the meantime a mayor was appointed with extraordinary powers, in the person of Buonaguida Lucari.

The bells of the Cathedral began to ring out and the bishop, having assembled all the clergy, exhorted them to pray barefooted in a procession, together with all the populace.

Buonaguida Lucari, as his first act, invited the Twenty-four to accompany him to the Cathedral and pray to the Madonna, offering her the keys of the city.

The ancient document narrates:

"Buonaguida, stripped his shirtsleeves, bareheaded and barefooted, marched to the Cathedral with the whole population of Siena that had armed itself at Piazza Tolomei behind him, and everyone prayed to the Virgin Mary: "help us in our hour of need, free us from these evil lions and dragons that desire to devour us". From the pulpit, the bishop exhorted the citizens to make peace with one another and commanded a procession be made with the cross and the image of the Madonna and San Cristoforo. For the whole of Thursday night, the Sienese set aside old grudges and resentments, embraced one another and made peace with their enemies.

The Twenty-four remained the whole night to organise the departure of the army the following morning. Long before dawn the citizens were assembled and the men followed their respective standards towards the gate of San Viene, nowadays called Pispini.

Those of the Terzo di Città quarter arrived first, followed by the Terzo di Camollia quarter, led by Bartolomeo Rinaldini, with a beautiful white standard placed on the war cart, and larger than the others as it

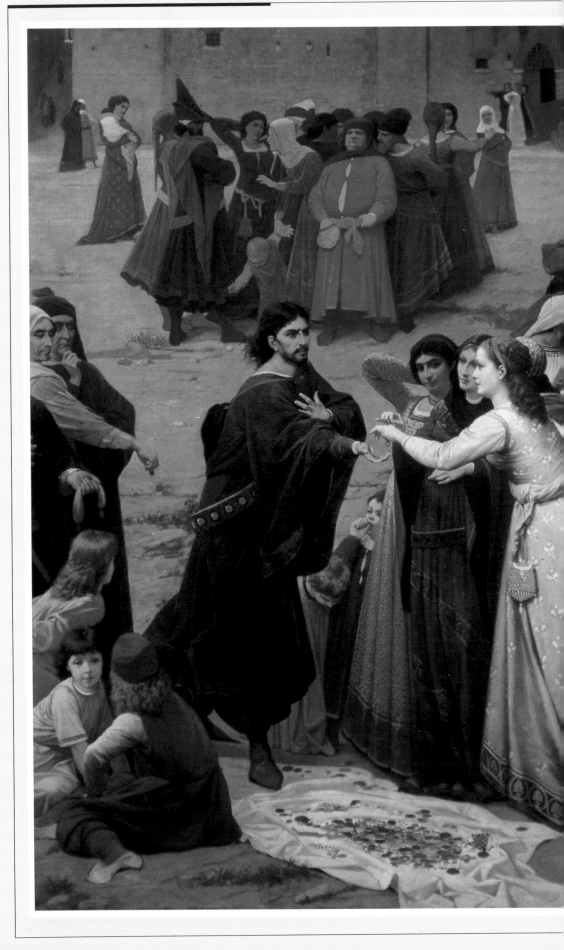

represented the mantle of the Madonna. To let the standard pass under the gate, the arch had to be cut. The army marched towards the Hill of Vignano, illuminated by lamps, lanterns and candles. It was

● Provenzano Salvani humbly collects the sum necessary for the ransom of an imprisoned friend in Piazza del Campo. This beautiful purist interpretation is by Amos Cassioli.

preceded by Count Giordano, representative of Manfred, with his eight hundred German horsemen, flanked by the captain of the army, Count Aldobrandino da Santa Fiora, with two hundred citizen horsemen. The standards followed with the infantry.
Back in the city, the Bishop, with the aged and the women, amidst prayers and tears, invoked the Virgin Mary. By dawn, the army had occupied the Hill of Ropole, opposite the Florentine camp. The various Sienese companies marched on the hill for a long time, continuously changing into different coloured clothes so as to give the enemy the impression that they were much more numerous than they really were.
The Captain of the Florentine army assembled his leaders to decide on their strategy. *"How have these foolish Sienese had the courage to face us on the battlefield?"* All throughout the day, the city continuously supplied the army with *"good and perfect wines... much roast meat, chicken and pheasant and all the best things that one could desire"* to refresh both body and spirit. At dusk, other people arrived from Siena, ready to fight and it

was therefore decided to attack on the following morning, 4th September, 1260.

During the night, continuous sorties were made against the enemy camp to keep the Florentines apprehensive and fearful. In Siena, those who remained, sat on the roofs or looked out from the highest towers onto the Arbia plain for the whole night. Suddenly, a great light was seen to illuminate the Sienese camp. A few watchers believed it was caused by the camp fires, but since the light remained perfectly still it certainly couldn't be natural. *"It is the mantle of the Madonna –* exclaimed others *– it is the Virgin that protects and defends the people of Siena"*, and everyone was much moved. From Montaperti, a light illuminating the city was seen equally well and the troops, too, imagined they could see the mantle of the Virgin. Thinking of Siena and of their homes, many men got on their knees, wept and prayed. At dawn, the Sienese captains saw the Florentines beginning to "prepare themselves and take down their pavilions". They therefore roused the soldiers and ordered the ranks.

For the first assault the most courageous were assembled together with Count Arese, German seneschal, with two hundred of Manfred's horsemen and two hundred of the most expert infantrymen.

The second wave comprised Count Giordano's men, six hundred German horsemen and six hundred infantrymen.

The third group was commanded by Count Aldobrandino with four hundred Sienese horsemen and another two hundred mercenaries bearing the

stem of Siena. Immediately afterwards came the war cart protected by three hundred horsemen commanded by Arrigo di Stimbergo and Messer Gualtieri. Finally, the companies of the populace followed with thousands of infantrymen.

The Sienese army numbered one thousand, four hundred horsemen and eighteen thousand, four hundred infantrymen in all.

Count Aldobrandino assembled the commanders and told them the Germans would attack first to secure the advantage.

"We, – continued the Sienese nobleman – *will entertain them until the sun beats in their eyes, we must not take prisoners, but make carnage of these evil people as it is not a sin to do unto those that which*

they wish to do unto us".
The first group of bold soldiers arrived at a cross bow's shot from the front lines of the Florentine army, in complete silence. Messer Gualtieri lowered his visor and threw himself at the enemy like an enraged lion. Meanwhile at Siena, from the tower of Palazzo Marescotti, a drummer boy called Cerreto Ciccolini was able to see what was happening. *The Sienese have moved and are streaming down the hill towards the Arbia... let us pray God that they will be victorious. They're attacking!, Messer Gualtieri has killed his foe, he has hit the Captain of*

● **Palazzo dei Mariscotti** (now Chigi Saracini), served as a privileged viewpoint of the battle. Cerreto Ciccolini, as an ancient chronicle informs us, continuously updated the Sienese on the course of the conflict.

Prato and is killing everyone he meets. Count Giordano is in the midst of the company of Arezzo, now Aldobrandino has arrived with the people of Siena and the standards".

The sun was already high, men fell everywhere as if the battlefield were *"a great slaughter house where beasts are butchered, except on Easter Good Friday".*

The Florentine war cart was taken and the slaughter became horrifying. The Germans and the Sienese did not spare the Guelfs. The Florentine standards and banners were taken *"with great anger, force and fury, and first of all the great standard that was on the war cart was thrown to the ground".*

In the meantime, Cerreto Ciccolini cried out: *"Pray, people of Siena!"* and the women and men at the foot of the Marescotti tower, put their hands together, kneeled down and invoked the Madonna.

The battle continued past the hour of Vespers. The dramatic account narrates that the Sienese were unable to fight any more for the exhaustion and the multitude of the dead. The survivors fled desperately, tracked and hunted down by the German horsemen. Count Aldobrandeschi, moved by compassion, ordered that the killing be stopped. At this announcement the men of Lucca threw down their arms and surrendered to the Sienese captain. Characters like the commoner, Usilia, who had reached the camp to supply the soldiers and to succour them, also took part in the battle. Seeing the Florentines escaping, she captured thirty-six of them.

The Sienese victory was impressive, the number of dead and prisoners exceeded thirty thousand and an incredible amount of material had been taken from the enemy army. On Sunday, 5th September, the victorious army returned in triumph to Siena. The Florentine ambassador who just a few days before had arrogantly pretended the surrender of Siena, opened the procession mounted backwards on an ass. Count Giordano, Count Aresi and the Germans with their heads crowned with olive leaves followed, and finally, the city companies with the Sienese war cart. Usilia, too, participated in the procession, dragging behind her donkey the thirty-six Florentines that she had captured the day before. For days on end, scenes of exultancy and enthusiasm were enacted all over the city. Every citizen thought only of celebrating and not of the dramatic struggle that had left the battlefield horribly covered with bodies. So dramatic was the situation at Montaperti that all the inhabitants had to abandon their houses transforming the area into a desert populated solely by ghosts that, five hundred years later, were to move Ugo Foscolo to write of it in his *The last letters of Jacopo Ortis.* ●

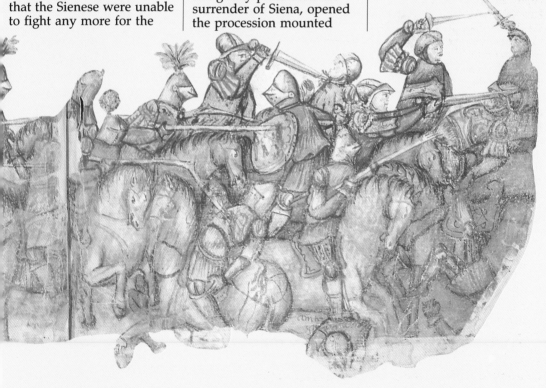

MONTALCINO:
THE FINAL HOURS OF THE FREEDOM OF SIENA

"Even if we have lost everything we possess, let us not at least lose our honour". These were the final words of Lelio Tolomei before being killed by Diego Mendoza, commander of the Spanish armed forces. The anger of the Sienese, faced with the overthrow of their fatherland, was tremendous: men, women, the old and the young, joined Blaise de Monluc, preferring exile to slavery. They had but one aim, the survival of the Republic and their liberty at any price or sacrifice.

On the 17th April, after a ferocious siege that had gone on for three years, the Sienese, worn out by much suffering and violence, were forced to yield to the relentless enemy. The losses had been enormous. Of the forty thousand inhabitants of Siena no more than eight thousand remained. There had been nothing left to eat in the whole city for some days and many people exposed themselves to enemy fire to pick weeds outside the walls.

Given the desperate situation, the Sienese government decided, against its will, to negotiate terms of surrender that included the departure of the French army from the city.

On the morning of Sunday, 21st April, 1555, the Imperial troops could be seen drawn up along the road to Porta Romana, from which the French soldiers left in a column led by a drummer and with their banners unfurled. Afterwards, Blaise de Monluc left, together with other gentlemen, and immediately went to meet the Marquis of Marignano, commander of the Imperial troops, who, regardful of the military traditions used on such occasions, accompanied him along a stretch of the road to Montalcino.

Over two hundred noblemen with their families and a further four hundred armed commoners, also with their families and servants, left Siena with the French. A few of them were so exhausted that they died during the journey. The Captain of the People, Mario Bandini, left, too, taking with him the seals of the Republic.

Monluc writes: *Never in all my life have I seen such a melancholy departure... even though our soldiers have suffered so much, they were*

bitterly distressed over this separation and I also felt sad for the people who had devoted themselves so much to save their freedom."
In the meantime, Marignano entered Siena in triumph but found the streets totally deserted. That evening, after attending mass in the Cathedral, the Marquis returned to his headquarters at Belcaro and then left for Florence, placing the command of the city in the hands of Count Sforza di Santa Fiora.
The imperial army celebrated the victory with fireworks and the ringing of bells. *"With this melancholy farce, dictated by fear and misery,* - wrote an illustrious historian - *the obedience of long centuries of slavery began".*
The sorrowful procession of the exiles reached Montalcino in desperate conditions the same day, 21st April, *"more like skeletons than men and more dead than alive",* as Monluc narrates in his *Commentarii.*

● During their forced exile at Montalcino, the Sienese did not suspend their institutional activities. In particular, the mint continued to beat coins, an evident indication of the hope of regaining their city.
Following pages: This beautiful painting by Pietro Aldi, preserved in the Palazzo Braschi Museum in Rome, illustrates "the final hours of liberty" before the exile in Montalcino.

Strozzi, a Florentine outcast, devoted to the Sienese cause for many years, went forth to welcome them with abundant victuals: *"Let us give thanks to God who inspired you to leave Siena so as not to see it subdued, but remember that you have not lost your territory, as you still possess a large part of it. Be sure then, that with the help of God, and the majesty of the Christian king, that you will soon come into possession of your city again."*
Then Strozzi entered Montalcino with the Sienese dignitaries: Mario Bandini, Fabio Spannocchi, Ambrogio Nuti and Giulio Vieri. On 3rd May, these men proclaimed that all the Sienese citizens in possession of political rights and resident in the territory not occupied by the Imperial army were to come as soon as possible to Montalcino. They were to present themselves to Cornelio Bentivogli, head of the

armed forces, and swear to contribute to the defence of freedom: *"We, the undersigned, swear and promise to strictly observe what is contained in this proclamation. We have made this oath in the presence of Signor Cornelio Bentivogli, Lieutenant of Marshal Strozzi in Montalcino and the lands of the mountains of the Orcia Valley."*
With this act, the Republic of Siena in Montalcino, the last supreme hope of the Sienese, was officially born.
Meanwhile in Siena, the Concistoro and the Balia (the organs of Florentine rule) were convened and it was decided to send an ambassador to Montalcino to try to persuade the exiles to return and perform their duties. They, however, completely ignored this intimidation and, on the contrary, as an immediate answer, sent back the ambassador to Siena. *"Being declared rebels by those who have no authority over us is a matter of small importance".*
In Siena, the reply was kept secret from the city, but the day after, a proclamation fixed to the door of the Palazzo Pubblico announced that if within a few days the thirteen Sienese citizens, considered responsible for the exodus to Montalcino, didn't present themselves before the Concistoro, they would be declared rebels. These were their names: Cornelio Bentivogli, military captain, Mario Bandini, captain of the people, Fabio Spannocchi, of the Signoria, Giulio Vieri, standard bearer, Ambrogio Nuti,

MONTALCINO CITTA e distante da SIENA M. IV

Mario Cacciaguerra, Ottavio Ottaviani, Marco Antonio Politi, Girolamo Spannocchi, Andrea Landucci, Deifebo Zuccantini, Carlo Nuti and Cesare Vajari.

In Siena, an atmosphere of suspicion and terror reigned. A further 44 citizens were publicly accused of conspiracy and numerous searches were made in the houses of those suspected. Meanwhile, the exiles organised themselves, both militarily and politically, so as to counterbalance the invasion of Siena with the firm control of the towns in the Orcia Valley. Important centres such as San Quirico, Pienza, Radicofani and Rocca d'Orcia were annexed to the new republic.

Power was assumed by an assembly of 150 citizens who chose the Palazzo Pubblico of Montalcino as their seat of government. Gold and silver coins were minted, ancient privilege of sovereignty and independence, with the impressions of the Virgin, the she-wolf, the stem, the lion rampant of the people and the writing "Sienese Republic in Montalcino".

But on 8th May, 1555, a small army, comprising almost six thousand men between infantry and cavalry, set out from Siena to overthrow the last bulwark of freedom. San Quirico, Rocca d'Orcia and Castiglioncello del Trinoro surrendered after a vigorous resistance. The Spaniards moved towards Port'Ercole, held by the Strozzi, and took it after a ferocious battle.

The Sienese, encouraged by the revolt of Rocca d'Orcia on 15th July, launched a counterattack, inconceivable in the eyes of the enemy, given they were so few in number, and regained most of the centres lost in the previous weeks.

The abdication of the Spanish Emperor, Charles V, in favour of Philip II, his son, suddenly changed the European political situation and the Peace of Vaucelles between France and Spain was signed on 3rd February, 1556. For the Sienese at Montalcino a period of relative peace followed that was used to build up morale and strength.

The truce didn't last long, however, as, in September, the Imperial armies reappeared in southern Tuscany. This caused the unexpected return to Montalcino of Blaise de Montluc at the head of the republican defence. The leader did not betray his fame as a bold and charismatic tactician. Montluc conducted the Franco-Sienese forces in a series of aggressive attacks right up to the walls of Siena, wreaking confusion and fear amongst the Spanish troops of occupation. As a result, the Florentine army marched once again towards Montalcino to put an end, once and for all, to a matter that, in their opinion, had been going on for far too long.

The Sienese territory, that had suffered the clashes between the opposing forces for so long and whose people were exhausted by the reprisals that the enemy constantly carried out, found itself in desperate conditions. It was not even possible to cultivate the land or raise cattle any more. Montluc desperately tried to obtain new loans and recruit fresh troops but the results were very modest. Notwithstanding this, he managed, at the price of a heroic attack, to regain Pienza. The coffers of the republic were by now sadly empty and there was no way, despite repeated appeals to the citizens, to obtain new funds.

In February, 1559, Spain and France, exhausted by a war that by now was being fought all over Europe, signed a peace treaty at Cateau Cambresis that, contrarily to the hopes of the Sienese, included the sale of the territory of Siena to Cosimo of the Medici as payment of the Emperor of Spain's debts.

The news arrived at Montalcino on 1st July, 1559, to the surprise and desperation of the government. At the same time, a letter was received from the King of France ordering the demobilisation of the French garrison, that for so many years had supported the Sienese cause. For three days, no one had the heart to tell the people the terrible news.

At first, the Sienese wanted to endure to the bitter end, but the menace of the Medici troops assembled at Buonconvento persuaded the people, by then incapable of any reaction, to negotiate an honourable surrender.

An atmosphere of doom spread through the streets and squares of the old Sienese citadel and bitter resignation entered the hearts of the heroic republicans.

By then, all was lost, but honour had to be saved. So the principal figures in the Sienese resistance refused with disdain the provisions with which Cosimo intended to buy the acquiescence of his old enemies. A proud silence greeted the enemy troops. A Florentine captain wrote to Cosimo of the Medici: *"It is most marvellous to me that, even though they have been without any form of government for four or five days, not one of them has come forward to obtain the clemency of the victor: this is the most evident sign of the feelings the Sienese have towards us"*.

And so ended, after so many centuries, the extraordinary story of the glorious Republic of Siena and its people who will remain *"for ever champions of freedom"*. ●

● *Facing page:* The signing of the treaty of Cateau Cambresis in a table of a Biccherna of 1559. The treaty put an end to the Sienese Republic and its territory was englobed in the Granduchy of Tuscany.

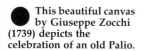

● **This beautiful canvas by Giuseppe Zocchi (1739) depicts the celebration of an old Palio.**

"It was in the light that follows dusk that, after going down a covered street, I found myself in the square and caught sight of the Torre del Mangia that seemed to shoot towards the stars in the night sky like a rocket.

Once you have seen the Mangia, all the other towers, obelisks, and columns seem miniscule, vulgar and tied to the ground; this tower, instead, seems to detach itself from the soil and has more the aspect of a flight than of a momument. The new moon, at the beginning of its journey, cast a glance from behind the battlements of Palazzo Pubblico, from which the tower rises, onto the façades of the ancient palaces that close off the vast semicircular space in front of it, and its silver beams lapped up the water from the most beautiful fountain in the world, whose dark and silent statues and bas-reliefs surrounded the basin.

There were shops at the bottom of some palaces and lamps all around the square; but it seemed that there was no-one there except ourselves and no figure could be seen on the ground that gently slopes towards Palazzo Pubblico from all three sides. When the time to go home arrived, I left the square in full possession of the situation, just as it was in the times of the ancient Republic".   ●

William Dean Howells "Tuscan Cities", New York, 1867

Il Campo: gracious town planning

Siena was founded and developed following a conception of town planning inspired by rules that were precise, but in many ways, "elastic". In fact, the walled city seems to recline on the irregular configuration of the ground, adapting itself with discretion and sweetness to its folds and respecting the variations in height.

The Campo is the most explicit example of this singular tendency. The "Square" of the Sienese, that probably represents the most emblematic and complex space in the whole world, if the number of painstaking analyses carried out by the architectural departments of every self-respecting university is anything to go by, is nothing but space taken from one of the many green valleys that insinuate themselves into the city, chosen for its strategic location and exceptionally well protected by a layer of bricks to ratify its decisive role as a privileged urban space. We are therefore in the presence of a sublime synthesis of space planned right from the start in the total respect of its natural geographical contours, avoiding traumatic operations and restraints, but intervening with slight alterations necessary to improve an area whose qualities were fully appreciated.

The Campo was the subject of one of the

first known urban by-laws that obliged those who wished to build round the square to respect certain rules.

This by-law dates back to 1297, probably in the moment in which the project for the town hall was decided and when, perhaps, the builders had already begun work.

It specifies that the windows of the other buildings should have "columns", in other words, that they should be mullioned with either one or with two pillars, and that the façades should not be weighed down by balconies, as the front of the town hall was to be built in this way.

This is a by-law made with exclusively aesthetic aims in mind, as even the largest overhanging balconies would not have compromised the functionality of such a large space. The town hall was the first building to rise in the square; in fact it became the primary element as it interrupted the view of the countryside behind it. The remaining buildings were placed in an orderly row along the old Francigena road and the street leading towards the Cathedral and the Hospital. They evidently belonged to the most important families of the city, and over the centuries, they were constantly embellished until radical changes were made in the eighteenth century involving three of the principal buildings: Palazzo Chigi Zondadari on the far left, Palazzo Sansedoni that was restructured in a highly evolved neogothic style and the Casino dei Nobili, where Ferdinando Fuga completely transformed the old façade of the Merchants' headquarters.

Such innovative fervour induced the borough government to cover, with an impressive façade, the modest buildings placed to the right of the town hall that housed certain "damsels" and "maidens".

At the end of the eighteenth century, the square reached its present day configuration and modern look.

The neogothic nineteenth century, so common in the city, did not produce important changes in the square, apart from the substitution of the Fonte Gaia

(the fountain) by Jacopo della Quercia, worn by time and the carelessness of men, with the emotionless copy by Sarrocchi.

The past, bristling with medieval towers and glorious events, is now far, far away, but the Campo today continues to be the space that it always was, witnessing not only the most important and significant happenings of city life but also the quieter and everyday moments. ●

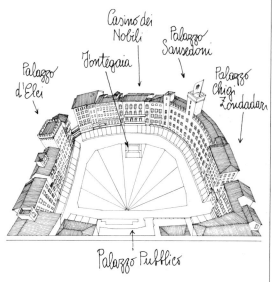

● In 1867, the purist sculptor Tito Sarrocchi realised a faithful copy of the ancient Fonte Gaia by Jacopo della Quercia, by then consumed by time and presently displayed in Palazzo Pubblico.

Following page: The regular pattern of bricks covering the Campo is interrupted by lines of stone that rebalance the irregularities of the ground.

Il Palazzo Pubblico

The Palazzo Pubblico, seat of government of the ancient Republic of Siena and now the town hall of the city, has always been the centre of the political life of the city and is associated with the most important happenings in the history of Siena. The most glorious events, the highest values and the noblest examples are immortalised in it. Images next to the divine, both reconciling and threatening, appear on its walls, depicting the most representative characters and moments of an eventful past whose importance surpasses the boundaries of the city.

It was the Government of the Nine that decided to build the new seat of political power, a palace that responded to the growing need of functionality of an oligarchy in continual expansion and to the aesthetic ideals of a political class confident of its role and of its future. Famous architects were probably not used to build it, but exceptional results were achieved all the same thanks also to a precise choice of town planning that involved the palace in the final organisation of that magnificent and disconcerting space called the Campo. The new building was sited in the point of escape, in other words, where one's eyes automatically turn on entering the square, no matter from what direction.

It is like a stage, then, a theatre backdrop, often exploited by the governors to demonstrate their power, like in the Spring of 1315, when the rivalry between the Salimbeni and the Tolomei families sparked off a kind of civil war and the Nine *"placed a candle outside the Palazzo Pubblico, proclaiming that if peace was not made between the two families before the candle went out, they and their possessions would be seized"*.

The Sienese have always displayed their joy in front of the Palazzo Pubblico. As a result of the construction of the new grandiose building, the Government of the Nine desired to free itself from its position of servitude, so dear to the nobility, who, certainly not by chance, preferred to carry out their public functions either shut up in their palaces or in the shelter of churches.

The decision of the Nine was not only made for reasons of pride and liberty, but it was also the result of a rational study to satisfy the most pressing needs of medieval society, like the prisons that contained those who did not conform to the rigid rules of common good, or the warehouses that contained the salt coming from the Maremma, an essential item to the economy of the times as it was the only substance that allowed food to be preserved.

Just as the façade of the Palace and its

● The *she-wolf* by Giovanni di Turino (1429) comes from the outside of Palazzo Pubblico, where it confirmed the important civic role of the building.
Facing page: The slender and austere Tower of the Mangia has for centuries observed the major events of Sienese history.

architectural composition were
conceived with the preciosity of a
miniaturist, so too were the decorations,
carried out by the many Sienese artists of
international standing, that were to
demonstrate the wisdom and refinement
of the new class of leaders.

In fact, the internal decoration of the
palace began almost
immediately,
proceeding at the
same pace as the
structural work. The
lands and castles
conquered by the
Republic began to
be recorded on its
walls, like a kind of
register of landed
property. The oldest
painting, to be
found in the sala del
Mappamondo (the
Hall of the Map of
the World), represents two people
and a castle that has surrendered to
Siena. It is the oldest fresco in the palace
but, strangely enough, it came to light
only very recently after having been
covered for centuries by layers of plaster.
Recent studies attribute it to Duccio di
Buoninsegna, due to the very high
quality of the painting that probably
represents the taking of the castle of
Giuncarico in 1314.

● The purchase of a castle on behalf of the State of Siena is depicted in this recently discovered fresco, attributed to Duccio di Buoninsegna. *Following page:* A detail of the "Maestà" (1315) by Simone Martini, the most elegant example of Sienese Gothic art, hung on a wall of the Room of the Mappamondo.

The first amply documented masterpiece
is the *Maestà (Majesty)* painted by
Simone Martini in 1315. The *Portrait
of our Lady* that takes up a whole wall
of the sala del Gran Consiglio (the Hall
of the Great Council), now the sala del
Mappamondo, was painted a few years
after that realised by Duccio for the altar
of the Cathedral. Compared with the
previous version, it contains new
stylistic techniques and iconographic
innovations, but, above all, it interprets
a different role: it principally intends to
admonish the Sienese citizens,
assembled in the hall below, concerning
the need to govern with justice and
humility: *"Oh, my loved ones, tell it to
the hearts of the people that I will answer
your devoted and honest prayers. But if the*

strong molest the weak or cover them with shame or injury, your prayers for these, as for all who deceive me, will go unheeded''. Right from the first decorative work in this hall, the most important in the palace, one can easily understand the objective that over the centuries inspired the choice of the patrons and the hands of the artists.

The recurring idea is, in fact, a balanced integration between civic pride, marked by the proud certainty of the role and power of government, and a fervid devotion towards the Virgin, patron and protector, and the other Sienese Saints. In the sala del Mappamondo, named after the enormous disc representing the territory of the Republic painted by Ambrogio Lorenzetti, we can find the most significant enterprises of the Sienese militia, together with the reassuring images of those saints and holy men that were closest to the devotion of the people. That which strikes us with innovative force is the mutated faith in the possibilities of mankind, by now protagonist of his own history, so perfectly depicted by the solemn gait of the captain of war *Guidoriccio da Fogliano*, of whom the recent controversy over his author has not deprived him of his restless and almost metaphysical aplomb.

But the highest expression of the politics of the Government of the Nine is to be found in the decoration of the sala delle Balestre (the Hall of the Crossbows), the ancient armoury of the palace, where, from 1337 to 1339, Ambrogio Lorenzetti painted his cyclic dissertation on good administration called *Good and bad government*. The theme of justice is the hub around which a series of visual documents of exceptional historical value rotates. In the well-governed medieval city, life continues tranquilly full of peaceful activity. In the warehouses, work continues without interruption, a teacher sits serenely behind his desk in front of attentive pupils, the shoe-maker negotiates with a customer

and the weavers are intent on their looms.

A little further away a group of girls is involved in a festive dance under the curious and entertained eyes of some citizens looking out from the windows. Similarly, the Sienese countryside is theatre of culture, trade and hunting. Faced with this picture, as much idyllic as realistic, the grim and menacing presence of the diabolic tyrant that symbolises *Bad government*, and around whom occurs a sad sequel of violence and abuse, manages to exalt the reassuring calm of the positive example. The palace had not yet been completed when the construction of the daring Tower of the Mangia was begun, a slender column of bricks ending

● *This page:* The portrait of Guidoriccio da Fogliano, the leader immortalised by Simone Martini. *Following pages:* Details of the cycle "Good and Bad Government" by Ambrogio Lorenzetti (1338-40), in the room of Peace that owes its name to the gentle allegory of this virtue. Of exceptional interest are the many details of daily life that enrich the painting.

unexpectedly in a crown of white travertine. Its exaggerated height manages to balance out the uneven profile of the city, until then dominated by the massive structure of the Cathedral. The solemn tolls of its bells, rung according to canonical and familiar rhythms, have always accompanied the important events of Sienese history. The relatively happy period of the Government of the Nine was suddenly interrupted by the outbreak of the black death in the middle of the fourteenth century. Conspicuous testimonies of this event are to be found in the Palace and also in the elegant chapel erected outside as a heartfelt prayer to the Virgin for the end of the tremendous epidemic. The event was the subject of a fresco by Lippo Vanni in the Sala di Biccherna, seat of the financial administration of the Sienese State, but it was destroyed a hundred years later when it was replaced by another fresco with a similar theme, *The crowning of the Virgin,* painted by Domenico di Bartolo and Sano di Pietro in about 1445.

At the beginning of the fifteenth century, the modified requirements of the Sienese government caused internal alterations to be made that included the building of a new Chapel and the sala di Balia.

The best artists that Siena had at that time, Martino di Bartolomeo and Taddeo di Bartolo, were called to decorate these surroundings but they were unable to free themselves from the influence of the memory of the great fourteenth century school.

Similarly, the only non-Sienese artist active in the Sala di Balia, Spinello Aretino, with his striking painting of the life of Pope Alexander III, was not able to break away from a late Giotto-like decorativeness.

In this hall, suggestive graffiti depict not only grim and politically significant events but also joyful ones inspired by everyday sentiments. Even the last great Sienese artist, Domenico Beccafumi, was called to leave an example of his work in the sala del Concistoro. Even if in this case the inspiring themes are similar to those that other decorations in the Palace

represent. Many new ideas can be appreciated all the same, above all, the iconographic programme inspired by the wisdom and value of the ancient Greeks and Romans, the daring perspective construction and the dazzling variety of colours.

After the fall of the Republic and the consequent loss of its freedom, the city did not cease to enrich its Palace. At the beginning of the seventeenth century, many important works by artists such as Ventura Salimbeni, Rutilio Manetti and Vincenzo Rustici,

● *L'Acca Larentia,* from the *Fonte Gaia* by Jacopo della Quercia, removed from the Campo at the middle of the nineteenth century, is still waiting for an adequate and final collocation in the museum.

representatives of a new school that owed its origins to the art of the first half of the fifteenth century, ennobled the halls of the Capitano del Popolo (Captain of the People), one of the oldest institutions in Siena.

The eighteenth century did not give birth to great talents and the last great decorative undertaking in the Palace took place in the nineteenth century with the painting of the sala del Risorgimento by masters of Sienese Purism who dedicated to the first king of Italy great scenes depicting the most significant episodes of the Italian Risorgimento.

In the adjacent halls, a crowded collection of pictures contains numerous examples of Sienese art between the sixteenth and the eighteenth centuries, as well as works by non-Sienese artists, coming mainly from the famous Spannocchi collection, partly housed in the Pinacoteca Nazionale.

A steep flight of stairs takes us to the Loggia, a hall built by the Nine where they were able to rest and refresh themselves during the months in which they had to stay at their post, almost like "prisoners" in their own palace. This hall now holds the remains of the *Fonte Gaia* by Jacopo della Quercia. A study is under way to find a more suitable location for this masterpiece to restore it to its former dignity, lost halfway

through the nineteenth century when the copy by Tito Sarrocchi was placed in the Campo.

The right-hand side of the Palace is connected to the massive structure of the ancient sala del Consiglio Generale della Repubblica (Hall of the General Council of the Republic), where, after many restorations over the centuries, the most recent of which is attributed to Antonio Bibiena (1753), the refined Teatro dei Rinnovati is located.

Aldo Cairola, in more recent pages, wrote: *"The Campo is the square of the people, the only Sienese square in which the crowd has always been the one and only protagonist; the Palazzo Pubblico filters the passion and the mood of the crowd, it takes its distance from popular facetiousness and places itself at the centre, above everything. The crowd, both in its composite and singular formation, searches the impulses of the sublimely absurd and is able to witness the fall of a country, knowing that it will not die. And the water bubbles out of the fountain to remind us of the power of determination and passion, the tower rises high and challenges the blue sky and the Palazzo Pubblico, immobile witness of a history that never stops, is the guardian of our most cherished treasures."* ●

● **The Room of Vittorio Emanuele II, or the Risorgimental Room,** represents the last great pictorial undertaking to be carried out in Palazzo Pubblico.

THE PALIO

The history of the Palio is interwoven with that of the city and for long periods of time they march along hand in hand, sometimes even overlapping. The same can be said for the Palio and the contradas: they were probably born together, then they lead separate lives only to find themselves triumphantly together again to share the same luminous destiny. We first hear of the Palio at the same time that the supremacy of Siena began to extend itself over an increasingly larger territory. At the beginning of the thirteenth century, the government, acquiring strength and prestige, began to organise regular religious events dedicated to various saints and especially to the Madonna towards whom there had always existed a special veneration even before the final and glorious consecration and donation of the city to the Virgin after the Battle of Montaperti. The Cathedral was also dedicated to the Madonna and the principle Sienese public ceremony, the offering of the candles, celebrated on Assumption Day, became increasingly important. Even if the event had a mainly religious matrix, it also contained strong political connotations. On that day of August the triumph of a governing class, aware of its role and confident in the future was celebrated, and the lords of the recently conquered

● The Palio is the feast of the people and is celebrated in Piazza del Campo. The painted standard assigned to the winning contrada is also called the Palio. The one shown above, won by the Contrada of the Aquila in 1719, is the oldest Palio still in existence.

castles were obliged to follow the magistrates in a procession, together with the populace, to offer symbolic gifts to the Queen of the Sienese.

The celebration was carried out according to a rigid ritual and whoever disobeyed the prescriptions of the government by not participating in the solemn procession, exposed himself to severe punishment. Furthermore, the procession was prepared with the closest attention to detail and no expense was spared for the sumptuous clothing of the participators and the decoration of the city streets along which the procession passed.

Very soon the event became famous outside Siena and began to attract a vast public, including illustrious visitors and official representatives of States and Courts. It was probably then that the feast of the Assumption began to be associated more and more with a horse race that was run along almost the whole length of the city, suggestively enriching the list of attractions that were offered to both Sienese and outsiders.

The contradas, small territorial nuclei linked to the various parishes and charged by the city government to carry out modest administrative functions, did not yet possess enough dignity to participate in the race that remained for a long time the exclusive right of the nobility and military captains who, either directly or entrusting their best horses to professional horsemen or promising and daring youths, competed to win a prize, generally consisting of a ''pallium'', a piece of valuable cloth - silk, damask or lampas - often padded with soft squirrel fur.

● The ancestors of the modern Palio were different and included popular representations such as the *Bull hunt* the theme of the painting shown to the right, by Vincenzo Rustici in about 1590.

Bloodier and more dramatic competitions were reserved for the people: the ''pugne'' and the hunting of bulls and other ferocious wild animals.

The Sienese participated in these ferocious and cruel fights divided into teams made up from the three city quarters called ''Terzi'' and the various contradas. Gentile Sermini, a jocular Sienese novelist, describes a ''pugna'' of 1424, giving us a kind of present day, detailed radio commentary and mentioning for the first time the presence in the square of the contradas of the Giraffa and the Chiocciola together with the other groups of contenders, whose names still referred to the zone of origin.

In the lively accounts of later events, the other contradas begin to show themselves in the square, until the famous bull hunt of 15th August, 1546, in which all the seventeen existing contradas participated.

We have a detailed testimony of this event written and published by Cecchino, a Sienese printer, and two detailed canvasses by the painter Vincenzo Rustici that allow us to fully penetrate the modality and spirit of that event. The competition was, in fact, preceded by a triumphal procession with robust carts built in the likeness of the animals of the contradas, well-equipped to shelter the hunters during the strange contest.

Even the most insignificant competition was aligned with the Assumption Day celebration, and even the representatives of the part of the population that watched the mid August procession

from the sides of the streets or from the windows were allowed to join in with all due pomp and circumstance.

Shortly afterwards, the Republic fell and was incorporated in the Medici State. The first step the Florentines took was to abolish the procession of the candles so cancelling what represented, at least symbolically, the triumph of the powerful and free Siena. The military companies, that could have been dangerous in that period of transition, were deprived of all their power. In this way the Palio run along the city streets in August began to lose importance while the competitions that were held in the Campo were intensified: the "pugne" and buffalo and donkey races were still organised by the contradas, to which the new regime recognised a role of primary importance in the life of the city and to which the birth in the territory of the lay companies, operating in the counter reformation, supplied new participating blood. These spectacular initiatives attracted an increasing number of citizens to the square who were more and more convinced that they were participating in real celebrations and new occasions of aggregation and transgression.

The first edition of the Palio run round the square, promoted and interpreted by the contradas and with precise similarities to the modern day race, was probably that of 1633. A refined engraving by Bernardino Capitelli proves the consolidated structure of the celebration, by then transferred to its most logical setting, the Campo, a valid natural scenario, invaded everywhere by a participating and tumultuous crowd, controlled with difficulty by the forces of law and order to ensure that the boundaries set by the law and good behaviour were not exceeded.

Although in 1656 the first Palio officially connected with the celebration of the miracle of the Madonna of Provenzano, that fell on 2nd July was held, the seventeenth century was, all in all, a period of settlement towards rhythms and habits that became more and more

● The "undertakings" of the contradas are illustrated in a vast series of engravings and picures, some of which of the finest workmanship and others of purely popular taste.

regular, thanks also to the direct intervention of the city government in the organisation of the principal aspects of the event, subtracting this role from the albeit efficient and willing spontaneity of the contradas.

At the beginning of the eighteenth century, thanks to the initiative of the Contrada dell'Oca, a second Palio began to be run on 16th August after the one run in the square in July and that of Assumption Day, run along the streets of the city.

In that century, the decisive consecration of the event was reached, thanks above all to Princess Violante of Bavaria, governor of Siena.

Probably moved by the triumphantly run Palio of 2nd July, 1717, instead of the ordinary one, postponed to the 4th of that month, Violante, also pushed by contingent necessities, issued in a short space of time, two decrees, both of which were fundamental in the codification of the Palio.

In 1721, twelve rules were made that rigidly ordered the way of competing in the race and that are still almost completely in force today.

A little later, in 1729, another decree fixed as seventeen the number of contradas, all of which survive to this day, and traced the territorial boundaries, ignoring the requests of some who intended to take possession of the ward of the Aquila, for many years fairly inactive in the life of the Palio.

All throughout the eighteenth century, many editions of the Palio were run that were memorable both for the sumptuous way in which the contradas always organised the pageant that precedes the race. Notable eye witness accounts, both by famous painters and willing citizens, document the vitality of the event and the high temperature that could be easily measured amongst the Sienese during the race.

From the eighteenth century to the present day, nothing much has changed. In 1701, as previously mentioned, the Palio of 16th August began to be run. The "sovatto", an old, complicated whip was substituted by the more modern leather whip in 1712. The contradas began to celebrate their victories with public celebrations for the whole city, competing even after their triumph in the square to surpass the other contradas in magnificence, too. A series of technical modifications also took place following the various lessons learned from unfortunate incidents.

● A few minutes before the race, the contradas wave their flags for the last time. The operation is called "sbandierata della Vittoria".

In the nineteenth century, the most important happening was the entrance of politics, so to speak, in the matters regarding the Palio that at times was taken as a pretext to promote one-sided demonstrations. But even this situation, certainly not pleasant for the rather introvert governors of that time, did not interrupt the continuity of the races and very few were unable to take place due to particularly violent disorders. After the Unification of Italy, the Palio took on greater and more well-defined importance and fascination. The season of the Kingdom of Savoy had just begun and the events that re-evoked the glorious era of the free medieval city states, of which the Palio is without doubt the most important and consolidated, were encouraged. The enduring medieval image of the city, "refreshed" by the purist restorations of the Architect Partini, is deeply interwoven with the Palio, so much so that in the 1970's, the city council was obliged to modify the costumes worn in the historical pageant under the severe direction of the professors of the Academy of Fine Arts. Attracted by this most noble revival, the Savoy royal family sent its representatives to Siena many times and all the members of the family became equally involved in the matters of the contradas, dispensing noble decorations

and Savoy knots that gracefully embellished their emblems.

Another important date for the Palio was 1928 when, thanks to the initiative of the mayor Fabio Bargagli Petrucci, the composition of the historical pageant was considerably renewed, adapting it, from a scenographic point of view, to the requirements of an event that increasingly met the public favour. Since then, there have been no important modifications and every year, on 2nd July and 16th August, the most spectacular event of the Sienese year is celebrated according to a ritual filtered down to us over the centuries.

Right from the time of the regulations of 1721, the first act in the horse race is the presentation of the horses. Early in the morning of 29th June and 13th August, the trainers bring their horses to the "Entrone", the entrance to the Palazzo Pubblico, where the clerks register them and the vets give them a check up. If they are judged free from imperfections that could prejudice their participation in the race, they are admitted to the trials. This decision is ratified by a progressive number that is marked on the thighs of the animals.

The jockeys that ride the horses during the trials are generally old glories hoping for the improbable opportunity of being taken on again or promising youths, anxious to catch the eyes of the managers of the contradas. The best jockeys do not usually participate in these trials as they consider them a useless kermess.

The city council provides the jockeys with a sober black and white uniform and a very modest pay but their job is fairly difficult. They have to try out the horses and verify from their qualities and form which will be the favourites, able to make the contradas dream of glory, and which have little or no possibility of winning, either because they are too young and inexperienced or too old and therefore unsuited to such a hard and intense contest.

After the trials the extraction takes place and the best horses are assigned to the contradas.

The "barbereschi" - the men that will look after the horses for four days with affectionate attention are dressed in great pomp for the solemn occasion and are full of superstitious gestures. Once the horse has been assigned, it is taken hastily to its stable, in the heart of the contrada, followed by the multitude of the members of the contrada, either cheering and exultant or down hearted and sad, according to the

● The dangerous curve of San Martino usually causes more than one contendor to come to grief.

form of the animal and its possibilities of winning. Whatever the quality of the horse, it is always venerated like an idol and is granted the role of absolute protagonist. The hopes of victory, however scarce, are always in the hearts of the people, even if their contrada has been assigned the worst nag of all. For this reason, the horse is housed in a stable that is often an elegant, well furnished place, more fitting for a gentleman than for a horse. After three days of trials, a grandiose propitious dinner is organised in all the contradas in which hundreds of people participate. On this occasion the directors of every contrada, torn between reticence and jest, announce the strategy they have chosen for the Palio, in naturally triumphal tones, so as to heighten the hopes of the members of the contrada.

The morning after, the horse is accompanied to the Oratory of the Contrada, a few hours before the race. In the church, the horse is blessed by the "correttore" - the priest - who wishes it the best of luck in the race that is now drawing nigh. This ritual, even in its atypicity, detains a solemn air of sacredness and, for the churches of the contradas, most of the year abandoned in their peaceful and shadowy loneliness, this a welcome moment to enjoy the sunlight and listen to the crowd of exalting people. After the blessing, the horse and the members of the contrada march towards the Campo

to participate in the historical pageant, so carrying out the final ritual before the definitive explosion of the passion of the race.

The historical pageant that precedes the Palio is opened by a formal fanfare highlighted by the agile sound of the clarions that set the dry rhythm of the ritual. The silvery blasts hit the nerves, set on edge by the increasingly long and frenetic wait, laying bare the most hidden fibres of the spectators. The official representative of the Republic march past, a suggestive summary of a series of historical events that have few equals, and the groups from the various contradas whose standard bearers compete for elegance and agility, carrying out complicated tricks with their banners. At the end of the procession, the war cart enters the square showing off the object of desire to the cheering crowd, the Palio, a cloth painted with the image of the Virgin to whom the event is dedicated and that will be triumphantly assigned to the victor.

Then a last excited waving of banners by all the contradas in front of the Palazzo Pubblico and a sudden roll of drums announce the arrival of the horses from the "Entrone" and their disorderly jostling at the starting point.

The thick hemp rope holds the anxious thrusting of the horses, urged on by the jockeys, with difficulty, and in the small space between the two ropes there is a melee of hooves and manes, a crowd of whips and helmets waiting impatiently for the race to begin.

At this point the horse chosen to start the race gets abreast of the others and the starter releases the rope that still divides the contestants from the fight and victory. After the start, the compact group of horses is rapidly transformed into a long single column dictated by the tight corners, while the jockeys create obstacles, collide with their rivals and raise their whips to contrast their adversaries or defend themselves from the attacks of their neighbours.

The race quickly draws to a conclusion on turf that boils as if it were molten metal, but there will be only one victor and its celebrating contrada will take home the "Palio". Victory celebrations begin when night has already fallen on the city and the defeated have gone home slowly and sadly.

The victors will march along the streets, self-confident and satisfied, waving flags and beating drums and looking forward to months of festivities. Only late in the night will the city regain its usual tranquillity, just a little disturbed by the euphoria of the few surviving revellers.

The darkness is interrupted only by the trembling flames of the torches that exalt the city, once again real protagonist of its history. ●

● **After the victory the main actor, the horse, is affectionately praised. At the end of Summer, the victorious Contrada celebrates its triumph with a great and solemn banquet.**

THE CONTRADAS

We would now like to present a synthetic summary of the Sienese contradas. The reader is invited to consult the books listed in the bibliography if he wishes to further learn about the complex nature of these active territorial organisms that have played such an important part in the history and life of the city.

The symbols of the contradas portrayed next to the summaries that follow are works by Icilio Federigo Ioni. They were, in fact, painted on five side panels of the war cart inaugurated, together with the new costumes for the historical pageant, on 2nd July, 1928.

The new war cart was characterised by very fine engravings and gilding and looked more like a real and proper "triumphal cart". The majestic oxen from the Chiana Valley were all that remained of the old war machine.

The tasteful allegories of the contradas realised by this famous "painter of old paintings" are worthy of a Renaissance miniaturist.

The fresh woods and ventilated river banks that provide a backdrop to the beauties in costume were, in fact, inspired by the later works of Sandro Botticelli.

THE NOBLE CONTRADA OF THE AQUILA (EAGLE)

The golden emblem bears a two-headed crowned eagle with imperial symbols (the globe, sword and sceptre) in its claws and the Savoy initials U.I. (Umberto I) at the centre. The colours of its banner are golden yellow with black and azure stripes. The military companies are those of San Pietro in Castelvecchio, Casato di Sopra and Aldobrandino del Mancino. The territory of the Aquila lies in the quarter of Terzo di Città and its motto, "From the Eagle its beak, its claw and its wing", symbolises combativeness. The Aquila was awarded the title of "Noble" for the particular welcome reserved by the population of the Contrada on the occasion of Emperor Charles V's visit to Siena in 1536. The headquarters and museum are in Casato di Sotto, next to the church dedicated to St John the Baptist, previously belonging to the Congregation of the Tredicini. The society of the Contrada, 'Il Rostro', lies in Vicolo del Verchione.

THE NOBLE CONTRADA OF THE BRUCO (CATERPILLAR)

The golden emblem depicts a caterpillar on a green leaf surmounted by a grand-duke's crown; the top section is quartered in red and silver. Its colours are yellow and green with turquoise stripes. The military company of the Caterpillar is that of San Pietro a Ovile di Sotto.
The motto of the Contrada, "My name is a revolution", symbolises industriousness. The Bruco possesses the title of "Noble" for having brought the Monte del Popolo to power in 1371 and for the courage shown by its militia in 1369 against Charles IV of Bohemia.
The ward of the Bruco is situated in the quarter of Terzo di Camollia, its headquarters is in Via del Comune and its oratory is dedicated to the Sacred Name of Jesus. The society of the Contrada, "L'Alba" is in Via del Comune, as are the church and the museum, and boasts a beautiful outside area that extends right up to the city walls.

THE CONTRADA OF THE CHIOCCIOLA (SNAIL)

The silver emblem bears a crawling snail surmounted by the letters U and M (Umberto I and Margherita of Savoy) interpolated with red roses. The colours of the Chiocciola are red and yellow with turquoise stripes. Its territory is situated in the quarter of Terzo di Città and its three military companies are San Marco, San Quirico and Monistero. The motto of the Contrada, "With slow and solemn steps the Chiocciola goes down to the Campo to triumph", symbolises prudence.
The historical headquarters is in Via San Marco as is the sixteenth century church, dedicated to St Peter and Paul Apostles, that rises on the medieval monastery of the Nuns of St Paul. The society of the Contrada, "San Marco", can also be found in Via San Marco right next to the Oratory of the Madonna of the Rosary.

THE PRIOR CONTRADA OF THE CIVETTA (OWL)

The emblem is divided in black and red and bears a majestic owl with two azure shields on the sides and the letters U and M (Umberto I and Margherita of Savoy). The colours of the Contrada are black and red with white stripes, while the motto, "I see in the night", symbolises astuteness. The three military companies of the Civetta are San Vigilio, San Pietro in Banchi and San Cristoforo. The ward is situated in the quarter of Terzo di San Martino. The Civetta gained the title of "Prior" for having hosted the first meeting of the Magistracy of the Contradas that assembles the seventeen Priors and deliberates questions of common interest. Its historical headquarters and museum are inside the Castellare degli Ugurgieri while the church, dedicated to St Anthony of Padua, is in Via Cecco Angiolieri. The society, that carries the name of the medieval Sienese poet, Cecco Angiolieri, who lived in the ward, is just a little further on in Vicolo al Vento.

THE CONTRADA OF THE DRAGO (DRAGON)

The silver emblem bears a green crowned dragon carrying an azure pennant with the Savoy initial U (Umberto I) in gold. The colours of the Drago are red and green with yellow stripes. "My burning heart becomes fire in my mouth" is the motto of this Contrada and symbolises ardour. Its military companies are Sant'Egidio and San Donato ai Montanini, while its historical centre is situated in Piazza Matteotti, under the oratory that is dedicated to Saint Catherine of Siena, previously owned by the Nuns of Paradise up to the end of the eighteenth century. The society of Camporegio, this is the name of the society of the Drago, is situated in Via del Paradiso. This Contrada is part of the quarter of Terzo di Camollia.

THE IMPERIAL CONTRADA OF THE GIRAFFA (GIRAFFE)

The silver emblem of this Contrada depicts a giraffe held by a moor dressed as a Turk, surmounted by a blue ribbon bearing the motto "UMBERTUS I DEDIT". Its colours are red and white and its military company is that of San Pietro a Ovile di Sopra. The Giraffa possesses the title of "Imperial" thanks to a decree issued by Vittorio Emanuele III on the occasion of its victory in the Palio of 2nd July, 1936, dedicated to the conquest of the Empire. Its territory is situated in the quarter of Terzo di Camollia. Its historical headquarters and museum lie underneath the Basilica di Provenzano and the entrance is in Via delle Vergini. The church of the Giraffa, also in the crypt of Provenzano, formerly belonged to the Congregation of the Suffragi. The motto of the Contrada, "The higher the head, the greater the glory", symbolises elegance. The society "della Giraffa" is also situated in Via delle Vergini, one of the most characteristic streets in the medieval ward of Provenzano.

THE SOVEREIGN CONTRADA OF THE ISTRICE (PORCUPINE)

Its silver emblem depicts an armed and crowned porcupine on a herbaceous background, surmounted by two red Cyprus roses. Underneath, there is an azure Savoy knot and the white octagonal cross of the Sovereign Military Order of Malta on a red background. The colours of the Istrice are white with black, red and turquoise stripes. The title of "Sovereign" was granted to the Contrada for having allowed the above-mentioned Order to have its headquarters in its territory in the fourteenth century. The motto, "I sting only to defend myself", symbolises shrewdness and the four military companies that were stationed in the Contrada are Santo Stefano, San Vincenzo, La Magione and San Bartolomeo. The Contrada lies in the quarter of Terzo di Camollia and its oratory, dedicated to St Vincent and St Anastasio, is in Via Camollia, as is its historical headquarters and the Society "Il Leone" that can be found a little further along the street, near Porta Camollia.

THE CONTRADA DEL LEOCORNO (UNICORN)

A silver emblem depicts a rampant unicorn on a herbaceous background, while the blue border bears a motto in gold, "HUMBERTI REGIS GRATIA".
The military companies of the Leocorno are San Giorgio, Pantaneto and Spadaforte and its colours are white and orange with turquoise stripes. The territory of this Contrada is comprised in the quarter of Terzo di San Martino. The motto "The weapon I have on my forehead both wounds and heals" symbolises science.
Its historical headquarters and museum are in Piazzetta Virgilio Grassi, as is the sixteenth century church of St John the Baptist "della Staffa" and the Society "Il Cavallino". The Contrada and the society both look out onto the beautiful Valle di Follonica which extends right up to the city walls.

THE CONTRADA OF THE LUPA (SHE-WOLF)

A silver emblem depicts a crowned Roman she-wolf with two twins and a pennant bearing the colours of the balzana, the black and white stem of the city, on a herbaceous background. The silver and red border is filled with red and silver crosses. The colours of the Lupa are black and white with orange stripes and its motto, "Et Urbis et Senarum Signum et Decus", symbolises loyalty.
Its military companies are those of San Donato and Sant'Andrea. Its territory lies in the quarter of Terzo di Camollia and its historical headquarters and museum are in Via Vallerozzi in the building that also contains the Church of St Rocco, a sixteenth century oratory that previously belonged to the Lay Confraternity of St Rocco. The society of the Contrada, "La Lupa", is situated right behind the church, in Via Pian d'Ovile.

THE NOBLE CONTRADA OF THE NICCHIO (SHELL)

Its blue emblem bears a silver shell surmounted by a grand duke's crown between two branches of red coral, three Savoy knots and two roses, one red and the other silver. The colours of the Nicchio are turquoise with yellow and red stripes, while its motto, "It is the red of the coral that burns in my heart", symbolises reservedness. The Contrada was awarded the title of "Noble" for the courage demonstrated by its soldiers at Montaperti (1260), at Porta Pispini (1527) and for having brought water to its ward in 1469 and to the Fonte dei Pispini in 1534. The territory of the Nicchio is situated in the quarter of Terzo di San Martino and its military companies are l'Abbadia Nuova di sopra and l'Abbadia Nuova di sotto. At the end of the seventeenth century, the Contrada dedicated an oratory that divides Via dei Pispini and Via dell'Oliviera to its patron saint, St Gaetano da Thiene. The historical headquarters, the entrance to which is in Via dei Pispini, lies next to the church. The society of the Nicchio, "La Pania", can be found in the same street and vaunts a beautiful green valley that extends right up to the city walls.

THE NOBLE CONTRADA OF THE OCA (GOOSE)

Its golden emblem depicts a white goose surmounted by a royal crown on a herbaceous background. It wears a blue ribbon round its neck from which hangs a Savoy Cross. The colours of the Contrada of Fontebranda are white and green with red stripes. Its military companies are Sant'Antonio and San Pellegrino. The Oca was awarded the title of "Noble" for the courage shown by its militia in the Battle of Montemaggio (1145), in that of Montaperti (1260), after which it was granted the title of "Governing", and in that of Siena (1552-1555). Even today, the Contrada is ruled by a Governor instead of a Prior like all the others. The motto of the Oca, "Clangit ad arma", symbolises shrewdness. Its territory lies in the quarter of Terzo di Camollia. The historical headquarters, museum and oratory - dedicated to Saint Catherine of Siena - can be found in Via Santa Caterina, in the birth place of the great Sienese Saint. The Society of the Contrada, la "Trieste", is in the same street and has a beautiful view of the Cathedral and the Church of San Domenico.

THE CAPTAIN CONTRADA OF THE ONDA (WAVE)

A silver emblem depicts a dolphin floating in the blue sea, surmounted by a royal crown. The colours of the Onda are white and azure and its motto, "the colour of the sky, the force of the sea", symbolises joy. It obtained the title of "Captain" thanks to its militia who used to mount guard at the Palazzo Pubblico which lies right on the boundary of the territory of the Oca. Its military companies are San Salvatore and Casato di Sotto and its territory lies in the quarter of Terzo di Città. Its historical headquarters and museum are situated in Via Giovanni Duprè in the crypt of the church dedicated to St Joseph, patron saint of this Contrada. The oratory of the Oca is of sixteenth century origins while the beautiful façade dates back to the following century. The society is named after the great nineteenth century sculptor, Giovanni Duprè, who was born in this Contrada, and is located in the Vicolo of San Salvadore.

THE CONTRADA OF THE PANTERA (PANTHER)

A silver emblem depicts a rampant panther with a white and azure quarter bearing the initial U (Umberto I) at the top left.
Its colours are red and azure with white stripes and the motto, "My leap overcomes all obstacles", symbolises audacity. The military companies of the Panther are Stalloreggi di dentro and Stalloreggi di fuori. The territory lies in the quarter of Terzo di Città. The museum, located in Via San Quirico, preserves, amongst other treasures, a magnificent fifteenth century multi-coloured wooden statue of the school of Jacopo della Quercia. The church of the Contrada of Stalloreggi is presently that of the Carmine del Piano dei Mantellini, officiated by the Carmelite monks and rich in artistic objects of great importance. The society of the Contrada, called "Due Porte", lies in Via San Quirico in the highest part of the city.

THE CONTRADA OF THE SELVA (FOREST)

A silver emblem represents a walking Rhinoceros at the foot of an oak tree on the trunk of which are hung hunting trophies. The whole image is surmounted by a radiant golden sun, bearing the initial U (Umberto I), on an azure background. The motto, "First the Selva in the Campo", symbolises power. Its colours are green and orange with white stripes, while its three military companies are: Vallepiatta, San Giovanni and Porta Salaria. The historical headquarters of the Selva forms part of the great building of the Church of St Sebastian, a splendid example of Sienese architecture of the first half of the sixteenth century, containing numerous extremely interesting works of art. The society of the Selva, "Il Rinoceronte", is situated in the same building as the ex-convent of the Jesuit Nuns. The territory lies in the quarter of Terzo di Città.

THE CONTRADA OF THE TARTUCA (THE TORTOISE)

A golden emblem shows a tortoise in a golden field, strewn with azure Savoy knots, alternating with daisies. Its motto, "Force and constancy dwell here", symbolises firmness. The colours of the Tartuca were originally yellow and black, but, as a result of the Risorgimental political situation, these were changed to white and yellow from 1847 until 1858, when the Tartuca definitely substituted them with the present day colours of yellow and turquoise. The military companies of the Contrada are Porta all'Arco and Sant'Agata. The territory is comprised in the quarter of Terzo di Città. The historical headquarters and the museum are in Via Tommaso Pendola, in the same building as the oratory built by the Contrada at the end of the seventeenth century, dedicated to their patron, St Anthony of Padua. The society called "Castelsenio" is next to the headquarters and the oratory.

THE CONTRADA OF THE TORRE (TOWER)

A golden emblem depicts a crowned elephant on a herbaceous background bearing a red saddlecloth with a white cross and a tower surmounted by a red, triangular pennant with a silver cross. The motto of the Torre, "After force, power", symbolises fortitude. Its colours are crimson with white and turquoise stripes and the four military companies of the Contrada are Salicotto di sopra, Salicotto di sotto, Rialto and San Giusto. The territory of the Torre lies in the quarter of Terzo di San Martino. Its historical headquarters and museum are in Via Salicotto and among the numerous historical and artistic objects on show, of particular interest is the bell bearing the emblem of the Contrada and the image of the Madonna realised in 1532 by Antonio da Siena using the bronze of the Florentine weapons captured during the Battle of Camollia (1526). The oratory, next door to the museum, was built shortly after the battle as an ex-voto for the glorious victory over the Medici and Papal armies. The society of the Torre, "L'Elefante', is also in Via Salicotto.

THE CONTRADA OF VALDIMONTONE (THE VALE OF THE RAM)

A golden emblem depicts a rampant ram, surmounted by an ancient crown while the top left corner bears the letter U (Umberto I) in gold, surmounted by a royal crown on an azure background. "Under my blow the great wall crumbles" is the motto of the Valdimontone and symbolises perseverance. Its colours are red and yellow with white stripes. It is the only Contrada whose jockey, during the Palio, wears a pink jacket and trousers to better distinguish his Contrada from the others with similar colours. Its territory lies in the quarter of Terzo di San Martino. The military companies of the Valdimontone are Il Borgo Santa Maria, Sant'Angelo a Montone and Samoreci (San Maurizio).

Its historical headquarters is located in the ex-oratory of San Leonardo, in Via Valdimontone, while the sumptuous church of the Contrada is that of the Holy Trinity, situated behind the Basilica dei Servi. The society "Castelmontorio" is in Piazza Manzoni, in the Park of the Servi, and from whose garden can be admired one of the most beautiful views of the city.

The Standard of the
Magistrate of the
Contradas, with the official
stems of each COntrada
and of the Terzi into which
the city is divided.

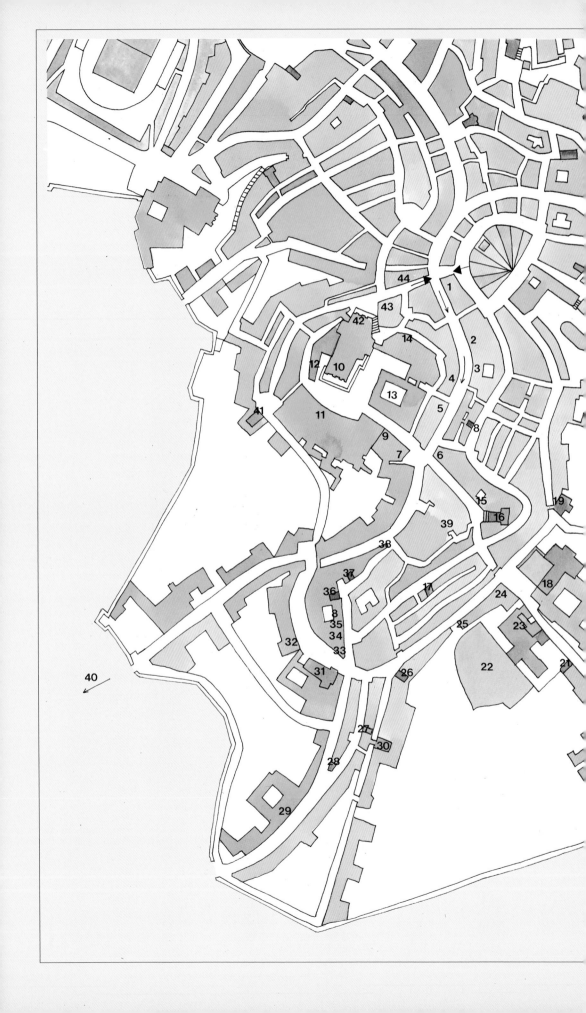

Terzo di Cittá

1 Palazzo d'Elci
2 Palazzo Patrizi
3 Palazzo Chigi Saracini
4 Palazzo delle Papesse
5 Palazzo Marsili
6 Palazzo Borghesi
7 Palazzo Chigi Piccolomini
8 Palazzo Borghesi
9 Palazzo del Capitano
10 The Cathedral
11 The Hospital of Santa Maria della Scala
12 Archbishop's Palace
13 Palazzo Reale
14 The Museum of the Opera Metropolitana
15 Museum of San Niccolò in Sasso
16 Pinacoteca Nazionale
17 Church of San Pietro alle Scale
18 Contrada of the Tartuca
19 Church of Sant'Agostino
20 Contrada Capitana of the Onda
21 Monumental Cemetery of the Misericordia
22 Church of the Maddalena
23 Orto Botanico
24 Accademia dei Fisiocritici
25 Palazzo Venturi Gallerani
26 Casa Bambagini Galletti
27 Church of the SS. Niccolò e Lucia
28 Contrada of the Chiocciola
29 Church of the Madonna del Rosario
30 Convent of Santa Marta
31 Convent of the Monache Trafisse (Sperandie)
32 Church of San Niccolò al Carmine
33 Palazzo Incontri
34 Palazzo Celsi Pollini
35 Chiesa di Sant'Ansano
36 Istituto Santa Teresa
37 Chiesa dei Santi Quirico e Giulietta
38 Contrada della Pantera
39 Madonna del Corvo
40 Castelvecchio
41 Cimitero Comunale del Laterino
42 Contrada della Selva
43 Pieve di San Giovanni (Battistero)
44 Palazzo del Magnifico
45 Palazzo Bindi Sergardi

20

Leaving the Campo by means of the Costarella dei Barbieri and turning left we find ourselves in the midst of Via di Città, the ancient Via Galgaria, that leads to the oldest part of Siena, the plain of Santa Maria with the Cathedral and the old Hospital of Santa Maria della Scala. A few yards further on, to the left, can be admired **Palazzo d'Elci** where, on the ground floor, the local Tourist Board has its Information Centre. The whole street is characterised by numerous, elegant shops and ancient, aristocratic palaces. Still on the left, we pass by another entrance into the Campo, Chiasso del Bargello, from which can be admired one of the most famous and appreciated views of the Mangia Tower, while, once more to the left, just a few yards further on, is **Palazzo Patrizi**, the home of the ancient and prestigious Accademia degli Intronati (see page 150).

This institution was born in 1525, even though it was probably derived from a confraternity founded in the fifteenth century by a group of learned men who had as their leader the great, Sienese, humanist Pope, Enea Silvio Piccolomini, Pio II. The emblem of the Accademia is a pumpkin, the inside of which is used to conserve salt,

Further along Via di Città, once more on the left, is situated one of the most prestigious patrician homes of the whole city: the ancient palace of the Mariscotti family, seat of the Council of the Republic of Siena before the construction of the Palazzo Pubblico. In the sixteenth century, the palace passed from the Marescotti family to the Piccolomini-Mandoli family, then, in the eighteenth century, ownership passed to the Saricini family, while in 1877, it was

protected from the damp, and refined with two pestles.

The medieval structure of Palazzo Patrizi was radically modified in the sixteenth century, thanks to the systematic rationalisation of the internal spaces and the construction of a magnificent hall on the piano nobile in which can be appreciated elegant plaster decorations by Marcello Sparti of Urbino and paintings by Bernardo Van Rantwyck of Flanders, realised in 1583.

Palazzo Marsili

V I A

Palazzo delle Papesse

D I

Palazzo Chigi Saracini

Palazzo Patrizi

This page: Palazzo Chigi Saracini (once called Palazzo Marescotti), nowadays home of a rich and original collection of works of art.
Facing page: The suggestive view of the Tower of the Mangia from Chiasso del Bargello.

acquired by the Chigi Saracini family (see page 138). Nowadays, the great building in Via di Città is the prestigious seat of the Accademia Musicale Chigiana.
Almost opposite **Palazzo Chigi Saracini**, one of the sisters of Pope Pio II, Caterina Piccolomini, had a palace built in stone designed by Bernardo Gambarelli, known as "il Rossellino", an architect in the service of the Sienese pope, also very active in Pienza, a jewel amongst Tuscan Renaissance cities.
The residence of Caterina Piccolomini in Via di Città is known as **Palazzo delle Papesse** and Antonio Federighi and Urbano da Cortona, amongst others, worked on its construction which lasted about thirty years, until 1495. The building, together with the other palace owned by the Piccolomini family in Banchi di Sotto, also built to a design by il Rossellino, is a rare example of fifteenth century Florentine-style palaces in Siena, characterised by powerful structures with large ashlars that, however, blend in well with the medieval urban architecture of Siena.
The inside of the palace still boasts many structural and decorative elements of the Renaissance, notwithstanding the substantial modifications carried out in the second half of the nineteenth century by the architect Augusto Corbi.
Next to this majestic palace belonging to the Piccolomini family can be seen **Palazzo Marsili**, prototype of the aristocratic, Gothic-style, Sienese palace.

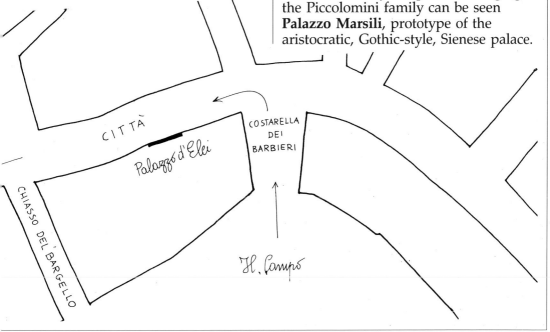

CITTÀ

Palazzo d'Elci

COSTARELLA DEI BARBIERI

CHIASSO DEL BARGELLO

Il Campo

The brick structure of the building has been conserved, although it underwent substantial modifications in around 1870, due to the purist taste of the architect Giuseppe Partini who was responsible for a real and proper neogothic conversion of vast areas of the city. The ancient Via Galgaria ends sweetly in the small Piazza di Postierla, surrounded by some imposing buildings. Up until a few years ago, the column in the square held a fifteenth century marble she-wolf, symbol of the quarter of Terzo di Città, now on display in the Magazzini del Sale, the ancient salt warehouses in Palazzo Pubblico. One of the buildings that look onto the square is **Palazzo Borghesi**, the façade of which was frescoed by the artist Domenico Beccafumi on his return from his first journey to Rome, in about 1512. Time and the elements have, regrettably, left no trace of this work.
The other important building in the square, on the corner with Via del Capitano, is **Palazzo Chigi Piccolomini**, today home of the Superintendence for the Artistic and Historical Heritage of Siena and Grosseto. The building dates

back to the middle of the sixteenth century and was designed by Bartolomeo Neroni, nicknamed "il Riccio" (A. Cornice), a Sienese painter, son-in-law of the more famous Giovanni Antonio Bazzi, known as "il Sodoma". Its state rooms were richly frescoed by Bernardo Van Rantwyck in about 1575, while the refined plaster decorations were realised by Marcello Sparti. Many paintings from all over the Sienese territory, by artists of the seventeenth, eighteenth and nineteenth centuries, are also conserved in the offices of the Superintendence.
A few yards before Piazza di Postierla, a steep slope leads down to Casato di Sotto where, surrounded by an intricate network of characteristic lanes, can be found the headquarters of the **Noble Contrada of the Aquila**. The church of the Contrada was where

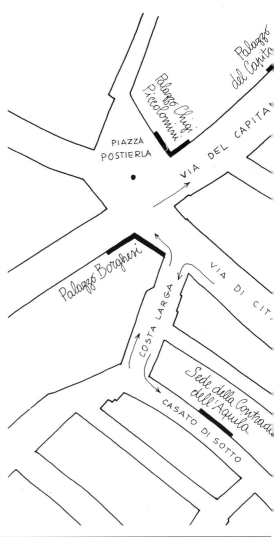

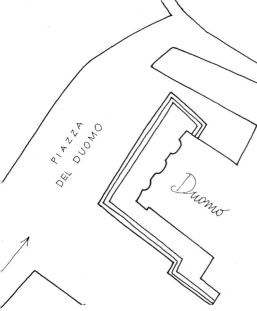

This page: The nineteenth century uniform of a drummer of the Contrada of the Aquila. *Facing page:* Piazza di Postierla and Palazzo Chigi.

the ancient Company of the Tredicini formerly officiated and houses canvases by Domenico Manetti, Bernardino Mei and Astolfo Petrazzi. Next to the oratory is the museum of the Contrada. Among the numerous works of art on display (sacred vestments, old costumes, objects in gold, inlaid wood), of particular interest is the oldest Palio conserved in Siena, won by the Aquila in 1719.

Climbing back up Costa Larga towards the Cathedral, along Via del Capitano, we can see, on the left, **Palazzo del Capitano**, built in the middle of the thirteenth century for the Captain of War and Justice. After various fifteenth century modifications, it was brought into line with neogothic taste by Giulio Rossi in the middle of the last century and it is in this state that we can see it today with its dignified façade divided in two by brick and stone structures onto which a row of mullioned windows opens. In the attractive internal courtyard, an old tablet commemorates the banquet held in honour of Eleanora d'Aragona, daughter of Ferdinando, King of Naples, who stopped off at Siena during her journey to Ferrara

to marry Duke Ercole d'Este.

Via del Capitano opens out into Piazza del Duomo, one of the most significant spaces of the city, surrounded by some of the oldest and most important buildings of Siena. The square is dominated by the superb black and white mass of the **Cathedral**, enriched by the elegant ornamentation of its Gothic spires (see page 130). The Cathedral rises on the site of a pre-existing sacred building and was unquestionably built by Nicola Pisano in the second half of the thirteenth century, reaching its present day disposition at the beginning of the fourteenth century. At that time, the Sienese conceived the ambitious idea of building the largest monument in Christendom by utilising the existing nave as a transept and constructing a new, enormous central body towards Via di Città. Various circumstances contributed to thwart the hopes of the Sienese, not least of all the precarious condition of the soil. Today, all that remains of the "New Cathedral" is a gigantic skeleton, surrounded by an imposing row of columns.

The façade of the Cathedral, although not perfectly homogenous from a stylistic point of view, due to the long time taken over its construction, is a majestic sight, intensely enlivened by the preciousness of the details and by the presence of numerous sculptures, many of which, as a precautionary measure, have been conserved in the Museum of the Opera Metropolitana and substituted with plaster casts.
The inside of the Cathedral of Siena immediately appears to us in all its extraordinary beauty. The space is divided by two rows of decidedly two-colour columns. The richly inlaid floor is probably the most exceptional aspect of the whole building. There are, in fact, around fifty scenes executed in marble inlay by fine Sienese artists such as Giovanni di Stefano, Neroccio di Bartolomeo and Antonio Federighi, or from cartoons by illustrious painters such as Pinturicchio, Beccafumi and Francesco di Giorgio.
The nave altars, too, although rebuilt between 1500 and 1600, host paintings of notable importance and great effect by proficient authors such as Francescesco and Raffaello Vanni, Pier Dandini and Carlo Maratta, that, unfortunately, substituted some of the most famous masterpieces of Sienese Gothic art including The Annunciation by Simone Martini, now in the Uffizi Museum in Florence, and the The Madonna of the Snow by il Sassetta, now in the Gallery of Palazzo Pitti in Florence. At the beginning of the right-hand transept is the Chapel of the Vow that exhibits a

● The Cathedral lies on a hill and dominates the city. The agile embroidery of its Gothic spires accentuates its thrust towards the sky.

painting dear to Sienese devotion, a Madonna with Child by an artist of the school of Guido da Siena (second half of the thirteenth century), that substituted the one that is now displayed in the Museum of the Opera Metropolitana. The chapel was wonderfully restored (around 1660) by Gian Lorenzo Bernini, on behalf of the Sienese Pope Alessandro VII. This celebrated figure of the Italian Baroque also realised the two extraordinary sculptures placed on the sides of the chapel, depicting the Madonna and St Girolamo. The statues of St Bernardino and St Catherine, sculpted in the same period by Ercole Ferrata and Antonio Raggi and placed beside the thirteenth century altar table, are also of great interest. Leaving the Chapel of the Madonna of the Vow, on one of the altars to the right, we can admire a sublime masterpiece by Mattia Preti, a canvas depicting The Sermon of St. Bernardino, executed around 1670.
In the middle of the Presbytery, on a slightly raised surface, the beautiful high altar, built to the design of Baldassarre Peruzzi in around 1530, dominates the surrounding area. The imposing bronze tabernacle placed on the altar was, instead, realised by Vecchietta (in around 1470) for the Hospital of Santa Maria della Scala and was transferred to the Cathedral at the beginning of the sixteenth century when it was decided to remove the Maestà by Duccio di Buoninsegna that no longer met the taste of the time. On the steps of the altar are two angels by Giovanni di Stefano and another two

marvellous statues by Francesco di
Giorgio Martini.

Eight angels, late masterpieces (around
1550) of the great Domenico Beccafumi,
placed on shelves attached to the
columns near the Presbytery, make
up a gallery of sculptures that has few
equals in the world.

The great stained glass window that
looks down onto the apse is of
conspicuous importance, too, as it is one
of the first Italian examples of this type of
workmanship.

The centre of the window, attributed to
Duccio di Buoninsegna, depicts scenes
from the life of the Virgin Mary with six
saints on the sides and is dated around
1290. Under this luminous "eye" are
arranged the elegant wooden choir stalls,
assembled in different periods but with
an altogether homogenous result. There

● **The majestic
inside of the
Cathedral houses
masterpieces of
inestimable value
realised by the greatest
interpreters of Italian
art of every era.**

are, in fact, stalls dating back to the end of
the fourteenth century and others
realised in the following centuries
by accomplished craftsmen such as
Domenico di Niccolò dei Cori and
Bartolomeo Neroni, known as "il Riccio".
Another important addition was made at
the beginning of the nineteenth century
with some extremely fine inlaid
woodwork by Giovanni da Verona, taken
from the monumental structure realised
at the beginning of the sixteenth century
at Monte Oliveto Maggiore. Next to the
choir stalls is the entrance to the vast
sacristy, furnished with some fifteenth
century altars and a series of frescoes
attributed to Benedetto di Bindo and
dated around 1410.

On the left-hand side can be seen one of
the most important masterpieces, not
only of the Cathedral of Siena, but also
of European art of all time, the pulpit by
Nicola Pisano and his son Giovanni with
whom collaborated, amongst others, a
brilliant artist of the second half of the
thirteenth century, Arnolfo di Cambio of
Colle Val d'Elsa. It is an extraordinary
work, even more magnificent and
analytical than the albeit splendid
pulpit in the Baptistery of Pisa. Octagonal
in shape and supported by nine pillars
placed on marble lions, the balustrade of
the pulpit is divided into seven
beautifully sculpted panels depicting:
*Visitation and Nativity, Journey and
Adoration of the Wise Men, Presentation
and Flight into Egypt, Slaughter of the
Innocents, Crucifixion, Last judgement of
the blessed, Last judgement of the damned.*
The presence among the authors of the
three most illustrious sculptors of the
period, contributed to create a monument
of the highest quality that remained
unequalled for over a century after its
execution.

Near the pulpit, in the left-hand nave is
the entrance to the Chapel of St John the
Baptist that preserves the precious
reliquary of the arm of the Saint, donated
by Pope Pio II. At the end of the Chapel
is situated a bronze statue of the Saint,
one of the most appreciated works of
Donatello, realised in 1457 by this great
interpreter of the Italian Renaissance.

The other two statues in the Chapel are works by Giovanni di Stefano *(St Ansano)* and Neroccio di Bartolomeo *(St Catherine of Alexandria)*, both realised in 1487.
Also of great interest are the eight scenes painted mainly by Bernardino di Betto, nicknamed "il Pinturicchio", in about 1505, and by Francesco Rustici, "il Rustichino", about a century later.

● This beautiful octagonal pulpit by Nicola Pisano is a wonderful example of thirteenth century sculpture.

Near the Chapel of the Baptist is the tombstone of Bishop Pecci, a splendid bronze bas-relief also by Donatello.
Opposite the nearby altar of St Ansano, enriched by a highly suggestive canvas painted by Francesco Vanni in the final years of the sixteenth century, can be admired the funeral monument of Cardinal Riccardo Petroni, realised by Tino di Camaino in 1317. It is one of the earliest examples of this kind of sepulchral monument.
The nephew of the great humanist Pope Pio II, Cardinal Francesco Piccolomini Todeschini, before becoming pope himself, even though for one of the shortest times in the history of the papacy, ordered that the life of his illustrious ancestor Pio II be commemorated in the Cathedral of Siena. Piccolomini took on a painter at the height of his career called Bernardino di Betto from Umbria (il Pinturicchio) to carry out this ambitious project. Between 1505 and 1507, the artist executed ten great paintings depicting the most important events of the life of the humanist pope in the Piccolimini Library situated on this side of the Cathedral.
They are in order:
1) *Departure of Enea Silvio Piccolomini for the Council of Basil*
2) *Enea Silvio before King James of Scotland*
3) *Enea Silvio crowned poet by Federico III*
4) *Enea Silvio and Pope Eugenio IV*
5) *Enea Silvio presides at the meeting between Federico III and Eleonora d'Aragona at Porta Camollia*
6) *Enea Silvio made Cardinal*

AENEAS FEDE... ...SPONSAM
EXHIBET ET... ...GVM
LVSI...

DEVM MAXIMVM ET POSTEROS OF
FEDI VTRISQ? DEBEO NE VTERMIHI

AENEAS SENEN
RICO IMP III
ET PATRVM PRIN

7) *Papal election of Pio II*
8) *Pio II assembles the Christian princes for the crusade*
9) *Santa Caterina da Siena canonised*
10) *Pio II awaiting the Venetian fleet at Ancona*

At the centre of the Piccolomini Library there is a marble statue depicting *The three graces*, a third century Roman copy of a Greek original. On the door of the library, sculpted by Lorenzo Marrina in 1497, is another marvellous fresco by Bernardino di Betto depicting *The coronation of Pope Pio II*.

 Francesco Piccolomini, the future Pope Pio III, commissioned Pinturicchio to decorate this beautiful room dedicated to the memory of the great humanist Pope Pio II, his uncle, and in which is conserved the precious family library.

The glass show cases arranged along the walls of the room contain an exceptional collection of chant books, illuminated by Liberale da Verona, Girolamo da Cremona, Sano di Pietro, Guidoccio Cozzarelli and others. Near the entrance to the library, Francesco Piccolomini had another extraordinary example of Renaissance art built, the gigantic marble altar dedicated to his family and commissioned to Andrea Bregno in 1481, holding, amongst others, four sculptures executed by the great Michelangelo Buonarotti in his youth: *St Pio* and *St Gregory*, not outstanding works, and *St Peter* and *St Paul* in which the dramatic force of the art of Michelangelo can be fully appreciated. A *Madonna with Son*, attributed to the young Jacopo della Quercia, was later placed in the largest niche, located at the top of the altar.

Moving back towards the entrance to the Cathedral, one of the most beautiful works by Pietro Sorri, depicting the *The Adoration of the Wise Men* and executed at the end of the 1580's, can be admired in the left-hand nave. Last but not least are the two beautiful holy water stoups by Antonio Federighi, bearing complex symbologies and rich in magical allusions.

Leaving this incredible repertoire of art of all periods, one's eye immediately falls on the ample and unusual front view of the **Hospital**. The great building of **Santa Maria della Scala** that rises in front of the Cathedral was constructed primarily to shelter pilgrims during their travels and to sustain the poor and abandoned children. The first document that mentions its existence is an act of donation dated 29th March, 1090. It was founded by the canons of the Cathedral even if a medieval Sienese legend talks of a mythical founder named Sorore, a shoemaker, who died in 898. It was only after a centuries old controversy between religious and civic power regarding the management of the Hospital that the city government won for itself the right to elect the Rector (D. Baestracci, G. Piccinni, 1985). Thanks to the bequests of the great Sienese families, from whose ranks most of the rectors of the Hospital originated, and to the conspicuous quantity of alms that constantly flowed into the coffers of Santa Maria della Scala, the institution played an increasing important role in the economy of the Republic, so much so that it was able to set up a subsistence fund for the city in case of famine or epidemic. It

● The severe façade of the Hospital of St Mary della Scala, occupies one side of the Cathedral Square.

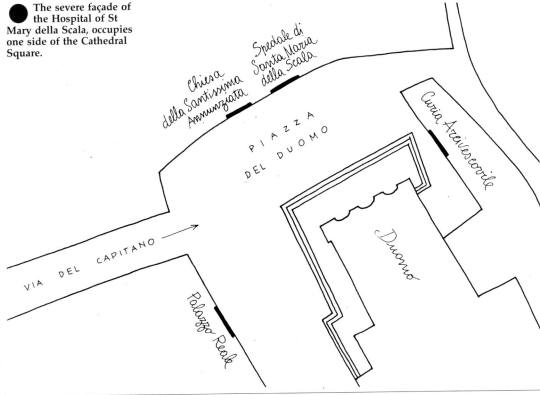

del Duomo. The church, dedicated to the Santissima Annunziata, was later enlarged and modified and still contains many works of art, amongst which a beautiful, fifteenth century, bronze statue, *Christ bearing the cross* by il Vecchietta (Lorenzo di Pietro) and the gigantic eighteenth century fresco by Sebastiano Conca depicting the *Probatica Piscina* (the biblical pool where animals were washed before being sacrificed). In around 1290, the Rector's palace was built to the right of the church, while a little later (1298), on the other side, rose the Casa delle Balie (Nurses Home). At the end of the thirteenth century, the Hospital extended to the city walls that confined with its possessions towards the underlying valley, the so-called Fosso di Sant'Ansano. Almost all the great Sienese artists worked on Santa Maria della Scala, so much so that it can be justly considered the third artistic pole of the city together with the Cathedral and the Palazzo Pubblico (L. Bellosi).

A prestigious work that bears out this affirmation is the Pellegrinaio (see page 144). Built in the second half of the fourteenth century, it is the oldest room with great lengthways development in the history of Italian hospital architecture, of Cistercian derivation, and corroborates the intense contacts that the city of Siena, lying on the via Francigena, held with the rest of Europe. The decoration of this great ward represents a systematic intervention of great artistic value, commissioned by the rector, Giovanni Buzzichelli, between 1439 and 1444. *He introduced a decorative style that was no longer wholly directed towards religious objects and practises, as had been the case in hospitals up until that time, inasmuch as they are places of suffering and pity. The iconographic programme conferred to the Pellegrinaio the role that belonged to the reception halls of the nobility, with the sole difference that the alternation of the guests was substituted with that of the pilgrims and patients so as to display the growth of Santa Maria from its legendary origins to the efficiency of the present"* (D. Gallavotti, 1985). Domenico di Bartolo, Lorenzo Vecchietta and Priamo della Quercia

owned numerous agricultural properties scattered over the length and breadth of the old Sienese Republic, many of which have survived to this day in their original architectural state. There are fortified farmhouses that still bear the stems of La Scala; two of the most famous and interesting are the "grancia" in Cuna in the Arbia Valley and that of Spedaletto in the Orcia Valley.

The complex organisation of Santa Maria was consolidated by a set of rules at the beginning of the fourteenth century. Their efficiency is corroborated by the interest they aroused in Gian Galeazzo Visconti, in 1399, and in Francesco Sforza, in 1415, both of whom sent their ambassadors to Siena to take this administrative organisation as a model.

The oldest part of the Hospital is the church that was built in the middle of the thirteenth century in cut slabs of travertine and which today constitutes the central body of the faade in Piazza

depicted the history of the institution and the daily life of the Hospital on the walls of the room. After the completion of the new city hospital, Santa Maria della Scala began to lose its sanitary functions. Some years ago, the city administration, together with important Sienese institutions, began to restore the old building, so undertaking one of the most important polyvalent cultural projects in Europe, capable of efficiently catering for the requirements of the great Sienese collections and for the growing needs of study, research and tourism.

Two lay confraternities of medieval origins that safeguard important collections and objects of great artistic value are still active inside Santa Maria della Scala: the Confraternità dei Disciplinati di Maria Santissima, nowadays called the Società di Esecutori di Pie Disposizioni , and that of Santa Caterina della Notte. At the end of the eighteenth century the Compagnia di San Girolamo, also housed under the roofs of the Hospital, was suppressed. Recently, the **National Archaeological Museum** that includes important examples from the Sienese territory and important aristocratic collections acquired by the Italian state (Bicchi Ruspoli Forteguerri, Bonci Casuccini, Bargagli Petrucci, Chigi Zondadari) was transferred here.

The collections include Italic and Etruscan vases, Etruscan and Roman urns, refined Etruscan gold objects, vases from Volterra and various important examples of ancient numismatics.

Of particular interest is the beautiful sarcophagus, nicknamed the *Muse Chigi*, and the *Testa dello pseudo Seneca* found in the city, a Roman copy of a Hellenic original.

On the sides of the square lie the **Archbishop's Palace**, a precocious example (early eighteenth century) of the imminent neogothic culture and the **Palazzo Reale** (Royal Palace), acquired and completely restored by the Medici after the conquest of Siena for their seat of government, as the grand dukes did not consider it suitable to occupy the Palazzo Pubblico, home of the republican independence of Siena.

The building, with its beautiful, late sixteenth century faades, now houses the Prefecture and the Provincial Administration. The very richly furnished interior boasts valuable decorations of the eighteenth and nineteenth centuries. Among the various objects, of special interest is a group of sixteenth century Medici tapestries, woven from cartoons by Giovanni Stradano and Alessandro Allori and hung in the Provincial Council Room.

On the right-hand side of the Cathedral, closed off at the bottom by an imposing wall of marble, the "facciatone" (the great façade), is piazza Jacopo della Quercia on which the "New Cathedral",

● *This page:* An ancient ceramic vase from the rich collections of St Mary della Scala.
Facing page: the gigantic fresco by Sebastiano Conca depicting the *Probatica Piscina* in the church of the Santissima Annunziata inside the hospital.

one of the great Sienese "Gothic dreams", was to have risen. The gigantic black and white columns that were to have separated the three naves of the Cathedral allow one to appreciate the vast dimensions of this "dream". Two of the naves were later incorporated into the Palazzo Reale and the **Museum of the Opera Metropolitana.**

● One of the admirable and powerful works of Giovanni Pisano, taken from the Cathedral and preserved in the rooms of the Museum of the Opera (Photo on facing page).

The entrance to this important museum is in the left-hand side of the square, near one of the ancient side doors that allowed access to the New Cathedral from Via Monna Agnese and from the steep flight of steps that leads down to the Baptistery of San Giovanni. Along the steps, built halfway through the fifteenth century, is the Crypt of the Statues, where sculptures and fragments from the outside of the Cathedral are displayed. The collection includes a beautiful marble statue sculpted for the portal by Giovanni di Agostino in the middle of the fourteenth century depicting the *Redeemer with two angels*. The one actually located on the portal is a copy.

The Museo dell'Opera Metropolitana, contained in the first three spans of the right-hand nave of the "New Cathedral", is one of the most prestigious museums in the whole of Europe and includes amongst its many masterpieces, the work most beloved by the Sienese, the *Maestà* by Duccio di Buoninsegna. Founded in 1870, the museum houses principally paintings and liturgical furnishings originally meant for the Cathedral and transferred here mainly for reasons of conservation and safety. Moreover, the Opera Metropolitana boasts extremely rich archives in which documents of fundamental importance for the study of the history and art of Siena are conserved.

A fifteenth century gate, originally made for the Hospital of Santa Maria della Scala, leads to the ground floor. On the walls are hung numerous

architectural fragments and bas-reliefs of various periods, transferred from the Cathedral and churches in the Sienese territory, amongst which the four marble reliefs of *the Annunciation, the Nativity, the Journey of the Wise Men and the Adoration of the Wise Men*, taken from the Church of St John the Baptist in Ponte allo Spino, sculpted by a pupil of Nicola Pisano in around 1265, and the beautiful circular painting called *the Madonna of Pardon* by Donatello, transferred from the homonymous door situated on the right-hand side of the Cathedral and substituted with a plaster cast a few years ago. Also worthy of mention is a bas-relief depicting the *Madonna with Child blessing Cardinal Antonio Casini presented by St Antonio Abate,* a real and proper masterpiece of the late maturity of Jacopo della Quercia (perhaps his last work) and other busts, blocks and figures realised by the sculptors that over the centuries contributed to the decoration of the Cathedral.

But the most important objects in the room are without doubt the statues sculpted by Giovanni Pisano for the façade of the Cathedral, of which the artist was author of the first project and director of works from 1284 to 1296. He sculpted the figures destined for the lower part while his pupils saw to the rest. The twelve statues executed by this great protagonist of medieval Italian sculpture are arranged under the arches and depict prophets, philosophers and sibyls of biblical and pagan times. The cycle is dedicated to the glorification of the Madonna and is unique among medieval European sculptures in that the figures, instead of adhering to the imposing architectural structures, swell out of their niches *"freely touching the surrounding space. This determined an extraordinary variety of structural solutions to which corresponds the powerful individuation of each single fold in the clothing not only from a psychological and dramatic point of view but also in its formal features"* (E. Carli, 1989). The series begins on the left with the impetuous and powerful folds of the

clothes of *(Moses)*, slightly offset by the serene spirituality of his face. The other statues continue in order with: *Mary, sister of Moses, Simeon, the Sibyl, the Prophet Isaiah, the Prophet Balaam, King David, Aristotle, the Prophet Abacuc, Plato, the Prophet Jesus of Sirach, King Solomon.*
The *Evangelists* and the *Patron Saints of Siena* were sculpted instead by the heirs to the art of Giovanni Pisano who remained after the master's departure from Siena in around 1296.
An interesting painting by Andrea and Raffaello Piccinelli, nicknamed i Bresciani, depicting *the Baptism of Christ*, realised in the 1530's for the Sienese Baptistery and transferred to the museum at the end of the last century, can be admired on the late seventeenth century altar, placed at the end of the room,
On the first floor, the suggestive obscurity of a room illuminated only be the precious reflections of one of the greatest masterpieces of all time, so creating an atmosphere of great emotional intensity, provides a suitable place of rest for the table of the *Maestà*, painted by Duccio di Buoninsegna for the high altar of the Cathedral from 9th October 1308 to 9th June 1311.

● The great table of the *Maestà* by Duccio di Buoninsegna (1308-11), realised for the high altar of the Cathedral, confirms the special veneration of the Sienese for the Virgin.

The table was commissioned to the painter by the Director of Works of the Cathedral, Jacopo di Gilberto Marescotti, for a salary of sixteen Sienese soldi for every day of work, as well as the necessary materials. The cost was very high even if it probably didn't reach three thousand golden florins as is reported in the Medieval Chronicles of Agnolo di Tura. We definitely know, however, that when the table was finished it was solemnly transported from the artist's studio to the Cathedral, accompanied by music and songs, with the great participation of the people and clergy and in the presence of the civic magistracy of Siena.
In 1260, on the eve of the victorious battle of Montaperti, the Madonna had been elected patron saint of the city and therefore the realisation of this masterpiece by Duccio also provided an important pretext to reiterate the great devotion of the Sienese towards the Virgin. Moreover, the inscription on the step of the throne *"Mater Sancta Dei-sis causa Senis requiei-sis Ducio vita - Te quia pinxit ita"* (Oh, Sainted Mother of God, bestow peace upon Siena, bestow life upon Duccio, inasmuch as he has portrayed you in this manner), seems,

GR. SCHOEI   SIS CAUSA SENS REQUEI SIS OLCIO ITA TE ODIA   PIRXIT ITE

as Enzo Carli points out, *"to reveal the artist's awareness of having created a masterpiece as he claims for himself a particular protection from the Virgin for having portrayed her so (well)"*.

The great altarpiece represents the Madonna enthroned with Child in Majesty surrounded by a celestial court of saints and angels. In the foreground, on their knees, are depicted the four patron saints of Siena interceding on behalf of the city: Ansano, Savino, Crescenzio and Vittore.

● A detail of the ancient back piece of the great pala by Duccio, depicting episodes from the life of Christ and his Passion.

The table was painted both on the front and on the back, as well as on the dais and the upper work. The dais illustrates seven episodes in the life of the Madonna and the Child; whilst the upper work depicts other scenes from the life of the Virgin. On the back of the table, Duccio painted his celebrated cycle depicting the life and Passion of Christ, divided into twenty-six episodes .

The table remained on the high altar, initially under the dome, until 1505, when it was transferred to the altar of San Sebastiano to make way for the ciborium of Vecchietta, removed from the nearby Church of the Santissima Annunziata. It remained there until 1771, when the two faces were divided vertically, then separated into seven parts and transferred to two different chapels from which they were transferred to the Museo dell'Opera in 1878.

Unfortunately, during these distressing episodes, the woodwork was destroyed and the upper work and dais were split up. Some panels were lost while another eight from the dais "emigrated" to various museums in Europe and the United States.

Notwithstanding these mutilations, the Maestà of Duccio is one of the cornerstones of European medieval art. *"Classical retrospection and Byzantine tradition appear marvellously renewed by Duccio in a language in which the most significant element of the new Gothic art*

of the West is by now fully manifested"
(E. Carli).
The fluent rhythm of Duccio, in fact,
manages to melt the residue Byzantine
rigidity with its warm, golden tonalities
and address itself towards the new
current of religious sentiment. The
concrete preciousness of the landscapes
and the harmonious arrangement of the
figures confer even to the most unsettled
and crowded little scenes, great
compositive stability and remarkable
psychological intensity.
The suggestive atmosphere of the room of
Duccio still contains two more wonderful
"surprises": another table by Duccio from
the territory of Siena, the *Madonna di*

Crevole, depicting the Virgin with Child,
and a table, signed and dated by Pietro
Lorenzetti in 1342, representing the
Nativity of the Virgin.
In the second table, the sacred subject
seems to give the painter the pretext for
describing the inside of a medieval
aristocratic house in great detail. In
particular, in the middle, can be seen
the refined coloured tiled floor, the great
bed surrounded by curtains, a trunk
decorated with precious inlays, while
the numerous other objects visible in the
scene seem to further underline the
socially elevated level of this fourteenth
century house, remarkable also for its
concrete spatiality within which the

elegant characters freely move.

In the adjoining room, dedicated to Jacopo della Quercia, five statues attributed to the sculptor (and his assistants), removed from the church of San Martino, are displayed : *Madonna with Child, St Anthony Abate, St Bartholomew, St John the Baptist, St John the Evangelist.*
Further along can be seen, amongst others, some designs referring to the construction of the Cathedral, the façade of the Parish Church of St John, the chapel in Piazza del Campo and a portico that was planned to be built in the great Sienese square in the fifteenth century. Some illuminated, fifteenth century chant books from Santa Maria della Scala are also conserved in the same room.
A beautiful, late fifteenth century, bronzestatue by Fulvio Signorini, depicting *Christ Resurrected*, the reconstruction of the floor of the Cathedral and numerous illuminated graduals and antiphons executed for the Cathedral of Siena can be admired in the stanza del Pavimento (room of the Floor). On the upper floor, instead, in the sala del Tesoro (Treasure Room), one can admire the *reliquary of the head of St Galgano,* in silver relief and enamel, originating from the Abbey of San Galgano, a beautiful silver urn containing the arm of John the Baptist, a gift of the Sienese Pope Pio II, an altar cloth in silk, gold and silver from Santa Maria della Scala, as well as many gold articles of various periods and a wooden *Crucifix* by Giovanni Pisano.
In the middle of the room of the Madonna del Voto di Montaperti (Madonna of the Vow of Montaperti) is situated the celebrated table depicting the Virgin and Child, called the *Madonna with big eyes*, or, more exactly, *Madonna of Grace*, that was replaced with the one that now stands on the altar of the Cappella del Voto (Chapel of the Vow) in the Cathedral.
This painting was executed in around 1230 and the Sienese, on the eve of the battle of Montaperti, pronounced their vows before it in order that the Virgin might protect them during the victorious conflict with the Florentines. Numerous paintings realised on tables, attributed to

This page: The reliquary of the *head of St Galgano,* a masterpiece of Sienese goldsmithery.
Facing page: The nativity of the Virgin by Pietro Lorenzetti (1342).

Ambrogio Lorenzetti, Benedetto di Bindo, Taddeo di Bartolo, Giovanni di Paolo, Sano di Pietro, il Sassetta (Stefano di Giovanni) and other Sienese masters of the fifteenth and sixteenth centuries are arranged along the walls.

The sala dell'Alfieri (room of Alfieri), commemorated by a tablet, displays other important tables and canvases by many artists, including Matteo di Giovanni, Matteo Balducci, Raffaello Vanni, Luca Giordano and il Riccio (Bartolomeo Neroni), but, above all, it contains a masterpiece by Domenico Beccafumi, *St Paul Enthroned*, an early work of the great Mecherino, originating from the demolished Church of San Paolo (St Paul) that used to stand next to the Loggia della Mercanzia. In the next room, as well as the numerous liturgical vestments, one can admire the two-sided standard of the Compagnia di San Giovanni (Company of St John), painted by Francesco Rustici, *Baptism of Christ* and by Rutilio Manetti and his son, Domenico, *Preaching of the Baptist*.

At this point, it's well worth the effort to climb up the rather arduous spiral staircase to the top of the "facciatone" from where one can admire another suggestive panorama of the city and the Sienese countryside and fully comprehend the "Gothic dream" of the New Cathedral.

Leaving Piazza Jacopo della Quercia by means of the doorway through the "facciatone", one enters the shaded and suggestive Via del Poggio that leaves from the church of **St Nicholas on the Rock** and joins up with Via del Capitano, passing in front of the thirteenth century hospice of Monna Agnese (nowadays the Ladies' Technical Institute) and behind Palazzo Marsili.

Turning left into Via del Capitano and continuing towards Via San Pietro, one returns to Piazza Postierla where, on the corner, through the windows of the Quattro Cantoni chemist's shop, can be admired the rigorously classical intaglios of the furniture and fittings designed at the beginning of the last century by the architect Agostino Fantastici (see page 148).

Fantastici, a very interesting character, worked in the fields of architecture, furnishing and fine arts and was also author of many dissertations amongst which the famous *Encyclopaedia of Architecture*.

A little further on, to the left, are two great buildings, Palazzo Buonsignore and Palazzo Brigidi that nowadays house the National Gallery (see page 134).

Palazzo Buonsignori, even though it was built in the fifteenth century, is directly linked to the façade of Palazzo Pubblico, thanks also to the "purist" restorations carried out in the second half of the last century, while **Palazzo Brigidi** (traditionally identified with the ancient residence of the Pannocchieschi family and, consequently, with that of the aristocrat Nello, husband of the famous Pia of the Tolomei family), is of fourteenth century origins, notwithstanding the numerous modifications that continued until its final transformation into a museum in 1932, worthy of housing part of the immense artistic heritage of Siena.

The **Pinacoteca Nazionale (National Gallery)** contains the biggest and most prestigious collection of pictures in gold leaf in the world and wonderfully documents the development of the Sienese school from its first examples in the thirteenth century until its decline in the eighteenth century when the city was no longer able to express an artistic production worthy of its ancient tradition. The oldest works are contained on the second floor (rooms 1 and 2), amongst which paintings by Guido da Siena, the greatest Sienese artist prior to Duccio. Of particular interest in the second room is *St Peter enthroned and six stories* (n. 15), that represents the splendid frontier between ancient art and what was to come from the innovator, Duccio di Buoninsegna. The following rooms (3-4-5-6) contain works by Duccio and his pupils, the first gleams of the precious Gothic dawn in Siena.

The most important painting is definitely the minuscule *Madonna of the Franciscans* (n. 20) where Duccio pays off his remaining debts to Guido da Siena and softens his painting with the tenuous development of the outlines that give an air of solemn monumentality to the scene,

● Palazzo Buonsignori, home of the National Portrait Gallery.
Facing page: The superb "facciatone" of the incompleted "New Cathedral" from which can be enjoyed a wonderful view of the city.

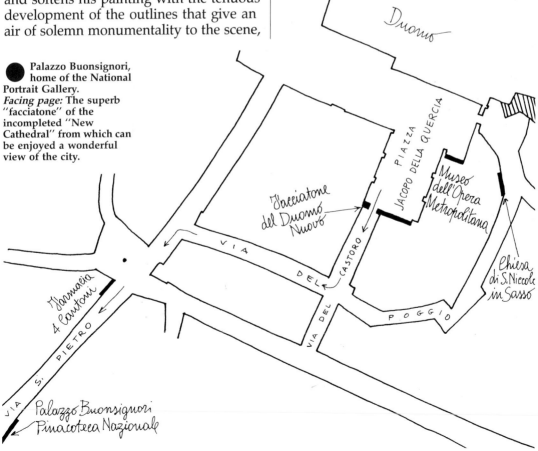

not contrasted, but exalted by the diminutive size of the work. Not to be missed is the *Madonna with Child* (n. 593) by the master from Badia a Isola and the *Crucifixion with St Francis* (n. 34) by Ugolino di Nerio. Tables attributed to Simone Martini and his closest pupils are displayed in the following rooms (6-7). The *Madonna of Mercy,* from Vertine in Chianti, is a remarkable work, recently attributed to the early years of Simone Martini, and the splendid cycle of the *Blessed Agostino Novello and his miracles,* of around 1330, is full of details of medieval life.

● *This page: Madonna with Child* by Simone Martini.
Facing page: A detail of the beautiful pala by Bartolo di Fredi depicting *The Adoration of the Wise Men.*

calligraphic detail as to constitute a rarity even in the refined context of Sienese art. The other masterpieces present in the room are, without doubt, *The Small Majesty* (n. 65) by Ambrogio Lorenzetti, a minute but luminous summary of the level of stylistic and executive perfection reached by Sienese painters in around 1340, and the great pala of the *Annunciation* (n. 88), also by Ambrogio Lorenzetti, from the Palazzo Pubblico. Room 8 contains works by authors active in Siena after the great catastrophe of 1348, the "black death", that mowed down the population and evidently reaped

Room 7 contains, amongst others, one of the masterpieces of Pietro Lorenzetti and of all fourteenth century art, the *Pala of the Carmine)* (1328-29), dismembered in the past but ennobled by the solemn austerity of the Virgin in the central compartment and enriched by the marked naturalistic representations on the articulated dais. The most fascinating paintings in the room are, without doubt, the two splendid landscapes: *A city on the sea* (n. 70) and *A castle on the shore of the lake* (n. 71), until recently attributed to Ambrogio Lorenzetti, so much so that it was supposed they belonged to the long lost "Mappamondo" (Map of the World), documented as being in the sala del Mappamondo in the Palazzo Pubblico up until the beginning of the eighteenth century. A recent convergence of studies brings forward the date of the pictures by a century, and attributes them to il Sassetta. The fact remains that the two tables offer strongly suggestive images, having been realised with such accurate

victims among the ranks of the most famous artists, too. Stupefying for its narrative articulation is the pala of the *Adoration of the Wise Men* (n. 104), a masterpiece by Bartolo di Fredi, active between 1350 and 1410.

The following rooms (9-10-11) display works by Taddeo di Bartolo, including the *Annunciation* that provides an introduction to early Renaissance, Sienese art, so well documented in the following rooms.

These rooms (12-13), in fact, contain authentic masterpieces of a period up till now not sufficiently considered but that is quickly acquiring increasing critical interest. They begin with the splendid *Madonna of Humility* (n. 206), a famous work by Giovanni di Paolo, where the delicate figure of the Virgin, lying on a soft damask cushion, competes for elegance with the orderly development of an almost mythical landscape. The next pictures, *The last Judgement, Heaven and Hell* (n. 172), where the characters

effectively appear to have been lowered into a sacred atmosphere, and the *Presentation of Jesus at the temple* (n° 211), dated 1447, and commissioned by the members of l'Arte dei Pizzicaiuoli (Guild of pork-butchers) as a pala for their altar in Santa Maria della Scala, are also by the same author. But the most important works are, without doubt, the six panels from the lost pala dell'Arte della Lana (Guild of wool-workers), originally kept in the church of San Pellegrino (St Peregrine), that now no longer exists. They depict *the Prophet Elijah* (n° 87), *the Prophet Elisha* (n° 95), the patron saints of Siena *St Vittore, St Ansano, St Savino, St Crescenzio* (n° 168) and *St Gerolamo, St Gregorio, St Ambrogio St Agostino* (n° 169). Not to be missed are the two little scenes, also from the dais of the lost pala, illustrating *The last supper* (n° 167) and *St Anthony beaten by the devils* (n° 166), set in a magical and rarefied morning landscape.

● A view of the National Gallery where the principal works of the old masters are preserved.

The fruits of the mature Sienese Renaissance, works by Francesco di Giorgio, his collaborators and the artists nearest to him, such as Matteo di Giovanni and Neroccio di Bartolomeo, can be admired in the following rooms (14-15). Of particular interest is the very fine *Nativity with St Bernard and St Thomas Aquinas* (n° 437), the only work signed by Francesco.

Rooms 16-17 are almost completely dedicated to Sano di Pietro, a very prolific author, not particularly innovative from a stylistic point of view, but a very correct interpreter of the Sienese figurative tradition and a realistic translator of extraordinary and sacred events in amiable, rustic settings. Worthy of note, by the way, is the beautiful panel from the Palazzo Pubblico depicting *The Virgin appearing to pope Callistus III* (n° 241) where a lively conversation is under way between the Madonna and the Sienese pope, the subject of which is the aim of putting an end to the famine that hit Siena in the middle of the fifteenth century, and

also the picturesque scene of the *Announcement to the shepherds* (n° 262), a late work and executed without a particularly brilliant technique, but remarkable for its numerous and precise realistic references.

The most important work of Domenico di Bartolo, the *Madonna of Humility*, is displayed in the adjoining loggia, signed and dated 1433, proof of the fact that, from an early age, Domenico frequented the great Florentine anticipators of the "perspective revolution".

In the following room (19), next to the *Arliquiera* (n° 204), by Lorenzo di Pietro (il Vecchietta), a rich gallery of Sienese saints, created as a door to the cabinet containing the precious reliquaries of Santa Maria della Scala, the magnificent *Coronation of the Virgin* (n° 440) is displayed, a crowded and spectacular assembly of adoring saints and angels, executed by the previously mentioned Francesco di Giorgio Martini, a great architect, painter and sculptor, in compliance with the humanistic conception that pretended from its interpreters total dedication in all fields of artistic activity.

Walking down to the lower floor, one can admire works of the Sienese sixteenth century. Together with other very worthy authors, paintings of great value by Giovanni Antonio Bazzi (Il Sodoma) from Vercelli and Domenico Beccafumi, the two artists of major importance in Siena in that century, immediately catch the eye.

Among the most remarkable pictures are the detached fresco depicting *Christ at the pillar* (n° 352) and the wonderful pala of the *Deposition* (n° 413), both painted by il Sodoma and rescued from the fires of the Basilica of San Francesco (St Francis). Works of fundamental importance by Beccafumi are also present, such as the *Birth of the Madonna* (n° 405), set in the shadows and animated by livid shafts of light, and the great pala of *St Michael expelling the rebel angels* (n° 423), executed in such a distorted and excited fashion as to appear unacceptably avantguard for the monks of the Carmine who had commissioned it.

On the third floor, the part of the Spannocchi Collection housed in the National Gallery (the rest is to be found in the Civic Museum) has recently been reorganised. This collection, probably the most impressive of the city, contains exceptional masterpieces, such as the *Nativity* (n° 643) by Lorenzo Lotto, signed and dated 1521, the *Sacred Conversation* (n° 500), an early work by Paris Bordone, *San Girolamo* (n° 501) by Albert Dürer and numerous other Italian and foreign works of excellent quality. Finally, worthy of admiration, is the beautiful, solemn portrait of *Elizabeth I of England* (n° 454), from the Governor's Palace, of uncertain attribution, but object of real and proper pilgrimages by numerous foreign visitors.

Back once again in Via San Pietro, on the left, at the top of a short flight of steps, is the **Church of San Pietro alle Scale,** of medieval origins but completely restructured at the beginning of the eighteenth century. Inside is an early polyptych by Ambrogio Lorenzetti and an important altarpiece depicting *The repose during the flight into Egypt,* a

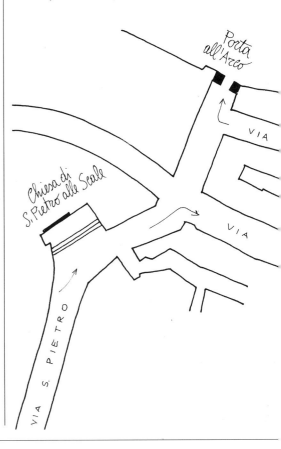

● The beautiful altar
of the Church of
St Anthony of Padua,
oratory of the Contrada
of the Tartuca.

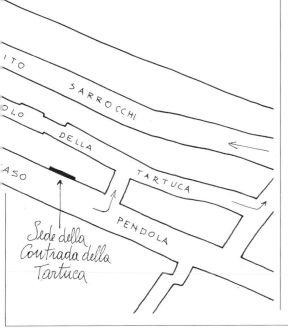

Sede della
Contrada della
Tartuca

masterpiece by Rutilio Manetti.
On the right, at the next cross-roads, is Via
Tommaso Pendola, (formerly Via delle
Murella), in the heart of the Contrada of
the **Tartuca**. Halfway along this street, on
the left, is the Oratory of Sant'Antonio da
Padova (St Anthony of Padua), entirely
built with the money and labour of the
members of the Contrada who erected it
at the end of the seventeenth century from
a design by Giacomo Franchini. Worthy of
interest is a bas-relief executed in 1686 by
Giovanni Antonio Mazzuoli depicting *The
appearance of the Madonna to St Anthony*.
Next to the church is the characteristic
museum of the Tartuca, rich, like all the
other contradas, in numerous war
mementoes, palios, costumes, vestments,
etc.. Not to be missed is a beautiful sketch
by the purist painter Luigi Mussini,
depicting a page of the Contrada.
Further down the street, on the left,
a few yards after the Oratory, is Vicolo
della Tartuca (a cul-de-sac on the left)
which leads down into the parallel Via
Tito Sarrocchi (formerly Via dei Maestri)

in which the house where the artist Domenico Beccafumi once lived stands.

At the end of the street, on the right, Porta all'Arco (an opening in the ancient city walls) leads to Prato di Sant'Agostino, from where one can enjoy a suggestive view of the area of San Martino.

On the right, under the great colonnade in front of the Collegio Tolomei (Tolomei College), designed by Agostino Fantastici, is the entrance to the **Church of St Augustine.** Of thirteenth century origins, the imposing structure of this church has undergone numerous and substantial modifications over the centuries, the most important of which was carried out following the ruinous fire of 1747, to such an extent that the actual internal configuration has completely covered the original medieval structure. Parts of the original walls are still recognisable on the outside of the apse. The violent fire that broke out inside the church practically destroyed the building. Immediately afterwards, on 17th July, 1747, a design was made by the great Luigi Vanvitelli who had been especially sent from Rome by the General of the Augustinians, and *"the foundations for the columns that were to support the new face of the Church of Sant'Agostino began to be dug, the work being executed by the religious order for a cost of ten thousand scudi"*. The work was entrusted to the master masons Sebastiano and Giuseppe Minocci. In 1748, Vanvitelli came to Siena to see how work on the building was progressing; in 1755, the restoration, after many difficulties, was finally finished. Sant'Agostino is one of the lesser known achievements of Vanvitelli, but, all the same, even though partly compromised by later modifications, it is a work of great spatiality and balance. In fact, one can still appreciate the restrained and radiant shapes of the moulded parts, taken from a baroque repertoire that, far from being oppressive in its details, is perfectly appropriate as regards its spatial substance. Vanvitelli

● **The imposing structure of the apse of the church of St Agostino.**

was evidently not at all satisfied with the work as in one of his letters he declared himself to be most displeased *"that the Church of Sant'Agostino was entrusted to ignorant builders who have mauled it so much that one can hardly see that an architect has designed it. One of my pupils who passed through Siena gave me all this information"*. The altars and the chapels of the church preserve tables, canvases, frescoes and sculptures by numerous important artists. Of particular interest is the *Crucifixion* by Pietro Perugino, the canvas depicting the *Adoration of the Shepherds* by Francesco Romanelli, the *Baptism of Constantine* painted by the "baroquesque" Francesco Vanni in 1587, the canvas representing *The temptation of St Anthony*, realised by Rutilio Manetti, and the high altar of Flaminio del Turco with the two beautiful angels on the sides, sculpted by the Mazzuoli family at the end of the seventeenth century. Also of great interest is the recent discovery of the frescoes of the Cappella Bichi (Bichi Chapel), attributed to Francesco di Giorgio and Luca Signorelli. Of equal interest is the fresco of Ambrogio Lorenzetti depicting *The Madonna enthroned with Child and Saints,*

conserved in the Cappella Piccolomini (Piccolomini Chapel), which also contains the beautiful *Adoration of the Wise Men* realised by il Sodoma in the mid 1530's. This chapel also contained the table depicting the *Slaughter of the Innocents* by Matteo di Giovanni, executed in 1482, nowadays displayed in the rooms of the Civic Museum. The previously mentioned, famous table by Simone Martini, depicting the *Blessed Agostino Novelli*, actually housed in the National Gallery, was originally kept in the Church of Sant'Agostino.

The Convent of the Augustinians, next to the church, was almost completely transformed at the end of the eighteenth century and, since the first half of the last century, it houses the Collegio Tolomei. To the left of Prato di Sant'Agostino is Via Sant'Agata, along which can be seen the faade of San Giuseppe (St Joseph), the oratory of the **Captain Contrada of the Onda**. The Guild of Carpenters paid for

Chiesa di S. Giuseppe
Sede della Contrada dell'Onda

FONTANELLA
DI

VIA G. DUPRÈ

Bottino di Fontanella

VIA

Arco di S. Agata

VIA S. AGATA

PRATO DI S. AGOSTINO

Basilica di S. Agostino

Porta dell'Arco

the construction of this church which began in 1521. The work was first entrusted to Baldassare Giusti and proceeded very slowly. Only in 1653 was the final project of the façade defined by Benedetto Giovannelli, who, with sagacious chromatic and compositive balance, modulated by bricks and travertine, managed to perfectly reconcile the two orders of the faade and the lateral scrolls. A bust of the Saint by Tommaso Redi is situated at the centre, while the great sixteenth century dome was inspired by Peruzzi and attributed

to a pupil of this great Sienese architect. The oratory contains a beautiful, early eighteenth century, wooden railing, numerous objects in silver, cloth, ceramics, plaster statues, canvases and frescoes of the seventeenth and eighteenth centuries as well as a late sixteenth century *Madonna with Child and Angels*, attributed to Francesco Bartalini.

The crypt, headquarters and museum of the Onda preserves the palios (that of 16th August, 1985, painted by Leonardo Cremonini, is of particular beauty), costumes and numerous mementoes of the Contrada. Of special interest are the plaster casts of many works of the nineteenth century sculptor Giovanni Duprè, Sienese and member of the Onda.

Tiredness permitting, it's worthwhile going down the steeply sloping Via Giovanni Duprè, strolling along the medieval lanes that open up on the left, going back up the same street towards the Arco di Sant'Agata (Arch of St Agatha), from where a beautiful view of the Tower of the Mangia can be enjoyed, and then going down the street in front, Via Fontanella (it's advisable to use the steps on the left). This street runs along the balza di Sant'Agostino (the precipice of St Augustine) on one side, and the valley of Porta Giustizia, that penetrates with its vegetable gardens almost up to the Palazzo Pubblico, on the other. At the end of the slope, on the right, a long flight of steps leads to a medieval well next to which is the entrance to a branch of the "bottini" (the famous medieval underground aqueduct). The bottino di

Fontanella is particularly suggestive for its walls that are almost completely covered with white lime deposits (permission to visit the bottini can be obtained from the Town Hall Technical Offices).

The Strada di Fontanella joins up with Via Pier Andrea Matioli, just a few yards away from the fourteenth century walls at Porta Tufi.

Outside the walls, to the left, on the site of the medieval Convent of San Benedetto (St Benedict), built by the monks of Oliveto and completely destroyed at the beginning of the last century, lies the **(Monumental Cemetery of Mercy)**. The project, by Lorenzo Doveri, was realised between 1835 and 1843, and the complex was later amplified by Giuseppe Partini in 1872. The chapels of the principal families of the city contained inside the Misericordia constitute one of the most important nuclei of nineteenth century Sienese artistic production. As well as the famous marble *Pietà* by Giovanni Duprè (1866, cappella Bichi Ruspoli Forteguerri), frescoes, sculptures, canvases and decorations by Alessandro Franchi,

● The baroque façade of the church of St Giuseppe, oratory of the Captain Contrada of the Onda.

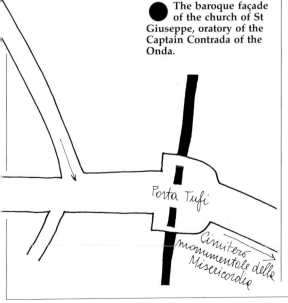

Porta Tufi

Cimitero monumentale della Misericordia

Tito Sarrocchi, Pietro Aldi, Cesare Maccari, Gaetano Marinelli, Paride Pascucci and many other interpreters of Sienese purism, are, in fact, conserved here.

Re-entering the city walls through Porta dei Tufi and going down Via Pier Andrea Mattioli, on the left can be seen the sober façade of the **Church of the Magdalene**, realised by Agostino Fantastici in around 1840. Of sixteenth century origins, the church was completely transformed at the beginning of the nineteenth century; some interesting furnishings and a canvas by Raffaello Vanni depicting *Jesus and the Magdalene* can be seen inside. The convent, part of the same building, has been gradually transformed and is now a secondary school. A few yards further on, still on the left, in the ancient convent of the Camaldolesian monks, is the prestigious **Accademia dei Fisiocritici**.

This Academy of the Sciences was founded in 1691 by an illustrious scientist, Pirro Maria Gabrielli, in the Hospital of Santa Maria della Scala. After a short while, the Academy was transferred to the rooms of the Studio Senese and a hundred years later, at the beginning of the nineteenth century, it was moved once more to the ex-convent of the Camaldolesians, also called "della Rosa". Of medieval origins, its original structure was radically transformed from the fifteenth century on, being modified according to the changing requirements of its occupants. Nowadays the Accademia dei Fisiocritici, apart from carrying out an intense activity of research, houses numerous collections that have given origin to the

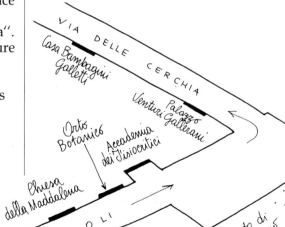

The Museum of the Accademia dei Fisiocritici contains large mineral, paleontological and zoological collections.
Facing page: The Botanical Gardens preserve the rarest and most important species of plants and flowers from all over the world.

Geomineralogical and Paleontological Museum and the **Zoological Museum.** The Fisiocritici also possesses an important library containing several thousand rare volumes of great scientific interest and publishes a periodical containing the results of the work of the Academy.
The chiesa di San Mustiola (Church of St Mustiola), nowadays used purely for didactic purposes lies next to the building. Of fifteenth century structure, but radically transformed in the eighteenth century, it still preserves its altars and some interesting plaster work of the same period, attributed to the Mazzuoli family and the Cremoni brothers, as well as some canvases, including a sixteenth century painting by Giomo del Sodoma depicting the *Madonna with Child and Saints*.
The space around the Accademia dei Fisiocritici also includes the university

Botanical Gardens (see page 154), the ancient "giardino dei semplici" (garden of the simples), also situated, since at least the end of the sixteenth century, in the Hospital of Santa Maria della Scala. In fact, in 1588, the Studio Senese set up a professorship for "the better understanding of Simples", reserved to the students, to allow them to get a first hand view of medicinal plants.
The Botanical garden was transferred to this site in the middle of the nineteenth century and nowadays carries out research in a vast area in which the rarest species of plants and flowers from all over the world are gathered in three great sectors.
Returning up the street to Prato di Sant'Agostino and bearing right, one enters Via della Cerchia where, right at the beginning, on the left, is **Palazzo Venturi Gallerani**, inside which are housed, amongst others, some interesting frescoes by Luigi Ademollo, depicting historical and mythological scenes realised by this Lombard painter during the last ten years of the eighteenth century. Further along, on the same side, is another interesting palace called **Casa Bambagini Galletti,** designed by Agostino Fantastici in around 1840. The street ends up in Piano dei Mantellini near the Arco di Santa Lucia (Arch of St Lucia), right in front of the **Church of St Nicholas and Lucia.**
The building, of medieval origins, was completely rebuilt at the end of the sixteenth century and frescoed at the

beginning of the following century by some Sienese artists, including Sebastiano Folli, *Triumph of St Lucia.* Of great interest is the painting on the high altar, a work by Francesco Vanni (about 1606), depicting the *Martyrdom of St Lucia.* Particularly significant are two great, late fifteenth century statues depicting *St Lucia and St Nicholas,* as well as four beautiful stretcher heads, realised by Rutilio Manetti in 1625 and kept in the side chapel adjoining the church *Madonna and Son, The Pity of Christ, St Nicholas, St Lucia.*

A little further on to the left is Via San Marco where, after a hundred yards or so, lies the chiesa dei Santi Pietro e Paolo (Church of St Peter and Paul), that in 1814 became the oratory of the **Contrada of the Chiocciola.**
The Church and Monastery of San Paolo (St Paul) are of medieval origins even if the actual structures are a result of

numerous seventeenth century modifications carried out by artists such as Flaminio del Turco and Giovanni Antonio Mazzuoli who worked on them for years. The building, whose entrance is protected by an iron gate, blends in perfectly well with the medieval surroundings, and is intelligently recessed with respect to the street, so as to create a space in front of it that allows one to view the church with the right perspective. A small fountain, characterised by a bronze figure of a child riding on a snail,

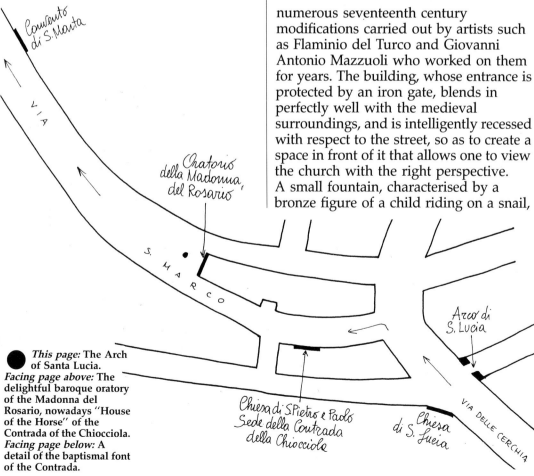

This page: The Arch of Santa Lucia.
Facing page above: The delightful baroque oratory of the Madonna del Rosario, nowadays "House of the Horse" of the Contrada of the Chiocciola.
Facing page below: A detail of the baptismal font of the Contrada.

is located in this space in front of the church. The children of the members of the Chiocciola are baptised into the Contrada with the water of this fountain (the rite is different from the religious one; each contrada, in fact, has its own fountain where, during the festival of the patron saint of the contrada, the Prior baptises the children born in that year).

The luminous interior of the church, built in the form of a Greek cross, houses many

paintings of the seventeenth and eighteenth centuries, among which, the exceptionally interesting *St Francesca of Rome* by Ventura Salimbeni. The most important work, however, is the great sixteenth century table on the high altar, painted by Andrea del Brescianino and depicting the *Coronation of the Virgin and Saints.* The museum, arranged on two floors, displays costumes, palios and numerous mementoes regarding the life of the Contrada, as well as a large collection of vestments, silver, furnishings, sketches, and a beautifully inlaid, gilded, wooden book-stand made at the end of the seventeenth century.

A few yards further along Via San Marco is the **Church of the Madonna of the Rosary**, ex-oratory of the Chiocciola and now the "casa del cavallo", the building where the horse of the Contrada is kept during the period of the Palio.

In April, 1655, the Chiocciola decided to build an oratory, at its own expense, in a house belonging to the Contrada, situated right at the cross-roads of San Marco, in front of the well bearing the same name. The work was finished quickly, but at the beginning of the eighteenth century (1722), the Contrada decided to build a new façade, entrusting the work to the Cremoni brothers, plasterers from Lombardy, who were active for many years in Siena. It is one of the rare examples of decidedly baroque architecture to be found in Siena.

On the right-hand side of Via San Marco, just before the gate, lies the great building containing the **Convent of St Martha.** The building, of medieval origins, as is the adjoining church, was transformed in the sixteenth century, especially in the part that runs along the side of the street. The internal courtyard contains some rather fragmentary frescoes depicting *Scene di vita eremetica (scenes from a hermit's life)* attributed to painters who were active at the end of the fourteenth century and the beginning of the fifteenth, such as Benedetto di Bindo. The church houses frescoes and canvases by some of the principal Sienese artists of the first half of the seventeenth century, such as

Francesco Vanni with his *The Coronation of the Virgin,* and Sebastiano Folli and Petro Sorri, responsible for the frescoes on the ceiling. In the choir, nowadays the sacristy, some fourteenth century frescoes have recently been restored, one of which, *the Burial of St Martha,* of extremely high quality, has rightly been attributed to the great Simone Martini. The others, realised at the beginning of the following century, are of inferior quality, but equally interesting.

On the left of Porta San Marco, at the beginning of Via delle Sperandie, one can enjoy a beautiful view of the Sienese countryside. The **Convent of the Transfixed Nuns,** commonly known as "le Sperandie", is situated after the bend, about a hundred yards further on. This building, also of medieval origins, has been completely transformed over the centuries and used as barracks, offices and university residences. The church was enlarged in 1655 and the choir was rebuilt in 1704. On that occasion, the great bridge that can be seen from the street was constructed. Some canvases, two of which are by Sebastiano Folli, *The Madonna and Saints* and Alessandro Casolani, *the Delivery of the Keys* are preserved inside.

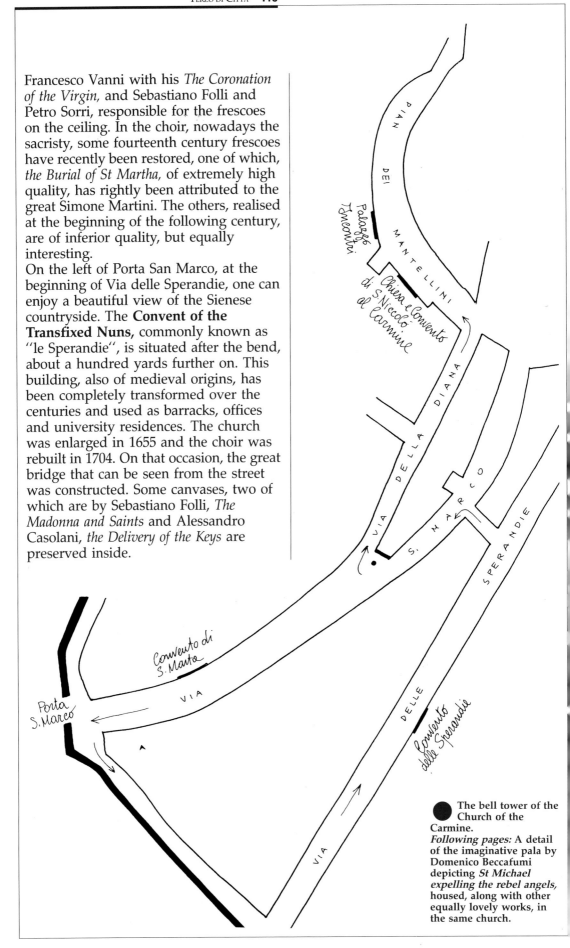

● The bell tower of the Church of the Carmine.
Following pages: A detail of the imaginative pala by Domenico Beccafumi depicting *St Michael expelling the rebel angels,* housed, along with other equally lovely works, in the same church.

Back in Via San Marco, to the right, next to the Madonna del Rosario, is the entrance to Via della Diana, which ends up in Piano dei Mantellini, where the great building containing the convent and church of the Carmelite monks stands. It was probably in the first half of the fourteenth century that the monks started to build the existing **church of St Nicholas** and the adjoining convent, an undertaking that, due to many difficulties, continued for about two centuries. The building was later progressively transformed and partially modified (the convent was used as a barracks until about 1960 and now houses various university institutes). Nowadays, San Niccolò al Carmine (St Nicholas at the Carmine) is also used by the Contrada of the Pantera for its religious functions. Notwithstanding the vicissitudes of its structure, the church still contains numerous and important works of art. One of the most beautiful works of the Sienese artist Alessandro Casolani, depicting *The Martyrdom of St Bartholomew,* painted in 1604, is hung on the left-hand wall near the high altar. A table painted at the beginning of the

sixteenth century by Girolamo del Pacchia, depicting *The Ascension,* one of the most convincing works of this artist, is also preserved here.
Another beautiful canvas by Francesco Vanni, especially realised in 1593 to hold the thirteenth century table representing the *Madonna of the Mantellini,* actually substituted by a photographic reproduction, depicts *St Stephen, Albert, Martha and Catherine of Alexandria,* and is placed to the right of the high altar. Halfway down the nave, on the same side, one of the most beautiful Sienese tables of the sixteenth century, painted by Domenico Beccafumi, *St Michael expelling the rebel angels,* is preserved. According to Vasari, this is a "revised" version of the previous one realised by Beccafumi depicting the same subject, originally in the Hospital of Santa Maria della Scala and now in the National Gallery. The Carmelite monks refused to accept it as they considered it *"unbecoming"* due to *"that fluctuating confusion of bodies, without a preplanned spatial framework"* (A.M. Guiducci, 1990). The Cappella del Sacramento (Chapel of the Sacrament), on the right hand side, contains a table depicting the *Nativity of the Virgin* by il Sodoma and a fresco by the same author representing the *Eternal Father.*
Other frescoes of the first half of the fifteenth century are preserved on an altar near to the table of Beccafumi, while seventeenth century canvases by Dioisio Montorselli, *Coronation of St Theresa* and Stefano Volpi, *Crucifixion* are hung on the walls. The convent, too, contains numerous canvases of the seventeenth and eighteenth centuries, including one of great interest, realised by Rutilio and Domenico Manetti, depicting the *Madonna with the Blessed Franco da Grotti* (P. Torriti, 1988).
The Piano dei Mantellini (the name is probably derived from the Carmelite monks who usually wore a short mantle over their tunics) is surrounded by various interesting buildings, such as the exquisitely neo-classical **Palazzo Incontri**, realised in the very first years of the last century by Serafino Belli,

abounding in elegant statues, niches and gigantic Romanic lesenas. Also of interest is the sixteenth century façade of the former **church of the Conservatory of the Derelitte**, attributed to il Riccio (A. Cornice).

The front of the sixteenth century **Palazzo Celsi Pollini,** one of the most beautiful works attributed to Baldassare Peruzzi, is situated right opposite the Carmine.

The building also runs along the right hand side of Via San Quirico and terminates right next to the **Church of St Ansano**.

Tradition has it that this was the site of the prison where the martyred Saint, protector of the city, was held (fourth century). The actual building, comprising the twelfth century tower and the fifteenth century church is of particular interest

● The ancient church of St Ansano next to the tower where tradition has it that the patron Saint of Siena was imprisoned. *Facing page:* the fifteenth century *Madonna of the Almond,* preserved in the Museum of the Contrada of the Pantera.

due to its elegant Renaissance windows and contains numerous frescoes, some of which are of the fifteenth century, depicting *The Adoration of the Wise Men* and *St Ansano,* attributed to Priamo della Quercia by Piero Torriti.

Next to the church of Sant'Ansano is the **Institute of St Theresa**, a neo-Renaissance work by Giuseppe Partini (about 1880), housing a series of paintings by the principal purist artists, depicting *Stories from the life of St Theresa.*

Shortly after, on the left-hand side of Via San Quirico, lies the **church**

dedicated to **St Quirico and Giulitta.**
It is a thirteenth century building, mostly rebuilt at the end of the sixteenth century, although numerous elements allow one to fully perceive its medieval origins. At the beginning of the seventeenth century, some of the major Sienese artists frescoed the ceiling and the walls and left some interesting canvases. Worthy of admiration are the *Pietà* by Alessandro Casolani, the fresco in the apse by Ventura Salimbeni depicting the *The Martyrdom of St Quirico e Giulitta*, and the canvases by Francesco Vanni *Christ at the pillar* and Pietro Sori *The crown of thorns.*

The area in front of the church opens out on the right towards the rooms of the Society of the **Contrada of the Pantera**, which boasts a beautiful view over the roofs in one of the highest points of the city. The Museum of the Pantera is situated a few yards further along Via San Quirico and preserves, together with mementoes, palios and some interesting liturgical vestments and furnishings, a fifteenth century statue of the highest quality belonging to the school of Jacopo della Quercia, called the *Madonna of the Almond*. It is a polychrome, wooden sculpture, (regrettably repainted in the last century) taken from the destroyed

Castelvecchio

church of the Arte della Lana, once situated in the square nowadays called Piazza Indipendenza), depicting the *Madonna with Child* gripping the fruit in his left hand.
At the end of Via San Quirico is the Madonna del Corvo, a place where, according to popular tradition, a crow fell in 1348 and spread the plague in the city. A tabernacle with a fresco by Giovanni Antonio Bassi (il Sodoma), depicting *Christ dead in the arms of the Madonna* was placed on the left-hand wall.

Before entering Via Stalloreggi, it's worthwhile turning right towards the hill of Castelvecchio, one of the oldest settlements of the city, characterised by a thick mass of houses, lanes and small medieval courtyards that have not undergone substantial modifications and are, therefore, of great interest to students of architecture and town-planning.
Returning to the Madonna del Corvo, the street to the left terminates in Due Porte, another opening in the ancient city walls from which can still be reached Piano dei Mantellini (for many centuries now, only one of the two great archways is accessible).
Inside Due Porte can be admired an early sixteenth century tabernacle depicting the *Madonna with Child and St Giovannino and Catherine of Siena* while, on the left, a tablet indicates the house where Duccio di Buoninsegna was supposed to have lived.
Outside the arch of Due Porte (on the right) is located another tabernacle representing the *Madonna with Child*.
It is an early fourteenth century fresco of great quality but, unfortunately, very

faded.

The street opposite is called Via Paolo Mascagni and terminates in the **city cemetery of the Laterino,** a few hundred yards outside Porta Laterina and from which one can return to Porta San Marco along a road that runs at the foot of the walls.

To the left of Due Porte is the Fosso di Sant'Ansano, a street where a tablet commemorates the first attempt to martyr the saint and patron of Siena who, according to the hagiography, got out unharmed from a boiling cauldron here. The saint was later beheaded on the banks of the River Arbia, a few miles away from Siena.

At the end of this street, dominated by the imposing structure of the back of Santa Maria della Scala and from where one can admire the suggestive view of the small valley enclosed by the city walls, is situated Piazza della Selva. The historical headquarters and museum of the **Contrada of the Selva** are in the Renaissance church of San Sebastiano in Vallepiatta.

The elegant profiles of Peruzzi culminate in the sober circular contours of the tambour that are a direct recollection of the lessons of the great Francesco di Giorgio. The inside of the ex-convent of the Jesuit nuns is in the form of a Greek cross and its walls show off numerous and admirable frescoes by various early seventeenth century Sienese interpreters, such as Giovanpaolo Pisani, *Presentation of Mary* and Pietro Sorri *Coronation of the Virgin.* Two fifteenth century tables, attributed to Benvenuto di Giovanni and the school of Cozzarelli, are located on the sides of the high altar. Another two seventeenth century canvases by Rutilio Manetti, *Crucifixion,* and Astolfo

Petrazzi, *The Epiphany,* ornate the beautiful side altars. The second painting, of excellent quality, has recently been restored and has allowed the Contrada della Selva to rearrange and make usable the numerous and precious sacred furnishings that are jealously preserved, as in all the contradas, in the sacristy and in the oratory. In the museum, as well as the usual, numerous mementoes, the palios won by the Contrada are displayed, among which the one painted by Mino Maccari in 1970 is of particular beauty.

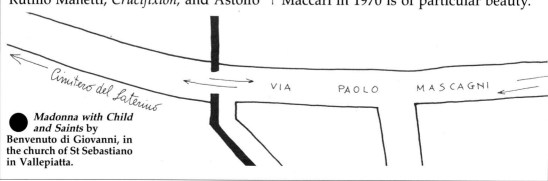

Madonna with Child and Saints by Benvenuto di Giovanni, in the church of St Sebastiano in Vallepiatta.

Right under the vast buttresses of the Hospital is the ancient Vicolo della balie that leads from the square back to Piazza del Duomo.

But it's worthwhile going along Via Franciosa, as halfway down on the left can be admired Via di Vallepiatta that leads to the steep slope of Via del Costone, an area that is especially evocative of Santa Caterina, and from which one can see the wild ravine upon which the majestic Basilica of San Domenico rises. Further along Via Franciosa, on the left, is the dark Vicolo delle Carrozze, a narrow and suggestive example of an uneven, broken, medieval, city street, dotted with rampant arches, small vegetable gardens and views towards the valley.

Via Franciosa opens out into Piazza San Giovanni where a flight of stairs leads to the entrance to the baptistery.

The **Parish Church of St John**, rectangular in shape, is subdivided into three naves by two great pillars, the vaults of which were frescoed by Lorenzo di Pietro (Il Vecchietta) and other fifteenth century artists, while, in the middle, is situated the baptismal font, one of the greatest masterpieces of Renaissance Italian sculpture, realised by Jacopo della Quercia, Lorenzo Ghiberti, Donatello and other distinguished artists.

Work on the baptistery began in the 1310's, shortly after the apse of the Cathedral had been lengthened (San Giovanni is situated right under the last two spans of the Cathedral), and terminated, under the direction of

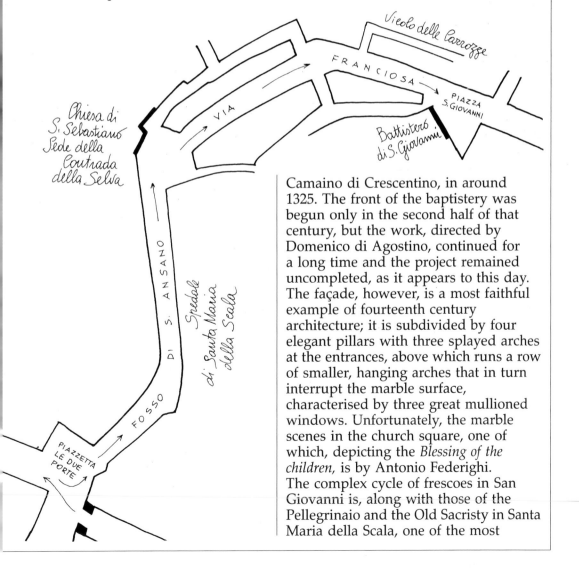

Camaino di Crescentino, in around 1325. The front of the baptistery was begun only in the second half of that century, but the work, directed by Domenico di Agostino, continued for a long time and the project remained uncompleted, as it appears to this day. The façade, however, is a most faithful example of fourteenth century architecture; it is subdivided by four elegant pillars with three splayed arches at the entrances, above which runs a row of smaller, hanging arches that in turn interrupt the marble surface, characterised by three great mullioned windows. Unfortunately, the marble scenes in the church square, one of which, depicting the *Blessing of the children*, is by Antonio Federighi.

The complex cycle of frescoes in San Giovanni is, along with those of the Pellegrinaio and the Old Sacristy in Santa Maria della Scala, one of the most

important pictorial accomplishments
of fifteenth century Siena.

The portions of the central vault, in front
of the entrance, depicting *four Apostles* are
attributed, as previously mentioned, to il
Vecchietta (around 1450), while the two
side vaults with *Saints and Apostles* were
probably realised by Agostino di
Marsiglio from Bologna. The other
three vaults that respectively represent:
the *Articles of the Creed*, on the vaults, and
Male and female heads and *Figures of
children and saints*, under the arches,
are also by il Vecchietta.

The Assumption of the Virgin is depicted on
the central arch while, underneath, can
be admired scenes representing *The road
to Calvary, the flagellation of Christ* and *The
Annunciation*. The "catino", the final
vault, divided into three parts, depicts,
at the centre, the *Crucifixion* with
the Bewailed at the sepulchre and *The
oration in the Garden* by Michele di Matteo
on the sides.

The two end walls depict, on the right,
The washing of the feet by Pietro di
Francesco Orioli (around 1490), and
on the left, *the Miracles of St Anthony*,
three frescoes by Benvenuto di Giovanni
(around 1460).

The great hexagonal font in the middle
can rightly be considered a perfect
synthesis of early Renaissance Italian
sculpture.

It took almost twenty years to finish from
when the Director of Works in the
Cathedral, Caterino di Corsino,
commissioned the marble part of the font
to Sano di Matteo, Jacopo di Corso and
Nanni di Jacopo in 1416.

The six gilded bronze panels depicting
The life of the Baptist are interposed with
statues representing *the Virtues*, also in
gilded bronze.

The scenes begin on the right with the
*Angel announcing the birth of the Baptist to
Zacharias*, by Jacopo della Quercia. The
following two scenes, by Giovanni di
Turino, represent the *Birth* and the
Preaching of the Baptist. The *Baptism
of Christ* follows, a work by Lorenzo
Ghiberti, who also realised the *Capture
of the Baptist*. The final, very famous panel
is by Donatello and represents the

*Banquet of Herod, "an extremely intense,
disturbing and dramatic creation that reveals,
at the same time, a rigorous perspective
structure of fundamental importance"*
(E. Carli).

Two of the six gilded bronze statues,
Faith and Hope, are also by Donatello.
The others are by Goro di Neroccio,
Fortitude and
Giovanni di Turino
*Justice, Providence
and Charity*.

● **The steep steps
that lead from
the Baptistery to Piazza
del Duomo above.**

The five bas-reliefs
in the niches of the
great tabernacle,
representing the
figures of the *Prophets* and that of
the *Baptist*, placed at the top, are by
Jacopo della Quercia, while the door
depicting the *Madonna with Child* is by
Turini (the version by Donatello was
refused by the Opera del Duomo). Two
of the six elegant bronze angels are also
by Donatello.

Outside the Baptistery, on the right,
is located the majestic Renaissance
building that once belonged to Pandolfo
Petrucci (see page 152).

Unfortunately, very little remains of the
ancient splendour of this suggestive
palace that was probably built by
Giacomo Cozzarelli (early sixteenth
century). In fact, as well as the numerous
modifications that have compromised its
spatial unity, the numerous paintings
that the building once contained have
slowly "emigrated" towards museums
and collections all over the world. A few
of them, luckily, have ended up in the
National Gallery of Siena.

At the beginning of the sixteenth
century, the residence of the
"Magnifico" was decorated by il
Pinturicchio (Bernardo di Betto), Luca
Signorelli, Girolamo Genga, Domenico
Beccafumi, as well as Cozzarelli, who
realised, amongst other works, the
elegant bronze rings (nowadays
preserved in the National Gallery) that
wonderfully embellished the faade in
Via dei Pellegrini.

In the same street, to the left, is another
prestigious sixteenth century palace that
once belonged to the Aristocrat Marcello

Agostini. Ownership then passed to Bindi Sergardi and finally to the Casini Casuccini family.

An extraordinary cycle is preserved on the vault of a room on the first floor, realised in around 1525 by Domenico Beccafumi, depicting episodes from ancient history and mythology. Shortly after, on the strength of this work, the artist was commissioned to paint the great vault of the room of Concistory in Palazzo Pubblico with a similar subject.

As has been confirmed in the recent study that accompanied the exhibition dedicated to the great Sienese mannerist (1990), the two cycles *"both share a geometrical pattern rich in illusory devices, both have an allegorical-paradigmatic setting, with subjects inspired by episodes and characters of ancient history"*.

At the end of this street is the Costarella dei Barbieri, right in front of the Campo, the starting point of the first of our three itineraries. ●

● *This page:* A bronze ring from the Palace of the Magnifico.
Facing page: The extraordinary baptismal font of the Church of St John the Baptist was realised by the most famous interpreters of the Italian Renaissance.

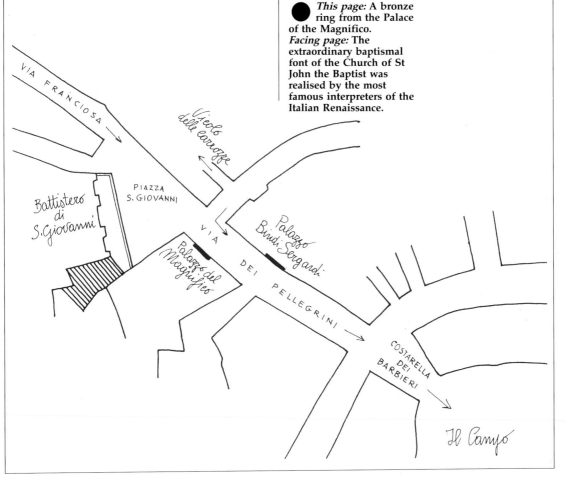

THE CATHEDRAL

● The balanced compositive structure of the Cathedral allows it to insert its powerful structure with grace and measure into the crowded urban surroundings.

"Even from afar, the Cathedral and the Palazzo Pubblico appear to us as the two emblems of spiritual and temporal power. The Cathedral, peaceful and majestic, dominates from the heights; it is covered in strips of light and dark marble, and this gives it a severe, cold and luminous appearance, standing out from the reddish colour of the city" (T. Burckhardt, 1988).

The Cathedral, like the Campo, is a cherished and famous place for the people of Siena. Just as the Campo is the setting for the outburst of the most spontaneous passions and sentiments, so too is the Cathedral, the place that traditionally inspires peaceful meditation and humble homage to the Madonna, to whom the city dedicated its glorious Cathedral.

Even in the most dramatic situations, the Sienese have always managed to overcome their hates and fears in this aulic and sacred space, recompacting souls and reacquiring awareness of a dignity that has never been extinguished, and faith in a future worthy of that of the past.

The story begins with a sacred representation, the procession of candles and riches, that forced the aristocracy and the middle classes to sacrifice a part of their power and wealth to the Madonna and to the city of whom She is queen, not in a reserved manner but theatrically, as if it were a scene directed by a shrewd producer. Even at the dawn of the most glorous day in the history of Siena, Montaperti, the Cathedral was chosen as the source of an impossible hope, pursued, however, with confidence and genuine insistence.

To penetrate the mystery that surrounds the origins of the Cathedral of Siena, one must start from the high Middel Ages, an era in which, according to a fragment of a parchment of 591, the bishop lived on the hill of Castelvecchio, the oldest nucleus of the city. Erudite scholars of the eighth century such as Giovanni Antonio Pecci and Vittorio Lusini, more recently, indicate instead the area of the Tufi as the seat of the diocese, in the second half of the eighth century. A few years later the construction of a new church was begun, coinciding with the removal of the body of San Crescenzio, one of the four patron Saints of Siena. The church with the

adjoining bishop's palace of which mention has been made, is the one that from 913 onwards was called Santa Maria and that was to be oriented towards Via del Capitano, in the area lying between the actual faade of Santa Maria della Scala and that of the Cathedral. A baptismal font was also located in the same area and was still in use in the twelfth century. A significant date for the history of the Cathedral was 1058, the year in which the Council that deposed the antipapa Benedetto X and elected pope Niccolò II, until then Bishop of Florence, was held.

As Enzo Carli points out, it was probably on this occasion that it was decided to build a new church in the present day position. using the previous one during the execution of the work.

Tradition has it that the Cathedral was consecrated by Rolando Bandinelli Paparoni, the Sienese pope Alexander III on 18th November, 1179. Still today, every year on that day, a standard bearing the papal emblems is lowered in the presbytery to commemorate the event. Specialised documentary investigations seem to confirm that the consecration of the Cathedral took place around that date, as the Spedale that previously had been qualified as a *"Xenodocxhium de canonica"*, in 1188 began to be called *"ante ecclesiam Santae Mariae Virginis"*, which signifies that the faade of the Cathedral was already pointed in its present day direction.

In fact, a few years later, documents talk of the Spedale as being *"ante gradus maioris Acclesiae"*,

meaning that it was located in front of the steps built to enter the Cathedral, still to be seen today.

The great "civic building site" of the Cathedral was directed, right from the start, by the Opera of Santa Maria by means of three "builders", directly nominated by the city government, principal financier of the great building.

In fact, the Consiglio della Campana (the Council of the bell) was called in to check the accounts and the various payments as a precautionary measure. The "builders" were initially chosen from among the canons of the Cathedral while, from 1258 up until the end of that century, they were sought for amongst the Cistercian monks of the Abbey of San Galgano who enjoyed such fame as good administrators that they were entrusted with one of the most important offices of the Sienese state: the Biccherna. The "builders" entrustd th work to first class workmen, those masters masons who totally dedicated their professionality and often their lives to this extraordinary undertaking. As part of their contract, the City government expected from them total dedication to their job, reserving the right to authorise them to absent themselves, even for short periods, from the site. The contract envisaged that they were to carry out their duties as *"if they were working for themselves"* and the magnificent result proves that they fully honoured their pledge.

The enormous building, with its varied and elegant use of two colours, was completed halfway through the thirteenth century. And it was from then on that the greatest artists of all time begin the centuries long task of enriching the Cathedral of Siena, finally transforming into a kind of enormous treasure chest, full of the finest and most appreciated masterpieces.

Probably, nowhere else in the world is it possible to follow with such detail the development of Italian art, especially that of sculpture. From the solid plasticism of Nicola Pisano, through the impetuous shapes of his son Giovanni, the tender and vibrant luminsity of the works of Jacopo della Quercia amd Donatello, the refined forms of the young Michelangelo Buonarotti, the story continues up to the precious sinuosity of Bernini, protagonist of the European baroque.

But how can one forget the delicate angels of Beccafumi and Franceso di Giorgio that crown the

monumental high altar? All this explains the emotion felt by Richard Wagner, so impressed, in 1880, by the Sienese Cathedral that he wished to set the most touching scenese of his *Parsifal* here.

If in the North of Europe the size of the Cathedrals did not take into account the image and overall structure of their cities, in Siena, much more so than in any other Italian city, this miraculous balance was achieved thanks to which an enormous and beautiful monument dominates the entire city due to its position and the glare of its candid structure, not with any pretence of supremacy, but as if wishing to defend it in a merciful embrace from the snares of time and its enemies.

A "Gothic dream", therefore, intensely desired and fully accomplished. ●

● The elegant two-coloured Sienese Cathedral has been portrayed both with ancient and modern images.

THE PINACOTECA NAZIONALE

The first nucleus of the great collection of panels in gold leaf housed in the Pinacoteca Nazionale of Siena was put together by a learned abbot, Giuseppe Ciaccheri, who, at the end of the eighteenth century, during the suppression of the lay confraternites decreed by Pietro Leopoldo I of Tuscany, managed to collect and donate to the library of the Studio a series of paintings by the early Sienese masters, together with other collections of designs, prints and manuscripts. The negligence of men and the scarce consideration given to the panels in gold leaf had already caused serious divisions and irreparable mutilations in the heritage of the city.

A few years later, in 1816, with the founding of the Academy of Fine Arts on the site of the ancient Sapienza, that in the meanwhile had moved to its present day site in San Vigilio, the collection begun by Ciaccheri was put in order and substantially added to by Abbot Luigi De Angelis, with the paintings from the Napoleonic supression of the convents on 1810.

Abbot De Angelis, who was also chief librarian, finally succeeded in setting up the first real and proper Gallery, in a few rooms adjoining the Academy of Fine Arts in Via della Sapienza and therefore *"on the evening of 26th September, 1816, the room in which the paintings of the ancient Sienese School are chronologically arranged*

● The great tradition of the ancient Sienese school is perfectly expressed by the works in the Pinacoteca Nazionale: from its beginnings with the altarpiece (above) by the Master of St Peter (about 1260) and the famous small panel (facing page) depicting the Madonna of the Franciscans by Duccio (about 1290).

exhibition was inaugurated with the exhibition of about 90 paintings".

In the following years the collection was enlarged thanks to the donation of the collection belonging to the aristocratic Sienese Spannocchi Piccolomini family and the works transferred here from the Hospital of Santa Maria della Scala, that still today constitutes one of the most significant nuclei of the great collection in Via San Pietro. Thanks to donations, bequests, purchases and recoveries from churches in the Sienese countryside, often abandoned and

semi-destroyed, the number of paintings grew to about five hundred in the middle of the nineteenth century. A few years later, in 1866, the gallery was renamed the "Provincial Gallery of Fine Arts". In 1872, a new catalogue of the collection was published following the one edited by Abbot De Angelis in 1816, and was brought up to date by further editions in 1852, 1860 and 1864. These were progressively replaced by further editions published in 1895, 1903, 1924, finishing with that edited by Cesare Brandi in 1933 and the latest catalogue of the Gallery by Piero Torriti, published in 1977-78. New works from all over the Sienese territory flowed into the gallery up until the first few years of this century. On 4th March, 1915, the Sienese aristocrat Niccolò Buonsignori died after establishing in his will that his palace, situated in Via San Pietro, be donated to the provincial administration *"on condition that a museum or gallery be set up there".* The provincial administration also purchased the adjoining Palazzo Brigidi in order that there would be enough space to adequately display the approximately one thousand paintings that, at that time, made up the collection. Finally, at a distance of 17 years from the death of Buonsignori, in 1932, the new rooms were inaugurated and the gallery took on its new name of "Royal Gallery of Siena".

The actual buildings have substantially remained as they were originally, apart

from certain technical modifications, the installation of security systems, the creation of modern restoration laboratories and the recovery of a few new display rooms on the upper floors. As is well-known, the Palazzo Buonsignori collection, notwithstanding its divisions, constitutes the most complete group of Sienese paintings on tables in the world, fruit of an extraordinary figurative culture that has proudly researched over the centuries, at an impetuous pace, precious stylistic refinement composed of soft lines and sinuous development within original, coloured, spatial perspectives.

This gallery-cum-treasure chest, where the paintings appear to be mounted like precious stones to the walls of the rooms that are definitely inadequate, but fascinating all the same, does not immediately suggest a particular itinerary to follow or a specific group of works to admire. However, after a first general visit, one can try to better understand the particulars of certain paintings as most of Sienese art is characterised by miniature refinement. An excellent atarting point could be the exceptional *Madonna of the Franciscans* that Duccio di Buoninsegna painted in his youth, in around 1290 and which seems to summarise *"the franco-gothic ascendancy that becomes the essential element of the celebrated lyricism of lines and colours with which the master succeeded in dominating and which pervades all the other components of his elaborate culture"* (G. Previtali). ●

● A detail of the beautiful *Nativity of the Madonna* (about 1530) by Domenico Beccafumi with vivid light and bright colours.

PALAZZO CHIGI SARACINI

"At sunrise, a drummer boy climbed up the Mariscotti tower so as to see all our people and also the people of the Florentine camp.... and most of the people that were at the foot of the tower were on their knees praying God and our mother Virgin Mary to give strength and vigour to our army in the fight against those cursed Florentine dogs, our enemies''.

As the ancient chronicles underline, the most glorious day of Palazzo Chigi-Saracini was certainly 4th September, 1260, when, to the sound of the drums, Cerreto Ciccolini reported from the top of the tower the exploits of the Sienese in the battle of Montaperti.

This event, though surrounded by the mist of legend, confirms the importance of the Marescotti family and the strategic role played by the palace, situated on the ancient Via di Galgaria.

The episode probably honoured the family so much that the city government, before the construction of the Palazzo Pubblico, chose to hold their assemblies in the residence of Via di Città. The family originally came from the Maremma and arrived in Siena halfway through the twelfth century.

Its members, small feudatories from near Montepascali, took on positions of primary importance almost immediately after their arrival in Siena.

Guido Marescotti was

● *This page:* **The emblem of the House of the Chigi Saracini.** *Facing page:* **The palace, precociously transformed according to Neogothic philosophy by Galgano Saracini.**

responsible for the construction of the part of the palace that boasted, as its distinguishing feature, the only row of Ghibelline battlements to be found in Siena.

He succeeded in overcoming the consolidated mentality of the Sienese nobles who mainly insisted on building imposing, protected and almost inaccessible city fortresses, and instead looked for solutions that, as well as defence, added elegance of form and building materials, anticipating the great season that was about to dawn.

At the end of the thirteenth century, the Marescotti family had abandoned much of its political activity, due mainly to the advent of the Guelf cause, and began to

dedicate itself to civil and religious work, as well as the constant improvement and expansion of their possessions in the city. Even though they did not play such an important role as in the past, the Marescotti continued to enrich their palace during the Renaissance period, following the example of Caterina Piccolomini, sister of Pope Pio II, who was forever refurbishing the so-called Palazzo delle Papesse, situated right opposite their home.

At the beginning of the next century, in 1506, the Marescotti, by now in decline and in serious financial difficulty, were obliged to sell their palace, the symbol of their lost splendour, to the Piccolomini-Mandoli.

The new owners did not alter the external architectural structure much, but, having at their disposal a great number of famous artists, concentrated on the embellishment of the interior.

These Renaissance interventions probably allowed the palace to go unscathed through the period following the fall of the Republic of Siena.

A new impetus to the valorisation of the building came from another of its great owners: Galgano di Marco Antonio Saracini, who, together with his father, bought it from the Piccolomini in the 1770's. Right from the beginning of that century, there had been a resumption in Siena of building work carried out

● The celebrated *Adoration of the Wise men* a masterpiece by Stefano di Giovanni, known as il Sassetta, from a dismembered and lost polyptych.

according to canons inspired by the highest peaks of architectural tradition of the previous centuries and upheld by the refined scholarship of historians and men of letters, such as Benvoglienti, Pecci and Gigli.

Galgano Saracini was faithful to this singular trend and carried out an enlightened restoration of the building he had recently purchased, so giving life to one of the first examples of the gothic revival.

He lengthened the façade, opened a second row of mullioned windows in addition to the original one and covered the whole of the first floor with stone. Galgano also began a conspicuous collection of works of art that are still today one of the most complete and original in the world.

The collection presents a complete view of Sienese and Tuscan artistic production, starting with the early works, represented by the *Madonna with Child* by the so-called Maestro di Tressa and the *Cross* attributed to Margarito d'Arezzo, one of the most famous painters of the thirteenth century.

Among the most representative authors in the collection is il Sassetta with some of his masterpieces subtracted by Galgano Saracini from the negligence of the monks of the Church of San Martino and, above all, the famous *Adoration of the Wise Men* originating from a polyptych that, as yet, has not been identified.

The Sienese Renaissance is also well represented by a triptych which is among the most significant of those painted by the Maestro dell'Osservanza and by some works of Sano di Pietro, while a consistent group of early sixteenth century paintings testifies the fertility of the Sienese school of that period. It's enough just to consider the *Sacred Family* by Marco Pino, the altarolo by il Brescianino, some fundamental works by Beccafumi, the *Virtues*, a masterpiece by an unknown but very fine Sienese artist of that period, to fully understand the importance of the Collection of Galgano. The seventeenth century, too, is amply represented inside the palace by some very fine canvasses by Francesco Vanni, Rutilio Manetti and his son, Domenico, and superb

works by Bernardino Mei. Galgano Saracini died in 1824 leaving everything to his son Alessandro Giulio Saracini, who in turn nominated as heir, in 1871, his nephew Fabio, son of Carlo Corradino Chigi, a brave soldier and hero of the battle of Curtatone. He made just one condition, that Fabio added to his surname that of the Saracini so as to perpetuate a line that otherwise was doomed to extinction. On his death, Fabio left the heritage to Guido Chigi Saracini. Guido, the last owner, continued and intensified the enlightened policy of his great forebears by adding to the art collections and carrying out major restorations and modifications to the palace, entrusting the work to Arturo Viligiardi, a Sienese painter and architect among

the most famous of his time, responsible for various important restorations in Rome.
Among the various arts, Guido preferred music above all and dedicated his entire life and a large part of his estate to give birth to the academy that bears his name and which constitutes one of the most prestigious and beloved cultural institutions of Siena, admired all over the world. The inside of the palace has been organised according to the requirements of the Accademia Musicale Chigiana that attracts young and promising musicians from all over the world to Siena every summer.
Many rooms have in fact taken the names of the musicians that frequented the Academy, such as the Casella room, or of artists who were valorised or even

rediscovered.
Every detail of the palace demonstrates refinement, well developed taste and a European-scale culture: fine curtains, precious carpets, furniture of the highest quality, together with the extraordinary collection begun by Galgano Saracini and enriched over the years by other significant purchases. All this makes Palazzo Chigi Saracini one of the best preserved and richest aristocratic residences in the world.
The great concert hall, thanks to the work of Count Guido and Viligiardi, underwent a profound and spectacular transformation that suited it more to the modern and growing requirements of the important institution that, right from its birth, had acquired qualified admirers from all over the world.
At the top of a great embroidery of plaster work and crystal, of neo-eighteenth century taste, is the imposing decoration by Arturo Viligiardi depicting *The return of the victorious Sienese from the battle of Montaperti*. The legendary episode of Cerreto Ciccolini has therefore been linked to the last great modification carried out in the palace, so tying the glorious past to the present in the respect of a historical memory that has never been allayed. ●

● *Facing page: La Fabiola* (about 1870) by the purist artist Cesare Maccari.
Above: Count Guido Chigi Saracini, founder of the Accademia Musicale Chigiana.
Below: The beautiful concert hall of the Academy.

Il Pellegrinaio:
the Rector's dream

Even today, many generations of Sienese are unable to fully appreciate this important pictorial cycle, a kind of "Good Government" of the Hospital, painted between 1440 and 1444. In fact, until a few years ago, this large room in Santa Maria della Scala was used as a ward of the orthopaedic clinic. It was probably not of great comfort for the patients to have the scenes frescoed for the rector Giovanni Buzzichelli by il Vecchietta, Domenico di Bartolo and Priamo della Quercia - notwithstanding their originality and quality - under their noses all day. Nowadays the frescoes have been cleaned and the great room is completely unfurnished. One is immediately struck by an atmosphere of rare intensity upon entering this suggestive penumbra. It almost seems as if the history of centuries that rotates around the pulsating world of Santa Maria must unravel itself slowly but surely with this cycle, through the daily stories of fearful, abandoned children, fed by abundant country nurses or of the archbishop on his majestic, dappled horse who, faced with an improbable dome-shaped model, bestows the "alms" necessary for the construction of the Hospital. However, it's nice to think that perhaps during the night in the uncertain bluish light of the ward, the patients will have asked themselves how come is

● The frescoes of the Pellegrinaio, realised principally by Domenico di Bartolo, but also by Vecchietta and Priamo della Quercia, give a detailed description of the historical events connected with the Sienese hospital and its sanitary functions in the fifteenth century.

present in all the scenese a figure dressed in black, that of the rector Buzzichelli, deviser of the cycle.
Good idea; however it seems a little exaggerated to want to be represented everywhere.
He bows before a great lord with a beard and a hat, perhaps it is he who arrived from Constantinople? We don't know, there's no time, he must get away to preside over the suture of an injury to the right leg of an unfortunate pilgrim. Don't worry signor Buzzichelli, you can keep calm, the surgeon is the famous Tura Bandini. Effectively, this surgeon, with the large grey

and red mantle and with that reassuring air manages to calm down the fearful stranger.
But the rector is alert, he doesn't lose sight of the large monk on the right who carefully listens to the confession of a patient just admitted, who, notwithstanding the suffering, doesn't seem altogether insensible to the fragrance of food coming from behind the gate where a servant is passing with a steaming plate.
Quick now, he must hurry to the "distribution of the alms". Hundreds of pilgrims and hungry citizens wait for the piece of "blessed" bread with the emblem of La Scala, that will allow them to arrive until tomorrow. In this excitement the only one to maintain his calm is that clever man called Celestino III who with his bull finally manages to calm the souls of oblates and canons in continual arguement for the control of the Hospital.
And that great copper basin placed by Domenico in a corner of the scene? It is a precise disposition of the rector; who doesn't wash his hands cannot sit at the table! Doctors and Rectors, servants and abandoned childrens must all indistinctly care for hygiene. Behind the grey Brunellescan colonnade one can make out the great hats of the gentlemen by Vecchietta and, a little further away, tender children who climb up, not really convinced, a flight of stairs in precarious balance. Suddenly the light has been

switched on, the stories of the Hospital immediately return to their rigorous perspective, the voice of the guide begins his illustration... ●

● The Pellegrinaio, ancient place of suffering, has recently been restored, much to the admiration of visitors to the studios of the specialists.

SIENESE CHEMISTS TORN BETWEEEN ASPIRIN AND SPICY CAKE

Nowadays, modern boxes of medicine look down from the austere, neoclassical-style shelves of the chemist's in Quattro Cantoni and the old vases and solid mortars have long been transfered onto the shiny furniture in the houses of well-off families or into the anonymous museum showcases. The sober compartments, designed at the beginning of the nineteenth century by the architect Agostino Fantastici, remind us of the fortunate Sienese school of furniture makers that reached its peak during the last century, especially thanks to Fantastici, who is generally remembered as a singular designer of furnishings rather than for his not banal achievements in private and religious buildings, and also to a large number of "purist" inlayers who affirmed themselves all over the world.

The chemist's in Quattro Cantoni is not the only shop in Siena that is finely furnished. It's enough to go to Piazza del Campo to admire the ancient spice shop with its shelves protected by panes of glass embellished with refined allegories by Giuseppe Pachetti, who in the last few years of the nineteenth century was the leader of the Sienese lawyers, but who was also afflicted with the virus of art, so much so that he won fame for himself as a graphic designer and painter of Palio cloths. The Sienese chemists, therefore, loved beautiful things and didn't hesitate to employ the best artists to furnish their shops. These keepers of medicinal and botanical science were heirs to the old spice merchants who had first introduced cinnamon and cloves to Europe and that had, for this reason, operated for some time also as cake-makers, inventing "panpepato", or spicy cake, that later gave birth to panforte, less spicy and more amiable, but now famous all over the world. Panpepato was believed to produce balsamic and medicinal effects and it was used during the siege of 1555 to give comfort to the

weak and injured.
It seems it was invented
by a nun called Leta who
first mixed together honey,
candied fruit, almonds and
spices with abundant ginger
for the stomach and as a
pick-me-up, but who paid
close attention to the
gastronomic side of things.
Its flavour, perhaps a little
too strong for most people,
was made decidedly milder
during the Risorgimento, so
giving life to the production
of a less specialised quality,
called "Margherita", in
honour of the queen of Italy,
who adored it.
Today, panforte is produced
on an industrial scale and
exported all over the world.

The alembics and boilers of
the pharmicists do not exist
any more, but some of the
modern factories have kept
the names of the ancient
spice merchants: Sapori,
Fiore, Parenti. And they
guarantee a unique flavour
and a traditional quality that
is a synonym of Siena
practically everywhere. ●

● For centuries, the
ancient chemists
have been depositaries of
the secrets connected with
the art of Sienese sweet
making, and especially the
exquisite panforte (the
beautiful tray is part of a
private collection in Siena).

L'ACCADEMIA DEGLI INTRONATI

MELIORA·LATENT

INTRONATI

DEVM·COLERE
STVDERE
GAVDERE
NEMINEM·LAEDERE
NEMINI·CREDERE
DE·MVNDO·NON·CVRARE
PATRIAE·SERVIRE

● The emblem of the
Accademia degli
Intronati comprises a
pumpkin surmounted by
crossed pestles, a complex
symbology that has given
birth to many different and
contrasting interpretations.

Among the numerous
academies that were
founded in Italy
during the sixteenth
century, the Sienese
Accademia degli
Intronati is among the most
famous and glorious. Its
origins have been object of
heated discussions between
men of letters and historians
for at least three centuries.
In particular, Girolamo
Gigli, at the beginning of
the eighteenth century, held
the Intronati to be the
natural continuation of a
fifteenth century academy

of the city, called "la
Grande", founded by the
humanist pope Enea Silvio
Piccolomini, who in his turn
had kept up the literary
conversations that were
constantly held in Siena
during the thirteenth and
fourteenth centuries.
The efforts of this earnest
scholar were naturally
aimed at documenting the
great age and prestige of the
Intronati, so as to prove that
the Sienese literary
confraternity was the oldest
in all Europe. Besides, the
*Preface concerning the origins
of the Ancient Sienese
Academy...* by Gigli had been
preceded by Luca Contile,
who, in his *Theories on the
ownership of the imprese*
("impresa" in this sense
means a symbol that
expresses, either
allegorically or synthetically,
a proverb or a sentence),
published in Padua in 1574,
considered the *"Accademia
Intronati the oldest of all"*. The
same view was also shared
by the components of other
Italian academies such as
that of the "Intrepidi" in
Parma who declared: *"may
the soul of the city of Siena be
for ever praised, as it is the true
root of the Tuscan language, a
great mother of Saints, Popes
and men of letters and whose
Accademia degli Intronati is the
oldest academic institution to
have become the owner of an
impresa"*.
We definitely know,
however, that the "ses viri
nobiles senenses", Marco
Antonio Piccolomini: the
Sodo, archbishop Francesco
Bandini Piccolomini: the
Scaltrito, Antonio Vignali:
the *Arsiccio*, Francesco Sozzi:

the *Importuno*, Giovan Francesco Franceschi: the *Moscone* and Alessandro Marzi, il *Cirloso*, founders of the Academy, began their activity in 1525 with the name of Intronati, so expressing the desire of the members to withdraw from the noise and confusion of the world, which so dumfounded them, and dedicate themselves to the study of language and literature.

From the moment of their entrance into the Academy, all the members of the Intronati were given a nickname to distinguish them.

The *Arsiccio* was responsible for the invention of the "impresa", comprising a pumpkin, inside which was preserved salt, a usage of Tuscan peasants to preserve it from the damp, surmounted by the motto: *"Meliora latent"*, taken from the *Metamorfosi* by Ovid. The pumpkin contains salt, the most essential of substances, refined by pestles. *"...And since pestles break up, crush and refine the salt, so too did the Intronati substitute these very same qualities with labour, vigilance and concentration on the liberal studies with the aim of further refining them and, by means of continuous virtuous acts, of perfecting them"* (G. Bargagli Petrucci).

The Intronati immediately won great fame thoughout Italy, even if they were forced to suspend their activity after the fall of the Republic due to the suspicion the Medici harboured towards all the Sienese institutions, so much so that the Intronati were hit by a decree that banned them for about half a century.

In 1603, their activity and studies began again, in competition with a new academy that had started up in the meantime, that of the Filomati, founded by Girolamo Benvoglienti. After half a century of literary controversy, the governor of the city, Mattias dei Medici, decided to merge the two confraternities and the Intronati so came into possession of the theatre built inside Palazzo Pubblico, in the room where, for centuries, the Great Council of the Republic had assembled. In 1688, the members had the brick stage built and, in 1670, performed *L'Argia*, a dramatic opera by the Florentine Marco Antonio Cesti.

In 1729, the Intronati chose as their meeting place the rooms of the present City Library at the entrance to which one can still read six of the fundamental rules of the association, taken from some maxims of Bernardino Bellanti, Sienese scholar, who died in 1522, around the time when the Academy was founded: *"Deum colere, studere, gaudere, neminem laedere, nemini credere, de mundo non curare"*.

To admit new members the Intronati compelled the candidates, that had to be over twenty years old, to undergo a "test of spirit": a composition approved by the censors and recited during "a public meeting". If he passed the test, a rigorous ceremony took place during which a ring was given to the candidate and a crown of heather was placed on his head. He was then made to sit in his place and his "nome intronatesco", in other words his nickname, was given to him.

The Intronati has distinguished itself over the centuries for its numerous publications and, in particular, those regarding the theatre and satirical texts. Still today, the Accademia degli Intronati, that resides in Palazzo Pubblico, edits important publications with constant zeal, and each year, publishes its prestigious *Bollettino Senese di Storia Patria*, a collection of research, essays and studies regarding various aspects of Sienese literature, history, and art of all periods. ●

PANDOLFO PETRUCCI: THE MAGNIFICENT TYRANT

● **The Palace of the "Magnifico" Pandolfo Petrucci has met the same fate as its ancient proprietor: the noble residence that was splendid in the sixteenth century has now been deprived of its works of art and undermined by an increasingly serious structural decadence.**

The story of the "Magnifico" Pandolfo Petrucci is one of the lesser known episodes in the history of Siena because scholars and men of letters, biographers and historians have never attached much importance to him. As a result, those dark years in the history of Siena have remained hidden in a corner of the fervid popular imagination. Even today, the Sienese themselves find it difficult to immediately associate, also due to its present state of degradation, the palace in Via dei Pellegrini with the ancient, prestigious residence of the "Magnifico" who ruled at the beginning of the sixteenth century, the only implacable despot that

Siena has ever had to put up with. Even the palace seems to have followed the same dire fate of its owner who entrusted its construction to Giacomo Cozzarelli in the first few years of that century.

Pandolfo, a member of the Monte dei Nove, the most authoritative party of the city, after having gained power in 1487, began to live in luxury and comfort, surrounding himself with all that could raise his image to the level of the greatest patrons and princes of the courts of Europe.

For this reason, he had the walls of his rooms painted by Genga, Signorelli and Pinturicchio, artists at the height of their fame in that period, fresh from other projects, including the Cathedral. He also had Cozzarelli realise some extraordinary bronze rings to decorate the principal faade in Via dei Pellegrini and some finely decorated ornamental pillars, while the majolica floors were covered with refined decorations. Unfortunately, the palace was gradually stripped of its decorations until it reached a state of almost complete ruin at the beginning of this century, when even the last objects were divided amongst private buyers and museums all over the world. His enlightened patronage did not hinder Pandolfo from killing the father of his wife Aurelia, Niccolò Borghesi, an old and esteemed Sienese citizen, who was stabbed to death at the Postierla while

returning from the Cathedral. He didn't hesitate to kill anybody, who in one way or another, constituted an obstacle to his pernicious "political design". Astute and deceitful, in 1502, he managed to elude the famous ambush of Senigallia, where by hand of Duke Valentino, many Italian princes, including Paolo Orsini and Gian Paolo Baglioni, found their death. Machiavelli wrote of him: *"He is a very prudent man and governs a state of great reputation and has not enemies of much importance, either inside or outside, as they are either killed or reconciled."* He was rather a playboy and fell hopelessly in love with a famous prostitute, Caterina di Salicotto, and kept her in his house for a long time, compelling his wife Aurelia to live with the woman and endure her tantrums. He had two sons, Fabio and Borghese, who were unable to match the political ability of their father, and, as a result, the Sienese Republic shortly fell into the hands of the Medici. ●

THE BOTANICAL GARDENS
AND ITS GHOST

Sodoma, a sixteenth century Sienese artist and a by no means mediocre pupil of the illustrious Giovanni Antonio Bazzi.

In fact, Giomo imitated his teacher not only in the stylistic sense but also in his dissolute conduct that was unbecoming to his position as a Camaldolesian monk. He was subsequently hung for his indecorous behaviour and it seems that, from that moment on, his spirit has continued to wander around the Church of the Rosa, dedicated to St Mustiola, for a long time occupied by the Camaldolesians and where the painter realised one of his most appreciated works, the *Madonna with Child and Saints*, placed on the first altar in the right-hand nave and whose dark colours perfectly demonstrate the restless nature of its author. ●

The ancient garden of the simples of the Academy of Science of Siena, called the Fisiocritici, is nowadays an exemplary botanical museum, full of rare species and exotic plants, by now acclimatised to the tufaceous soil of this valley to the south-east of the city.

Rare examples of trees of Judas grow from the neatly arranged flower beds, interrupted by the rough profile of pointed agaves with large, intensely green, veined leaves. But the peace of this urban "Eden" is disturbed by a presence that has aroused the popular imagination of the Sienese for centuries. At the Botanical Gardens

"you can hear it"! In the last century, the phenomenon was put down, with reassuring optimism, to the trampling of the horses that were kept in the nearby stall of St Augustine. But the noises can still be heard today even though the horses have been replaced by taxis for ages. Especially in the first years of this century, the so-called "ghost" of the Botanical Gardens raged in this part of Siena, avoiding all the ambushes of its hunters and even succeeding in driving some of them completely mad. It seems that, during some spiritualistic seances, held in that period, contact was made with a mysterious entity that turned out to be the spirit of Giomo del

● It seems that a fastidious ghost wanders among the rare essences of the Botanical Gardens that, naturally, many people have heard but none have ever seen.

Terzo di Camollia

1   Accademia dei Rozzi
2   Nobile Contrada of the Oca
3   Church of the Crucifix
4   Portico of the Municipalities of Italy
5   Fontebranda
6   Basilica of St Domenico
7   City Library of the Intronati
8   Church of St Pellegrino alla Sapienza
9   Palazzo Tolomei
10   Palazzo Bichi Ruspoli
11   Palazzo Cinughi de' Pazzi
12   Palazzo Gori Pannilini
13   Palazzo Spannocchi
14   Rocca Salimbeni
15   Church of St Maria delle Nevi
16   Palazzo Pozzesi
17   Palazzo Sergardi
18   Contrada of the Drago
19   Medici fortress
20   Italian Wine Centre
21   Church of St Stephen
22   Palazzo Bernardi Avanzati
23   Oratory of St Anna in St Onofrio
24   Church of St Andrew Apostle
25   Sovereign Contrada of the Istrice
26   Church of Fontegiusta
27   Church of St Pietro alla Magione
28   Chapel of the Holy Sepulchre
29   Fortino delle Donne
30   Church of St Girolamo in Campansi
31   Villa Rubini Manenti
32   Church of St Sebastiano
33   Consuma
34   Palazzo Franci
35   Fontenuova
36   Contrada of the Lupa
37   Noble Contrada of the Bruco
38   Basilica of St Francis
39   Oratory of the Company of St Bernardino
40   Imperial Contrada of the Giraffa
41   Basilica of Provenzano
42   Church of St Pietro a Ovile
43   Church of St Donato
44   Palazzo Bandini Piccolomini
45   Church of St Vigilio

Leaving the Campo from Vicolo di San Paolo and turning right, one immediately comes across the palace of the **Accademia dei Rozzi** situated in Via di Città, Via delle Terme, Piazza Indipendenza and Via Diacceto.

The building, of notable size, has undergone numerous and substantial internal and external transformations, incorporating various constructions, among which the medieval tower of the Codenacci family and the rooms of the Wool-workers Corporation.

The Company of the Rozzi was founded in the early years of the sixteenth century and was transformed into an academy in 1665.

The entrance to the rooms of the Teatro dei Rozzi is in Piazza Indipendenza. Built to a design by Alessandro Doveri at the beginning of the last century (1814), it was later enlarged by Augusto

Corbi following a series of positive experiences acquired by the purist architect who was present at Milan and Rome during the reconstruction of great theatrical spaces and from which he was able to glean ideas from the new styles and decorations utilised in these European-scale surrroundings. The horseshoe-shaped theatre has three tiers of boxes and a gallery overhanging the stalls; their partitions are decorated with acanthus leaves in gilded plaster work. The theatre, closed in 1945, should shortly begin its activity again as soon as the restorations, under way for some years now, are finished.

A nineteenth century loggia, supported by three great arches, characterises Piazza Indipendenza, a space redesigned by Archimede Vestri at the end of the last century on the site of the destroyed medieval church of St Pellegrino and of the Wool-workers chapel, demolished in 1777, from which came the famous, but fragmentary, polyptych bearing the same name, painted in 1423 by Stefano di Giovanni, il Sassetta.

As well as the loggia, the project envisaged a new façade for the buildings situated on the sides and a flight of steps on top of which was to have been placed the monument by Tito Sarrocchi (1879) depicting *Italy* (now situated in the modern zone of San Prospero).

One of the most suggestive streets of the city, Via della Galluzza, leads from

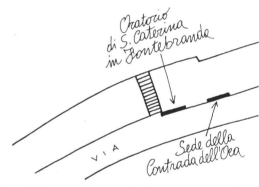

Via di Diacceto towards Fontebranda. Its medieval aspect has remained completely unchanged, the first part of the street is characterised by a forest of small arches that buttress the surrounding walls and almost block out the light, so creating an intricate pattern of light and shade.

The steep slope is dotted with small lanes, the first of which, on the left (Costaccino), leads towards Via Fontebranda, while the second, on the right (Macina), and the third, also on the same side (Forcone), rise again towards Via delle Terme.

Via della Galluzza leads directly into the heart of the **Noble Contrada of the Oca**, birthplace of St Catherine of Siena. The oratory of the Contrada was formerly the old workshop of Catherine's father, Jacopo Benincasa, a dyer of wool.

The Saint was born in Fontebranda (see page 208), on 25th March, 1347, from Jacopo and Monna Lapa Piagenti.
The name of Catherine and her short but intense life are particularly linked to the tormented events of the papacy, at that time in Avignon, and to her famous correspondence, by means of which she communicated, with mystic passion and great force and efficacy, with the rulers and kings of all Europe. She died in Rome on 29th April, 1380. The cult of Catherine of Siena rapidly spread, together with her apostolate of peace and love, and, almost immediately after her death, pilgrims came from afar to visit her birthplace.
In 1461, the Saint was canonised by the Sienese Pope Pio II, and, a few years later, the inhabitants of Fontebranda decided to build an oratory, called the

Dye-works, as it was to be built on the bottom part of the Saint's birthplace to venerate their great fellow citizen.
The people of Fontebranda, supported also by the city government, nominated Corso di Bastiano to design the oratory which was built between 1465 and 1474. Francesco di Duccio del Guasta, Antonio Federighi and Urbano da Cortona also

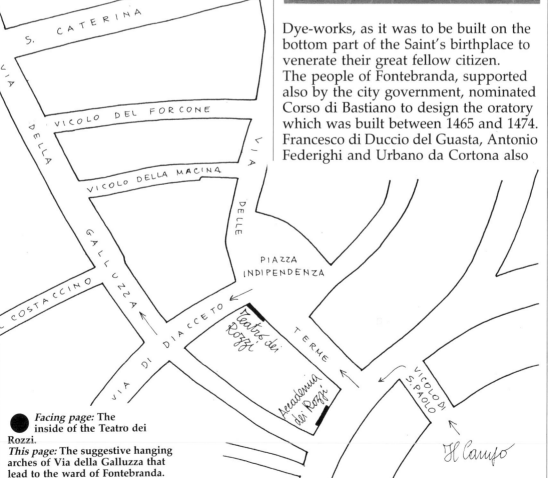

Facing page: The inside of the Teatro dei Rozzi.
This page: The suggestive hanging arches of Via della Galluzza that lead to the ward of Fontebranda.

worked on the building; the latter was also the author of the bas-relief on the façade depicting the *Madonna with Child and Angels.* The architectural part of the outside of the building was completely restored by Giuseppe Partini, Pietro Marchetti and Giuseppe Maccari in 1877, after the numerous lesions caused by the earthquake of 1798.

The inside, with one nave, is divided into two spans, surmounted by ribbed vaults and all the walls are frescoed with numerous stories of the life of Catherine. The recently restored cycle was begun in around 1520/25 by il Sodoma, who frescoed five beautiful angels holding a red curtain hanging along the whole length of the wall of the high altar. The artist, who at that time enjoyed great fame in Siena, quickly abandoned the commission and the rest of the wall was completed by Giacomo Pacchierotti with the *Stigmatas of the Saint".*

The other scenes are works by Girolamo del Pacchia, Vincenzo Tamagni, Ventura Salimbeni and Sebastiano Folli. But the real masterpiece in the oratory of the Oca is the wooden statue, sculpted by Neroccio di Bartolomeo in 1475, that

dominates the high altar, built in 1679 by Austo Cini.

The work is justly considered one of the masterpieces of the Sienese fifteenth century and manages to combine a very solid structure with flowing lines and the tenderest of forms that recalls the great traditions of the previous centuries.

In the Chapel of the Madonna, adjoining the oratory, another beautiful wooden statue of Catherine, dating back to the beginning of the fifteenth century, wears the scarf of the Contrada around her neck, a sign of the popular devotion of the members of the Oca.

The rooms underneath the oratory, reached by means of a steep flight of travertine steps, are where Catherine, according to a consolidated tradition, performed the miracle of the multiplication of the wine.

Since then, every fragment of earth in this "miraculous cellar" is considered a precious reliquary. Right in front of the Chapel of the Madonna is the entrance to the room of the Victories and the Museum of the Noble Contrada of the Oca.

Apart from the numerous palios, some of which are worthy of particular note such as that of the painter Marte, won in the extraordinary Palio of September 1969, run to commemorate the landing on the Moon, or that by Ernesto Treccani with its magnificent graphics, won by the Contrada in August, 1977, the museum also displays a vast collection of ancient sacred vestments and numerous objects in silver of the seventeenth and nineteenth centuries, donated by the members of the Contrada to their patron. One can also admire various paintings by Massimo d'Azeglio, Alessandro Mafei, Vittorio Giunti, Paride Pascucci, as well as the recent tabernacle depicting the *Madonna of the Oca,* by Riccardo Tommasi Ferroni, situated in the adjoining Vicolo del Tiratoio.

Climbing up an imposing seventeenth century staircase one reaches an elegant mid-sixteenth century loggia, in the style of Peruzzi, but attributed

This page: The beautiful wooden statue by Neroccio di Bartolomeo, depicting *St Catherine,* a masterpiece of the Sienese Renaissance.
Facing page: The front of the oratories dedicated to St Catherine in Via Santa Caterina, nowadays home of the Contrada of the Oca.

to one of his pupils.

From the white travertine balustrade of this loggia, one can enjoy a splendid view of the countryside, the Cathedral and the majestic and ancient building of the Tira, situated right next to the Sanctuary.

On the left, is the entrance to the oratory of the Kitchen, presumably built, if the blackened remains of a wall situated behind the high altar are anything to go by, in the kitchen of the Benincasa family. This oratory was also the first place of prayer of the confraternity, before a table depicting the *Stigmatas of Catherine* by Bernardino Fungai. Halfway through the sixteenth century, the oratory was enlarged, incorporating other small rooms, and a gilded decoration was carved by Bastiano di Girolamo from a design by Bartolomeo Neroni, il Riccio. The walls, articulated with ornamental pillars bearing the same type of decoration, depict the most important episodes of the life of the Saint, realised by some of the principal protagonists of the late-mannerist revival in Siena: Alessandro Casolani, Pietro Sorri, Cristoforo Roncalli, Lattanzio Bonastri, Arcangelo Salimbeni, Francesco Vanni and Rutilio Manetti. The polychrome majolica floor, was extended and largely restored at the beginning of the seventeenth century by Girolamo di Marco, a Sienese potter. On the other side of the loggia is the entrance to the **Church of the Crucifix,** built on the land of the nearby church of St Antonio, demolished at the end of the 1920's to make way for the portico of the Municipalities of Italy.

The church, consecrated on 23rd April, 1623, was built to house a twelfth century *crucifix,* from Pisa, which was supposed to have given the stigmatas to the Saint in the church of Santa Cristina in that city, in 1375.

The painting, placed on the high altar realised by Tommaso Redi, is of the School of Pisa, with the evident influence of Lucca. Two tables depicting *St Catherine* and *St Girolamo,* attributed to il Riccio, are placed on either side of the work.

The frescoes on the vault, depicting the *Glory of St Catherine,* were painted by Giuseppe Nicola Nasini in the first years of the eighteenth century. The works on the walls and the other two altars of the church are by Rutilio and Domenico Manetti, Giuseppe Nasini, Liborio Guerrini and Sebastiano Conca.

⬤ The episode of *St Catherine cutting her hair,* by Alessandro Franchi (1895), is part of the pleasant cycle of frescoes in the oratory of the church built on the site of her bedroom.

Some episodes in the youth of the Saint, realised by the purist painters Alessandro Franchi and Gaetano Marinelli (1896) are located in the oratory of the Bedroom, built right underneath that of the Kitchen. In the same chapel can be admired a beautiful little sixteenth century table by Girolamo di Benvenuto, depicting *The stigmatas;* some reliquaries are preserved in the adjoining little cell, including the lantern that Catherine used during her journeys to visit the sick at night, the bag in which her head was transported from Rome to Siena in 1348, and a fragment of her veil. An elegant well in travertine, the only original object dating back to the end of the fifteenth century, is still visible nearby the Peruzzi-style loggia.

Outside the gate, to the right, is the suggestive Vicolo del Tiratoio, at the end of which, to the left, is the oldest and most famous well in Siena: **Fontebranda** (see page 212). An inscription of 1193 'attributes the design of the new well to Bellamino as a replacement of a previous one. Fontebranda, characterised by three great arches, has always been the real power behind all the productive activities of the area, as well as being one of the principal junctions of the medieval aqueduct of Siena, the famous "bottini", which, as previously mentioned, supplied water to the city by means of suggestive, underground, capillary tunnels up until a very short time ago.

From the plain of Fontebranda, a flight of steps in bricks and travertine, lying along the precipice of tufa at the

foot of the hillock of San Domenico, passes behind the buildings of the Sanctuary of St Catherine and leads to the zone of Camporegio from which one can admire one of the most beautiful views of the Cathedral and the city. This beautiful panorama also allows one to carefully examine and appreciate the town planning of Siena and the architectural styles of numerous medieval buildings.

Right in front of this great natural terrace lies the massive building of the **Basilica of St Domenico** (see page 200).

The construction of the church was begun in around 1225 by the Domenican fathers after the visit to Siena of their founder, Domenico Guzman, on land donated by Fortebraccio Malavolti, with the contribution of the city government and the alms collected by the friars. Approximately forty years later, the church and the convent were completed, even if around the middle of the following century St Domenico was

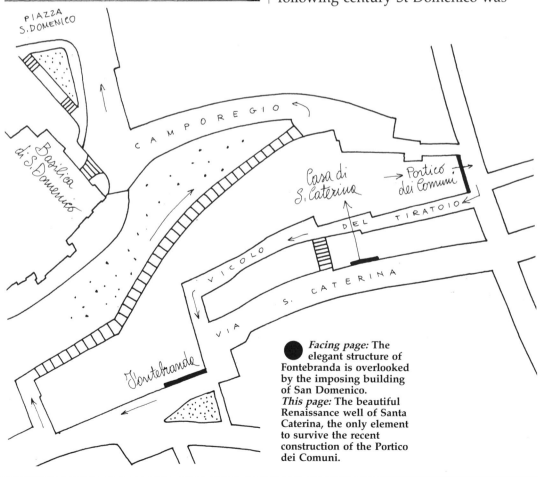

● *Facing page:* The elegant structure of Fontebranda is overlooked by the imposing building of San Domenico.
This page: The beautiful Renaissance well of Santa Caterina, the only element to survive the recent construction of the Portico dei Comuni.

greatly enlarged, practically assuming its present form.

Inside the church, among the numerous historical and artistic objects, is the Chapel of the Volte, formerly the oratory of the Mantellate Nuns of Catherine, where almost all the miracles of the Saint were performed. Catherine was said to have offered her mantle and exchanged hearts with Jesus in this chapel.

A fresco depicting *St Catherine with a believer*, painted in around 1375 by a Sienese artist, Andrea Vanni, a fervent follower of the Saint of Fontebranda, is also preserved in this chapel.

This fresco is probably a true likeness of the Saint as it was painted when

Catherine was still alive.

The other chapel dedicated to the cult of Catherine is to be found on the right-hand side of the great nave, built by the Bensi family in the second half of the fifteenth century, in which is located a beautiful marble altar by Giovanni di Stefano (1469) containing the head of the Saint. Many of the greatest Sienese artists, such as Girolamo di Benvenuto, Matteo di Giovanni, Francesco di Giorgio, il Sodoma, Francesco Vanni, Alessandro Casolani, Ventura Salimbeni, Rutilio Manetti, Franceso Rustici, as well as Benedetto da Maiano from Florence and Mattia Preti from Calabria, worked in St Domenico.

Halfway down Via della Sapienza that leads off from Piazza St Domenico, is the **City Library of the Intronati,** situated on the right-hand side of the street after the cross-roads with the steep Costa di Sant'Antonio, from which one can admire another suggestive view of the Cathedral that, like a precious marble crown, dominates and envelops the radiant brickwork of the imposing pillars, houses and palaces gathered around it.

The first nucleus of this important library was formed by a donation from Archdeacon Sallustio Bandini in 1759. It was initially called the Library of the Sapienza (the whole building, that extends up to the Church of the Sapienza, was originally occupied by the Studio senese), and later it took on the

⬤ *This page:* The ancient Vicolo di Camporegio, a suggestive "Catherinian journey" towards San Domenico. *Facing page:* The reading room of the Biblioteca degli Intronati, the most important library of the city, full of rare and precious works.

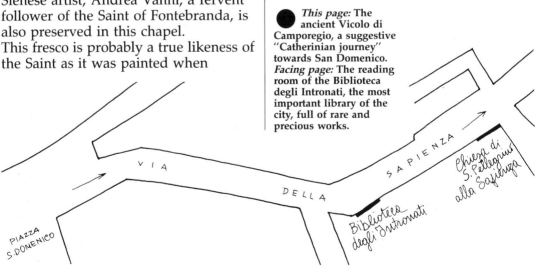

name of the sixteenth century Academy of the Intronati that inherited the building.

The library presently contains about 500,000 volumes including 5,000 manuscripts and 1,000 incunabula. Numerous codices were illuminated by Sienese artists between the thirteenth and fifteenth centuries, such as Lippo Vanni, Lippo Memmi, Pietro Lorenzetti, il Sassetta, Giovanni di Paolo and Sano di Pietro. The collection of designs and prints is one of the most important in the whole of Italy. Also worthy of note is the precious cover of a Greek evangeliarium from the Hospital of Santa Maria della Scala, a refined work in gold and probably dating back to the twelfth century.

The Studio senese was founded in the same building in around 1240, and later, at the beginning of the sixteenth century, it moved to the Hospital of the Misericordia: a fairly important medieval institution that was supposedly founded by the blessed Andrea Gallerani in the middle of the thirteenth century and suppressed to make way for the university, with a lot of space available to put up students coming from all over Italy.

It remained there until 1816, when it was transferred to the ex-convent of San Vigilio (now the Rectorate), and the rooms of Via della Sapienza became, by decree of Ferdinando III of Tuscany, seat of the **Institute of Fine Arts**, at that time the "stronghold" of Purism led by Luigi Mussini who, halfway through that century, instituted an important school from which emerged artists such as Alessandro Franchi, Giuseppe Partini, Cesare Maccari, Amos Cassioli, Pietro Aldi and others who renewed the great Sienese artistic tradition at the beginning of this century.

The thirteenth century church has been restored various times. The actual version was realised by Giovanni Marchetti who worked on the whole building during the second half of the eighteenth century, while, in 1783, it became a parish church and took on the name of St Pellegrino, substituting the one that had been suppressed and then demolished in Piazza Indipendenza.

A few precious tables by fourteenth and

fifteenth century Sienese artists are still preserved in the church, together with other significant works of the seventeenth and eighteenth centuries. Right in front of the **Church of the Sapienza** is the entrance to one of the many suggestive lanes of Siena, Vicolo della Pallacorda, halfway up which, hidden from indiscreet glances, is the stall of the Contrada of the Drago.

Leaving the penumbra of Vicolo della Pallacorda and going along Via delle Terme and then Vicolo della Rosa, one reaches the rear of **Palazzo Tolomei**, one of the oldest and most prestigious noble residences of the city, facing Piazza Tolomei and the Church of St Cristoforo.

The palace (see page 204) was built at the beginning of the thirteenth century by Jacopo and Tolomeo Tolomei and the façade at the front was finished in around 1270, after the defeat and death of the Ghibelline, Provenzano Salvani, in the battle of Colle Val d'Elsa, an episode that marked the return to the city of the Tolomei family, supporters of the Guelf cause. Originally, the building probably possesed another floor surmounted by a crown of battlements. The travertine palace is characterised by two rows of five, elegant, mullioned windows on the façade and is now the headquarters of a banking institute. Inside, arranged along the walls of the first floor hall containing great brick pillars, are numerous architectural and sculpted fragments from the thirteenth and fourteenth centuries, originating from recent restorations. On the right hand side of the palace, in Vicolo della Torre, a tablet commemorates the verses of Dante dedicated to Pia dei Tolomei: *"Remember me, my name is Pia, and Siena compelled me to leave the Maremma"*.

Via Banchi di Sopra is dotted with various important palaces belonging to ancient noble families. On the right hand side, towards Piazza Salimbeni, can be admired **Palazzo Biche Ruspoli**, a building in tufaceous stone, restored in the first half of the sixteenth century. Some precious paintings by Alessandro Franchi and Giorgio Bandini (nineteenth century) are visible in the lunettes of the hall that gives onto the street.

A few yards futher on, after the Arch of the Rossi that crowns the entrance to Via dei Rossi, is situated the massive structure of **Palazzo Cinughi de Pazzi**, built, at least in its actual form, at the

● Vicolo della Pallacorda, one of the many secret lanes of Siena. *Facing page:* the façade of Palazzo Tolomei, decorated with elegant mullioned windows.

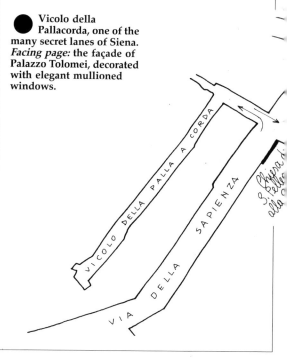

beginning of the fifteenth century. Directly opposite lies **Palazzo Gori Pannilini,** restored in the second half of the sixteenth century, incorporating numerous buildings belonging to the Galli Family.

The eighteenth century decorations inside extol the *Glory of the Gori, Pannilini and Savini families.*

Between 1472 and 1475, Giuliano da Maiano was commissioned by Ambrogio Spannocchi to build one of the most beautiful palaces of the Sienese Renaissance, situated right next to Palazzo Cinughi de Pazzi.

The façade overlooking Banchi di Sopra still preserves its original lines, while, in the second half of the last century, a neo-Renaissance prospect was added to the part in Piazza Salimbeni by

Partini, who also reorganised the inside where numerous fifteenth century objects are, however, still preserved. The Spannocchi were originally a family of small landowners from Spannocchia, a castle situated in the thick woodland lying towards the Maremma at about fifteen miles from Siena. They came to the city in the first half of the thirteenth century and, two centuries later, thanks to the enterprise of Ambrogio di Nanni Spannocchi, became the most important

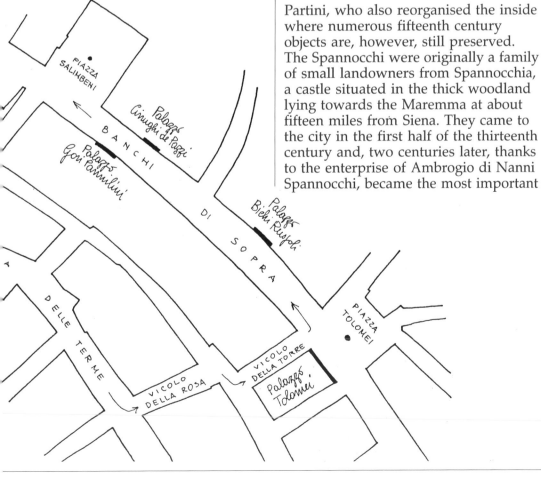

merchants and bankers of the city.
In 1871, Giuseppe Partini completely restored the area in front of the ancient **Rocca dei Salimbeni**, headquarters of the oldest banking institution in the world: **Monte dei Paschi** (see page 196). The project included the demolition of the garden of **Palazzo Spannochi** that ran along Banchi di Sopra, repeating the architectural model of the front of the Rocca along the whole façade of the palace, the internal decorations and furnishings of which were, on that occasion, largely modernised and integrated. In the same period, another building confining with this area, the sixteenth century headquarters of the ancient Dogana which subsequently passed to the **Tantucci** family, was restored by Partini, so integrating the various parts of the new square, called Piazza dei Salimbeni.
The Salimbeni family arrived in Siena at

the end of the twelfth century and, in a short time, gained great prestige in the city for their ability in concluding business deals with merchants and bankers in France, Germany, England and Spain. They were tax collectors for the papacy and administrated the tenders for the imperial revenues. Their prestigious residence, or more precisely, the network of buildings owned by them - now completely transformed - are situated in the area that incorporates the ancient ring of medieval walls that used to run along the stretch of Via Francigena corresponding with Banchi di Sopra, the demolished Church of St Donato and

Piazza dell'Abbadia.
In a short while, the residence of the Salimbeni became the fulcrum of the Sienese economy, remaining such until 1419, the year in which the city government confiscated all the possessions of the family and set up the Dogana del Sale and the Revenue Office in that area. On 27th February, 1472, due both to the changing economical and political situations and the need to kerb

● Piazza Salimbeni, "invented" at the end of the last century, is the headquarters of Monte dei Paschi, the oldest bank in the world.
To the left: A particular of the Renaissance Palazzo Spannocchi, another part of the headquarters Monte dei Paschi of Siena.
To the right: Rocca Salimbeni that once belonged to one of the most important families of the city.

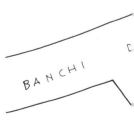

the usury practised by the merchants and jews of the city, the government set up the Monte Pio, an institution similar to a pawn merchants, with the aim of attenuating what was becoming a big problem for the Sienese community. The Monte Pio continued its activity until the beginning of the sixteenth century, that is, until it became caught up in the political and economic crisis that lead to the downfall of the Republic. Shortly after the fall of Siena, however, the bank

continued its rapid development, to the extent that the Medici government also allowed it to effect operations of agricultural credit, mainly to the Maremma cattle-raisers. But the definite, "modern" reorganisation of Monte dei Paschi began in 1624 with the participation, as guarantor, of Grand Duke Ferdinando II, who maintained that the revenue from the grazing lands of the Maremma was the safest in all the Sienese state. With the death of Gian Gastone dei Medici and the advent of the Lorena, Palazzo Tantucci was purchased in 1770 and the new space was redistributed into offices, up until

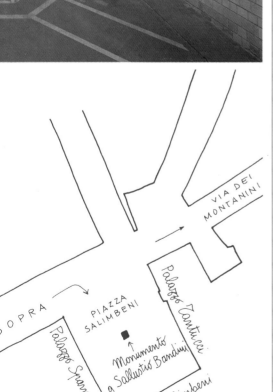

then, most insufficient.

In the meanwhile, Pietro Leopoldo began a series of reforms, encouraging the granting of loans to entrepreneurs who *"pledged themselves to increasing production by taking on new labour"*.

Fundamental for the city, for example, was the financial support of Monte dei Paschi in the retrieval of Pian del Lago, a marshy plain to the north-east of the city. The increasingly close bond with the government of the Grand Duchy distinguished Monte dei Paschi as the real *"instrument of actuation of the vast plan of reforms devised by Pietro Leopoldo"* (G. Catoni).

● *Above:* **The Madonna of the** *"Vetturini"* **by Giovanni di Paolo (about 1440)** *Facing page: Bewailing the body of Christ* **by Arcangelo Salimbeni (1577).**

few years after its foundation (1481), the administrators of the Monte commissioned to Benvenuto di Giovanni a great fresco depicting the *Madonna of Mercy* on the sides of which Bernardino Fungai later added the two great Sienese saints *Bernardino* and *Catherine, St Antonio and Mary Magdalene.* The stems of the city and people of Siena were also added. In the second half of the sixteenth century, yet another fresco underlined the recovery of the banking institute; this time il Rustico was commissioned to paint *The Pity of Christ* (1572).

In the same period, works were commissioned to Arcangelo Salimbeni and Francesco Vanni, who painted a canvas depicting the *Madonna with Child,* crowned with a magnificent carved gilded frame, and numerous paintings were also entrusted to other Sienese artists.

With the incorporation of Tuscany into the Kingdom of Italy, institutional conflicts cropped up in which the city administration of Siena, that, already on 17th August, 1862, had been authorised to approve the resolutions of the Board of Directors of Monte dei Paschi, a body instituted in 1786, assumed a leading role.

On 14th May, 1863, following a proposal by the city council, the privilege held by the Sienese nobility of monopolising the jobs and offices of the Institute was abolished and it was resolved that the nominations to the board of directors be made by the city council.

The Sienese bank is also the only institute of its kind that, right from its birth has paid close attention to the world of art, playing a leading role as patron of the arts in the city. Today, its collections are of great significance to the entire figurative civilisation of Siena. A

Recently, the bank has begun a precise artistic policy.

In this century, in fact, it has found and brought to Siena many masterpieces kept in private collections all over the world, so creating a large collection of works, dating from the fourteenth to the twentieth centuries, by authors such as Pietro Lorenzetti, il Sassetta, Jacopo della Quercia, Antonio Federighi, Sano di Pietro, Domenico Beccafumi, il Riccio, Alessandro Casolani, Francesco Vanni, Rutilio Manetti, il Rustichino, Bernardino Mei, Luigi Mussini and Alessandro Franchi, just to mention the most important names. Furthermore,

Monte dei Paschi has purchased numerous objects belonging to the so-called minor artistic fields, such as furniture, tapestries, objects in majolica, etc., all works of great quality that constitute an important part of the great collection housed in Rocca Salimbeni.

Further along Via dei Montanini, to the left, is a marvellous fifteenth century religious building: the **Church of Santa Maria delle Nevi,** built by the Bishop of Pienza, Giovanni Cinughi, in 1471. The church was owned by the Cinughi family up until a few years ago when it passed to the Italian state. Inside is preserved the great table by Matteo di Giovanni depicting *The Madonna enthroned with son and angels,* nicknamed, in fact, the Madonna delle Nevi.

The balanced Renaissance proportions of the building in Via Montanini, formerly thought to have been built by Francesco di Giorgio, have recently been very closely studied, and now the design of the building has been attributed to Corso di Bastiano, the author of the Church of St Catherine in Fontebranda.

Further along the same street, to the left, is the Piazzetta degli Alberghi where the first Sienese inn-cum-hostel was built along what was, in fact, a stretch of the ancient Via Francigena.

There are also numerous palaces of medieval origins, belonging to the Malavolti family that dominated the whole area towards the Hill of Malavolti (Piazza della Posta), that were quite often transformed, such as Palazzo Turamini that then passed to the Grisaldi del Taja, as a stem points out. Also of importance is **Palazzo Pozzesi**, now called Palazzo Griccioli, with a beautiful stone façade, transformed in the second half of the nineteenth century.

The brick palace once belonging to the Spannocchi is also of interest, while the prestigious **Palazzo Sergardi**, is a great achievement of Paolo Posi (1763). This building, like Palazzo De Vecchi in Pantaneto, realised by the same author, confirms the stylistic trend of this period that harks back to the sixteenth century but uses a lighter technique that makes it less rigorous but equally recognisable.

At the other end of Via del Cavallerizzo is the street that leads to Poggio dei Malavolti. On the left is Piazza Matteotti (Piazza della Posta), an area that was completely redesigned at the beginning of this century. The hill where the houses belonging to the Malavolti family were situated was levelled, Palazzo della Posta was built (1910) and the **Church of the Suore del Paradiso** was equipped with a flight of steps as this building, untouched during the reconstruction work, remained at a higher level than the square. The convent of the Suore del

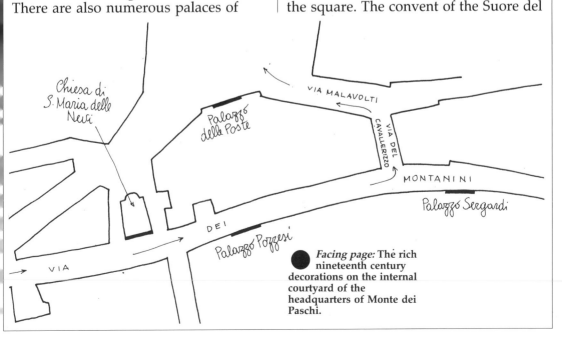

● *Facing page:* The rich nineteenth century decorations on the internal courtyard of the headquarters of Monte dei Paschi.

Paradiso, built at the beginning of the sixteenth century by the Mantellate of St Catherine, was suppressed by the Grand Duke in 1787, while the oratory passed to the Contrada of the Drago.

Inside can be admired a canvas of great quality, depicting the *Pietà and Saints*, placed on the high altar. The painting is a work by Francesco Rustici, il Rustichino, and dates back to about 1614. Also of interest are beautiful canvases on the side altars by Domenico Manetti and Raffaello Vanni. Another interesting object is a polychrome, earthenware bust of St Catherine, realised by Marrina in the 1410's.

At the foot of the steps leading up to the church can be admired the fountain used to baptise new members of the Contrada, realised by Vico Consorti in 1977. Also in the same building is the Victory room. Among the numerous mementoes and objects reminiscent of the life of the Contrada, one can admire a particular Palio, that of 2nd July, 1921, painted by Maria di Maria, the first one to be realised by a woman. Furthermore, Virginia, the first woman jockey to run a Palio, at the end of the sixteenth century, rode for the Contrada of the Drago.

At the end of the gardens of the Lizza, created during the last century from the reconstruction of the area where cavalry manoeuvres were held, is the **Medici Fortress,** a ponderous symbol of the lost liberty of Siena. The Emperor Carlo V ordered the commander of the Spanish garrison, Don Diego de Mendoza, to build a fortress in this area, in around 1548, entrusting the project to Giovan Battista Pelori. The Sienese rightly saw that fortification as an attempt to deprive them of their liberty and autonomy, so much so that, in 1552, they managed to drive the Spaniards from the city and destroy the military citadel. In 1561, however, Grand Duke Cosimo I received the city in feud from the Spaniards and ordered that the great fortification be rebuilt by the architect, Baldassarre Lanci, from Urbino.

The new fortress was built using the

foundations of the previous one and was oriented towards the hill of San Prospero. The rectangular shape also embodies great bulwarks on each of the four corners. The cost of the project amounted to 41,250 ducats and almost a million bricks, eighty thousand paving stones and fifteen thousand litres of mortar were used to build it. In 1567, the two great Medici stems, realised by Francesco Camilliani, were added. The interior of the vast fortress is nowadays

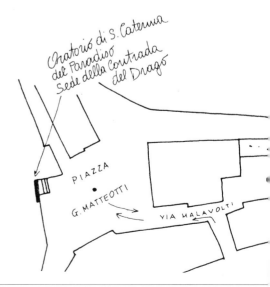

● *Facing page:* The extraordinary *Madonna della Tegola,* object of great devotion of the members of the Contrada of the Drago. *Facing page:* In the butresses of the Fortress of the Medici is the home of the Italian wine-tasting centre in which are conserved the principal wines of every region of Italy.

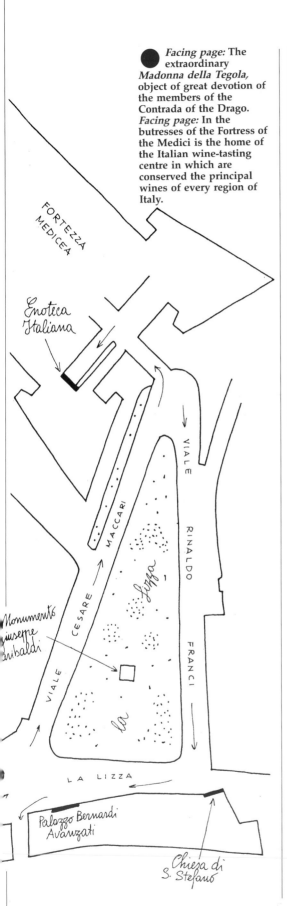

used as a public garden while the vaults of one of the bulwarks contains the **Italian Wine Centre.** This suggestive ''cellar'', established to valorise and accumulate the best national oenological products, is now famous all over the world for the numerous promotional activities conducted with the aim of diffusing and making better known one of the most important products of the Italian economy.

An equestrian monument to Garibaldi by the sculptor Raffaello Romanelli, realised at the very end of the last century, is situated in the middle of the gardens of the Lizza, while, on the left, is the **Church of St Stephen,** of Romanic origins, but completely restored at the end of the eighteenth century. Inside, on the high altar, can be seen a great polyptych depicting the *Madonna with Child and Saints Stephen, James, John the Baptist and Bartholomew,* realised by the Sienese artist, Andrea Vanni, and dating back to 1440.

Of undoubted quality and interest is the dais by Giovanni di Paolo where scenes of the life of St Stephen are represented, with the *Crucifixion* at the centre. A

seventeenth century canvas by Rutilio Manetti, depicting the *Visitation*, is placed on the right-hand altar.

The palaces in front of the gardens were built in the sixteenth century, but have either been substantially modified or completely transformed, such as **Palazzo Bernardi Avanzati** that was totally modernised at the beginning of the nineteenth century. A curvilinear decoration was added to the upper part of the façade at the back (overlooking the Lizza), while an original subdivision comprising ornamental pillars and small cornices, was envisaged for the other façade. The whole of this area became increasingly important in the eighteenth century as it was used for the transit of pedestrians and coaches through the Lizza, towards the fortress.

Right in front of Via del Sasso di San Bernardino, traditionally indicated as the point where the Saint preached to the people of Siena for the first time, is situated the **oratory of St Anna in St Onofrio**, restored in the eighteenth century, containing a canvas by Sebastiano Folli depicting the *Death of St Onofrio* and an earthenware bust of St Bernardino, attributed to the school of Cozzarelli (late fifteenth century). On the left-hand side of the church, at the top of a flight of stairs, is the medieval **Church of St Andrew the Apostle.** This ancient parish church, lying on Via Montanini, was probably built in the middle of the twelfth century and was totally transformed in the eighteenth century, the façade and the floor being repaired. The bell tower and the courtyard behind have recently been totally restored.

Inside the church is a beautiful polyptych, dated 1445 and signed by Giovanni di Paolo, depicting *The coronation of the Virgin between Saints Andrew and Peter.*

A few yards to the right of St Andrew's Church, the name of the street changes into Via di Camollia, the final urban stretch of the Via Francigena before Porta Camollia and the North.

The street is lined with palaces of medieval origins, many of which have been almost completely transformed, even if they frequently preserve unmistakable stylistic and morphological elements. The headquarters and church of the **Sovereign Contrada of the Istrice** is situated on the left, after the cross-roads with Via dei Gazzani and Via Campansi. The oratory of the Contrada of Camollia is the medieval (early fourteenth century) church of Saints Vincenzo and Anastasio. Numerous works of art are displayed in the museum that, naturally, contains the palios won by the Contrada. A table by Sano di Pietro, depicting *The Madonna with Child and Saints Bernardino and Girolamo,* an early sixteenth century Sienese pala-cum-standard, also depicting the *Madonna with Child and Saints* and an early fourteenth century fresco, recently

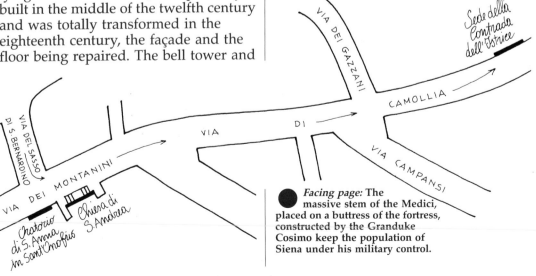

● *Facing page:* The massive stem of the Medici, placed on a buttress of the fortress, constructed by the Granduke Cosimo keep the population of Siena under his military control.

Madonna with Child, dating back to the end of the fourteenth century.

Porta di Pescaia was later blocked off and such was the popular devotion towards the image of the Madonna that an oratory was built against the walls and was named after the well with portico that at that time was situated nearby. The church was dedicated to the Madonna as thanksgiving for the victory obtained by the Sienese at Poggio Imperiale in 1479 and assumed the name of Saint Mary in the Portico of Fontegiusta. It was built to a design by Cristoforo Fedeli of Como between 1482 and 1484. The central part of the brick façade is artificially raised to form a triangle and the inside of the church, square in shape, with three naves, has no apse and the great marble columns support the cross vaults.

Numerous interesting works of art are preserved inside, such as, for example, the famous sixteenth century fresco depicting the *Sibyl prophesying the coming of Christ to Augustus* attributed to Baldassare Peruzzi, a beautiful, fourteenth century, wooden *Crucifix,* frescoes by Ventura Salimbeni depicting the *Birth, Annunciation and transit of the Madonna* (about 1600), the marble altar that surrounds the image that gave origin to the church, a great work by Lorenzo Mariani, nicknamed il Marrina, realised in the 1510's, and the splendid canvas depicting the *Blessed Ambrogio Sansedoni imploring Jesus, the Madonna and St Bartholomew to protect the city of*

detached from the outside of the church, depicting *the Blessing of Jesus,* are worthy of mention. Also of interest are some seventeenth and eighteenth centuries canvases, the impressive collection of sacred drapes and objects in gold, as well as various works by Sienese artists who lived and worked at the end of the last and the beginning of this century, such as Pietro Aldi, Vittorio Giunti, Arturo Viligardi, etc..

A little further ahead, on the left-hand side of Via Camollia, a detour can be made to the *Church of Fontegiusta.* Before the construction of the oratory, the revenue booth of Porta di Pescaia was situated against the city walls next to the gate, together with an image of the

This page: The refined *Madonna with Child and Saints* by Sano di Pietro, preserved in the Museum of the Contrada of the Istrice. *Facing page:* In the beautiful table by Francesco Vanni (1590) contained in the Church of Fontegiusta, the *Blessed Ambrogio Sansedoni invokes the protection heaven on Siena,* accurately illustrated in the bottom half of the painting.

Siena by Francesco Vanni (1590). Some small trophies that were supposed to have been offered by Christopher Columbus during his stay in Siena at the local university, consist of a helmet, a harquebuse, a whale bone and a painted wooden shield, all preserved in the small museum in Fontegiusta.

Back in Via di Camollia, to the left, is the **Church of St Pietro alla Magione.**
The Magione was built near Porta Camollia to put up the pilgrims in transit and dates back at least to the year 1000.
At the beginning of the fourteenth century, when the order of the Templars was suppressed, the Magione passed to the order of Jerusalem and later to the Knights of Malta. The façade of the Romanic church dates back to the fourteenth century, even though recent and useless additions have been made.

The church contains a canvas by the Spanish painter Diego Pesco (1760) depicting the *Madonna in Glory and Saints,* an interesting fifteenth century synopia representing the *Madonna and Angels* and a marble tabernacle, also of the fifteenth century. A few yards further on is Piazza Guido Chigi Saracini from which can be admired the mighty walls of Porta di Camollia. Unfortunately the whole inside area was redesigned and therefore, to admire the elegant decoration of the gate, one must pass through it towards Viale Vittorio Emanuele II.
The famous phrase written at the centre of the fortification by the Medici reads ''COR MAGIS TIBI SENA PANDIT''.
A few yards outside the gate, to the right, is situated the elegant seventeenth century chapel of the **Holy Sepulchre** while further along the same street is the Antiporto di Camollia: an extra defensive barrier against the Florentines, built in stone in around 1270. The antiporto was originally joined to the gate by two high walls that ran along the sides of the

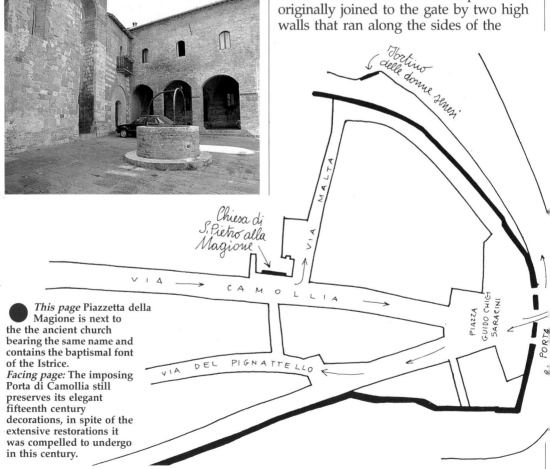

● *This page* Piazzetta della Magione is next to the the ancient church bearing the same name and contains the baptismal font of the Istrice.
Facing page: The imposing Porta di Camollia still preserves its elegant fifteenth century decorations, in spite of the extensive restorations it was compelled to undergo in this century.

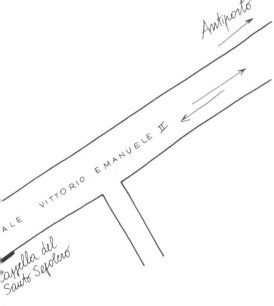

Back through the gate, on the left, one can admire a beautiful view of the Sienese countryside and enter, on the right, one of the most characteristic medieval streets of the city: Via del Pignattello.

Along this street lies the ex-convent of the Convertite, now almost completely transformed, even if a part of the original façade can still be seen. At the end of Via del Pignatello is one side of the great complex of **St Girolamo in Campansi,** now used as an old people's home. This ancient Franciscan convent was built in around 1420 but was modified in different periods. The actual church, built during the decisive restoration carried out at the end of the nineteenth century, contains some canvases by Pietro Locatelli, while works by Sano di Pietro, Pietro di Domenico and Domenico Beccafumi are preserved in the ex-monastery.

Back in Via di Camollia, along a lane on the left that once led to the ancient Convento of the Umiliati, is to be found

present street. On the opposite side, in Via Biagio di Monluc, can still be admired the remains of the **Fortino delle donne**, a bulwark built by Baldassarre Peruzzi between 1527 and 1532, and defended by the women of Siena during the dramatic siege of the city.

the entrance to **Villa Rubini Manenti,** now used as an old people's home, and its splendid centuries-old park, from which one can enjoy a pleasant view of a large part of the city (see page 215). Right in front of the entrance to the villa is Piazza del Sale, completely transformed, at the end of which, however, can be perceived architectural elements pertaining to an old monastery. Via Garibaldi, that now leads towards the railway station, was completely redesigned during the last century to suit it to modern day traffic conditions, but this "improvement" so strangled the pre-existing urban structure that the **Church of St Sebastiano,** in fact, lies under the level of the street. The church, restored in the seventeenth century, contains some particularly interesting frescoes by Sienese authors of the seventeenth century such as Casolani, Folli, Volpi and Manetti.

In the same street, on the left, just before the Barrier of San Lorenzo, is situated the **Consuma,** the legendary headquarters of the "brigata spendereccia", mentioned by Dante, where many young, wealthy Sienese noblemen were said to have wasted away their entire fortunes in feasts and banquets.

The Barrier of San Lorenzo, a breach made in the wall at the end of the last century to make the railway station easier to reach, replaced the old gate of San Lorenzo and its desirability was the object of heated debate at the time.

Pian d'Ovile, the street in front of the Consuma that runs down the side of **Palazzo Franci,** the centre of a thriving trade in wrought iron in the nineteenth century, leads to **Fontenuova,** situated on the left.

This medieval well is one of the most significant examples of the care taken by the Sienese, during the centuries in which the economy of the city underwent its greatest expansion, over the necessity of rationalising a precious commodity such as water. Fontenuova is one of the most beautiful wells of Siena and its majestic lines are a suggestive example of the usual synthesis between functionality and

harmony sought for by the Sienese. Right opposite can be admired the apse of the sixteenth century church of St Rocco, the present headquarters of the **Contrada of the Lupa.** This building houses both the oratory and the museum of the Contrada. The church of St Rocco contains a large number of paintings by the Sienese masters of the sixteenth and

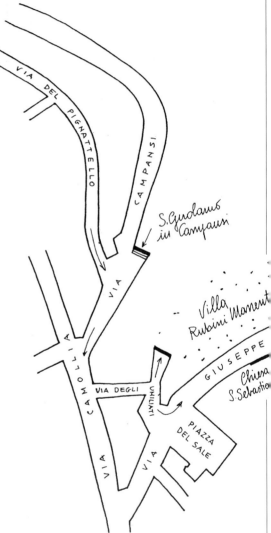

seventeenth centuries. Of particular interest are the frescoes of the "Cappellone" by Rutilio Manetti depicting the *Stories of St Rocco*, the frescoes by Bernardino Mei and Simondio Salimbeni and also some canvases by Raffaello Vanni and Ventura Salimbeni.

At the foot of Via di Vallerozzi, heart of the Contrada of the Lupa, is Porta

Ovile, a city gate that dates back to the fourteenth century but which was later modified.

On the right hand side of the gate is Via del Comune that, together with Via degli Orti and Via di Mezzo, comprises the territory of the **Nobile Contrada of the Bruco,** one of the largest and most active contradas of the city.

Halfway along the steep slope lie the museum and the oratory of this Contrada that counted mainly wool and

Fontenuova, an example of the importance attached by the Sienese to the distribution of water.

silk workers among its members, who, in 1371, gave life to one of the first episodes of "class struggles" of European history, led by the commoner, Barbicone, that even managed to provoke, if only for a few days, the

fall of the government of the Republic.
The oratory contains a beautiful,
fourteenth century table by Luca
di Tommè, depicting the *Madonna
with Child.*
At the top of Via del Comune and along
Via dei Rossi is situated Piazza San
Francesco with the great **Basilica of
St Francis** that closes off this suggestive
space like an enormous curtain behind
which lie the Chianti hills.
The ancient Franciscan convent,
nowadays headquarters of the Faculty of
Economics and Jurisprudence of the
University of Siena, was founded at the
beginning of the thirteenth century and
was enlarged more than once in the
fifteenth century due to the increase
in the number of monks.
The majestic gothic building, however,
has been frequently modified down the
centuries due to the various disasters
that have damaged the church, among
which the tremendous fire of 1655 that
almost completely destroyed the
furnishings.

However, St Francis still contains objects
of exceptional interest, such as the
celebrated cycle of frescoes by Ambrogio
Lorenzetti, depicting *Episodes in the life of
the Franciscans,* and a splendid
Crucifixion by his brother Pietro.
These paintings are reminiscent of
the masterpieces of the Lorenzetti
brothers realised for the Palazzo
Pubblico in Siena and the Basilica
of St Francis in Assisi.
Other objects of great value include a
great polyptych by Lippo Vanni and a
remarkable funeral monument to
Cristoforo Felici, realised by Urbano
da Cortona in 1460.
Also worthy of attention is the portal by
Francesco di Giorgio that was
transferred to the inside of the church
during the purist restoration of the
building, begun by Giuseppe Partini
and concluded at the beginning of this
century by Vittorio Mariani who was
also responsible for the questionable
reconstruction of the façade.
On the other side of the square lies one of

the most significant religious buildings of the Sienese sixteenth century: the **Oratory of the Company of St Bernardino.** This building comprises two small oratories; to be admired on the ground floor are the lunettas that were frescoed at the end of the sixteenth century by Sienese authors, such as Ventura Salimbeni and Rutilio Manetti. Perhaps the most prestigious work conserved there, however, is the bas-relief by

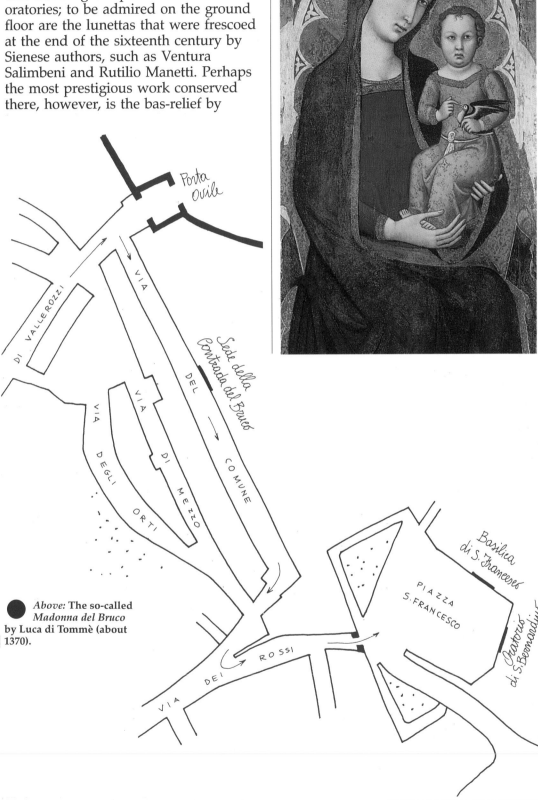

Above: **The so-called** *Madonna del Bruco* **by Luca di Tommè (about 1370).**

Giovanni d'Agostino, realised in the 1330's, one of the most appreciated works of Sienese sculpure.

On the upper floor, instead, is an exceptional cycle, realised by the most famous artists of the early sixteenth century, such as Beccafumi, il Sodoma and il Pacchia, who, in the first thirty years of the sixteenth century, enriched the oratory with the *Stories of the Virgin*. Leaving the square, Via dei Baroncelli, to the left, leads, through a maze of narrow and suggestive lanes, to the headquarters of the **Imperial Contrada of the Giraffa**, situated in Via delle Vergini, at the foot of the magnificent structure of the **Basilica of Provenzano.**

● The Oratory of St Bernardino contains a magnificient cycle of frescoes dedicated to the *Stories of the Virgin,* realised by the greatest Sienese painters of the early sixteenth century.

The oratory of the Contrada is dedicated to the *Madonna del Fosso,* a fifteenth century fresco, detached from one of the streets in the ward and, after a pilgrimage that lasted centuries, found its final resting place in the chapel of the Giraffa. By a singular series of circumstances, the headquarters of the Contrada boasts some palios painted by the most famous contemporary artists in Italy, such as Renato Guttuso, Renzo Vespignani and Riccardo Tommasi Ferroni.

At the top of the steps, along the side of the room of the Victories of the Contrada, is the great Piazza di Provenzano, dominated by the imposing white mass of the basilica, dedicated to a miraculous image of the Madonna, damaged by a Spanish harquebuse halfway through the sixteenth century, right on the site where the church now stands.

The Palio of 2nd July is dedicated to the Madonna of Provenzano and, immediately after the race, the winning Contrada takes the palio to the church where the ''Te Deum'' of thanksgiving is sung and where the devotion to the sacred reliquary is renewed.

The basilica was one of the first buildings of architectural significance to be constructed in Siena after the conquest by the Medici. The church was built where the palaces belonging to the noble Salvani family, from whose ranks the famous Provenzano came, once stood. Work began in 1595 from a design by Damiano Schifardini, a Sienese monk at the Certosa of Florence, although the building operations were directed by Flaminio del Turco. The project was finished in 1604, but the church was only consecrated in 1611, when, with a solemn procession, immortalised by

various images of the Sienese iconographic tradition, the miraculous image of the Madonna was translated into the church.

The beautiful façade reminds us of Roman models, such as the Church of Jesus del Vignola, and the imposing dome is reminiscent of the basilica of St Peter. The inside is richly furnished and includes a series of canvases of great interest by Bernardino Mei, Rutilio Manetti and Francesco Rustici. The altar was realised by Flaminio del Turco

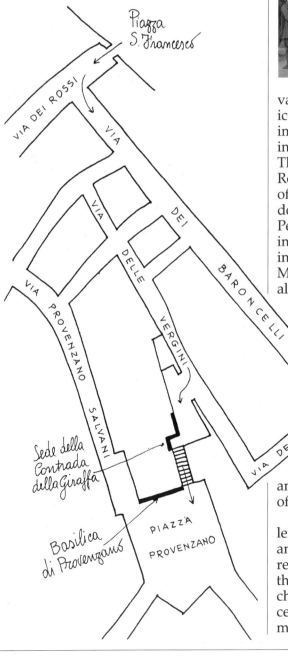

● *This page:* A detail of the Biccherna depicting *The Translation of the Madonna of Provenzano* (1613). *Facing page:* The majestic prospect of the Basilica of Provenzano.

and displays a marked and elegant sense of monumentality.

Along Vicolo di Provenzano, to the left, is the **Church of St Pietro a Ovile,** an important example of medieval religous construction, notwithstanding the eighteenth century modifications. The church contains the remarkable, fifteenth century *Annunciation*, inspired by the more famous pala realised by Simone

Martini for the Cathedral of Siena, now preserved in the Gallery of the Uffizi in Florence. Also to be admired is a fresco, also depicting the *Annunciation,* situated in the apse and attributed to Bartolo di Fredi, and, at the bottom, a magnificent *Cross* by Giovanni di Paolo, realised in about 1440.

Leaving San Pietro a Ovile and back once again in Via dei Rossi, a little further on, to the right, is Piazza dell'Abbadia, where, in front of Rocca Salimbeni, is situated the **Church of St Donato,** a medieval building that has been greatly modified over the centuries. Inside, among the numerous works of art belonging to various periods, is to be admired the beautiful *Cataletto* by il Sodoma, comprising four coffin heads.

Returning along Via dei Rossi and Via del Refe Nero, at the cross-roads with Via Lucherini, built in the nineteenth century, one can enjoy a beautiful view of Piazza Provenzano and the façade of the church. A few yards further on, still to the left, is the beautiful fifteenth century building, ennobled by a great stone tympanum, attributed to Antonio Federighi, that once belonged to the Bandini Piccolomini family (it is now the headquarters of the University administration). Right opposite is Via San Vigilio with the **Church of St Vigilio** that formed part of an ancient convent and now belongs to the University of Siena. The building was probably built by the Ugurgieri family between the eleventh and twelfth centuries. Ownership then went to the Camoldesian monks, then to the Jesuits until their suppression by Leopoldo and then to the monks of Vallombrosa. In the eighteenth century, many restorations were made on the building, including the façade of the church by Antonio Matteucci, as well as the addition of a double flight of steps. Among the many works of art preserved here are to be mentioned a marble altar by Tommaso Redi and Dioniso Mazzuoli, a canvas depicting the *Glory of St Ignazio* by Mattia Preti, a bronze *Crucifix* attributed to Pietro Tacca, some sculptures by Giuseppe Mazzuoli and a canvas depicting *St Anna teaching the Madonna to read* by Romanelli.

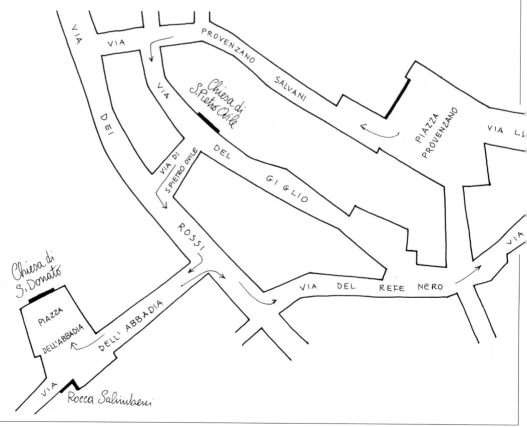

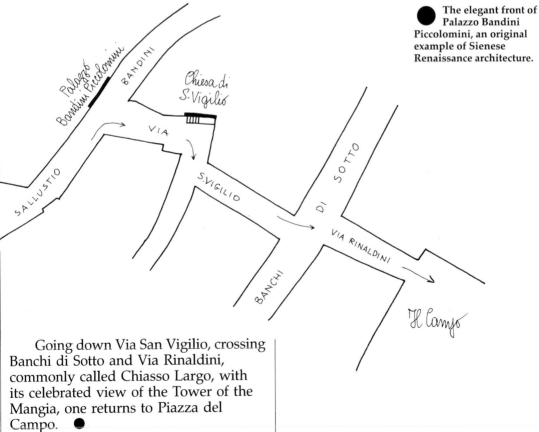

● The elegant front of
  Palazzo Bandini
Piccolomini, an original
example of Sienese
Renaissance architecture.

Going down Via San Vigilio, crossing
Banchi di Sotto and Via Rinaldini,
commonly called Chiasso Largo, with
its celebrated view of the Tower of the
Mangia, one returns to Piazza del
Campo. ●

IL MONTE DEI PASCHI:
REFINED PATRONS OVER THE CENTURIES

If the word "city" implies the organised place of community life, where the people who live there use their labour and creativity to construct as admirable and comfortable an environment as possible, this definition of the word explains the reason why a great bank like Monte dei Paschi has prospered in the singular city of Siena for over five centuries.

It was precisely its ancient foundation (1472) and, consequently, its development hand in hand with that of the city over the centuries, that ensured that a tightly woven link was formed between the bank and the Sienese community, an authentic symbiosis that often exceeded its institutional functions to reach the more complex spheres of civic life, touching the most hidden fibres of the connective tissue of the city.

Furthermore, as one of the peculiar characteristics of Sienese society is the love

● The *Madonna della Misericordia* by Benvenuto di Giovanni was the first painting to be commissioned by Monte dei Paschi (1481).
Facing page: The elegant figure of *Sant'Antonio Abate* by il Sassetta, one of the most important works among those present in the collection of the bank.

of art and beautiful things, the ancient Monte Pio could not but emulate this tendency that struggled to embellish every corner of the city, including even the most anonymous government ledgers.

It was with this spirit that, in 1481, the governors of Monte Pio, recently founded by the government to curtail the despotism of the usurers, commissioned a *Madonna della Misericordia* to the painter Benvenuto di Giovanni, that, significantly, depicts the Madonna sheltering under her soft mantle whoever in Siena needed to be helped by the

new charitable institution. Shortly afterwards it was decided to add other Saints to the figure of the Virgin, the two most venerated by the Sienese, *St Bernardino* and *St Catherine,* and also *St Antonio of Padua* and *St Mary Magdalene.* The *Achievements of the Government and people of Siena* by Bernardino Fungai was also placed under this sacred composition so as to testify not only the strong link existing between the bank and the city and its government, but also with its most deeply-rooted traditions.

In the second half of the sixteenth century, while the bank successfully pursued a solid future, partially compromised by the downfall of the free Republic, a fresco depicting *The Pity of Christ* was commissioned to Lorenzo Rustici, a typical subject for the financial institutions of that time.

The painting is one of the greatest works by the founder of a successful family of artists that worked in Siena between the sixteenth and seventeenth centuries.

Monte dei Paschi also possesses the two most famous works by Lorenzo's son, Vincenzo: *The procession of the contradas* and *The bull-hunt* that constitute a document of exceptional value, accompanied by a very analytical description of the Palio of 15th August, 1546, written by Cecchino, a paper merchant.

Significant in this sense is the presence in the collection of Rocca Salimbeni of two eighteenth century canvases by Giuseppe Zocchi, depicting *The celebrations held in Siena in honour of Grand Duke Francesco I* and one painted in the middle of the last century by Francesco Nenci, depicting *The procession of the contradas held in 1818 in honour of Grand Duke Ferdinando III.*

Around this important original nucleus, especially in this century, thanks to a courageous and pioneering policy that has created a trend now followed by others, Monte dei Paschi has carefully studied the international market and collected various glorious examples of the great figurative civilisation of Siena, not limiting itself to its most famous periods, thereby creating one of the most prestigious collections in the world.

A series of masterpieces by artists such as Pietro Lorenzetti, Sano di Pietro, Sassetta, Giovanni di Paolo, Andrea del Brescianino,

Bartolomeo Neroni (il Riccio), Alessandro Casolani, Francesco Vanni, Rutilio Manetti, Raffaello Vanni, Bernardino Mei, by sculptors such as Jacopo della Quercia, Domenico di Niccolò dei Cori, Antonio Federighi and Benedetto da Maiano, have been thus preserved.

This suggestive summary of Sienese and Italian art of the most flourishing centuries of our civilisation is displayed in a modern setting in the especially restored rooms of the ancient church of San Donato, adjoing Rocca Salimbeni, where, as well as the masterpieces of the major masters, important examples of the so-called minor arts are also preserved. To be particularly admired are the

● The Madonna enthroned with Child, otherwise known as the "Madonna of Chiusdino".
Sienese sculptor of the middle of the XVth century
Facing page: A detail of the painting by Rutilio Manetti *Jesus admonishing the Magdalene.*

refined sixteenth century tapestries of Tournai and Brussels, some fifteenth century sacresty furniture and other carved objects of the fifteenth and sixteenth centuries.

This perspicacious policy of Monte dei Paschi has led to the retrieval of important works of ancient Sienese art, dispersed at the end of the last century by improvident owners. At the same time, it has not omitted to collect works of art of periods closer to our time, especially those of the fortunate purist season led by the famous Luigi Mussini, and a series of paintings by some of the most brilliant artists of the Italian school of this century such as Ottone Rosai, Ardengo Soffici, Mario Mafai and the Sienese Dario Neri. ●

SAN DOMENICO:
A DIALOGUE WITH THE CATHEDRAL

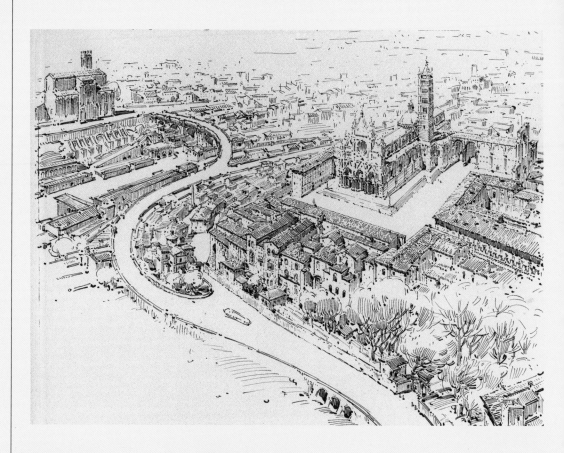

This page: The ambitious project, of the first years of the twentieth century, by Arturo Viligiardi, that reproposed the medieval idea of connecting the Cathedral with St Domenico across the Valley of Fontebranda by means of a gigantic bridge.
Facing page: The majestic interior of the building of St Domenico.
Following page: A detail of the *Fainting of St Catherine,* a celebrated fresco by il Sodoma.

Probably not even Fortebraccio Malavolti, the Sienese nobleman, who, in 1225, donated his land on the hill of Camporegio to the Domenican monks to allow them to build their church and convent, imagined that a gigantic structure such as that which overlooks the Valley of Fontebranda would shortly arise and that this building would be capable of "conversing" on an equal footing with the refined lines of the Cathedral that faces the great building of San Domenico.
At the end of the fourteenth century, the hypothesis of

joining the two areas of the city with an enourmous bridge was discussed. This very same hypothesis was reconsidered also at the beginning of this century by Arturo Viligiardi who, thankfully, never got past the design stage, but realised a beatiful sketch that is now displayed in the City Museum.
Thanks to the support of the Sienese nobility and the alms that constantly flowed into the coffers of the convent, the church, dedicated to the founder of the order, Domenico di Guzman, who probably visited Siena at the beginning of the thirteenth century, was finished after approximately forty years

work (about 1262). Towards the middle of the fourteenth century, the structure was modified with a series of additions, mainly to the apse and the central nave.

The following centuries were instead marked by numerous dramatic and destructive fires, additions and "free and easy" restorations, almost up to this day and age. The last restoration, in neo-purist style, was begun in 1941 and finished at the beginning of the 1960's. In particular, apart from the two fires of 1433 and 1531 (the latter almost destroyed the head of the Saint, the most precious reliquary of the cult of Catherine), San Domenico was one of the buildings worst hit by the disastrous earthquake of 1798. Some parts of the building were reduced to a mass of rubble, so much so, that the idea of demolishing the whole structure and starting from scratch was considered. The convent and the church had been previously occupied for about five years by the Spanish soldiers of Don Diego de Mendoza, who, in the middle of the sixteenth century, used many of the vast rooms in San Domenico not only as his headquarters but also to store powder and provisions.

Notwithstanding the numerous transformations of the building (an interesting comparison can be made between the church as it stands today and the plan of Siena designed by Francesco Vanni at the end of the sixteenth century in which one can note a gothic bell tower and the original proportions of the building), San Domenico is particularly fascinating for the strong tie it has with the life and cult of Catherina Benincasa, nun of the third order of the Domenicans, who right in the Chapel of the Vaults, performed some of the miracles that are described in detail by her biographer, the blessed Raimondo da Capua in his *Legenda Major*.

Notwithstanding the tormented history of the building, San Domenico contains a great quantity of works of art of the highest level realised by major Sienese artists. An exceptional example is the chapel dedicated to St Catherine, situated halfway down the great nave with its refined marble altar, a fifteenth century work by Giovanni di Stefano and with the frescoes on the sides realised by il Sodoma in 1526. They depict *The fainting* and *The ecstacy* of the Saint while, on the other side, the same artists painteded the perturbing fresco representing the *Beheading of Tuldo*. Seventy years later, on the opposite side, Francesco Vanni realised *The liberation of a possessed person by St Catherine*, a work with very lively colours and a notable perpective layout.

The walls and the chapels of San Domenico reserve many pleasant "surprises", and compel one's eyes to wander along a suggestive pictorial journey, even though it is not in perfect chronological order. One cannot, for example, help stopping to admire the exceptionally beautiful table realised by Francesco di Giorgio, depicting the *Adoration of the Shepherds*, one of the few paintings by this distinguished protagonist of the Renaissance.

The upper lunetta of the painting of the *Pietà* is instead a work by another great fifteenth century artist, Matteo di Giovanni, while the lower dais was realised by Barnardino Fungai, an excellent illustrator of the same period.

Other two tables by Matteo di Givanni, of great originality and compositive refinement, represent *St Barbara enthroned with Angels and Saints* and the *Epiphany*. Among the "surprises" to be found in San Domenico is a youthful fresco by Petro Lorenzetti depicting the *Madonna with Child, St John and a horseman*, a *Madonna with Child* by Francesco di Vannuccio, a great table with *The Madonna enthroned with Child, Angels and Saints*, by Benvenuto di Giovanni, a ciborium and two candlesticks in the form of angels realised at the end of the fifteenth century by Benedetto da Maiano, as well as numerous other tables by various authors.

Later periods are also well represented with works by artists such as Mattia Preti, Fancesco Rustici, Rutilio Manetti, Alessandro Casolani, Stefano Volpi, Crescenzio Gambarelli, Deifebo Burbarini and others.

One of the fundamental works of all Sienese painting, the thirteenth century *Madonna enthroned with Child*, by Guido da Siena, now in the rooms of the City Museum, was originally painted for the Church of San Domenico. In the underlying crypt, the entrance to which is on the right hand side of the church, can be admired a beautiful gold cross painted by Sano di Pietro in around the middle of the fifteenth century and two interesting canvases by Ventura Salimbeni and Sebastiano Folli, depicting the *Crucifixion* and a *Vision of St Catherine*. ●

Palazzo Tolomei

This palace was the home of that frail heroine, celebrated by many romantic authors: the tender and defenceless Pia, whose distressing story even Dante, who placed it in an anonymous part of his Purgatory, was unable to interpret, even though he betrays a delicate sentiment of sympathy towards her. She probably enlivened the austere rooms of the beautiful stone palace with her youthful freshness before leaving on that final, tragic journey that led her to die among the miasma of the marshes of the Maremma. From the elegant mullioned windows of the palace, Pia was able to observe the never ending column of pilgrims that winded its weary way along Via Francigena, driven by spiritual fire and thankful to finally find themselves in the safety of a hospitable city, far from the dangers and suffering of the road. But while the surname of Tolomei evokes the desperate ghost of Pia described by Dante, it is also the name of a family that boasts a genealogical tree crowded with important personages in the history of Siena and Italy. Hagiographers have struggled for centuries to trace the fabulous origins of the family. It is commonly assumed, however, that the first person of any importance was a certain Baldistricca Tolomei, who reached Siena with Pipino il Breve, whose name clearly betrays his German origins

and whose surname may have been derived from his studies of the astrological art and the teachings of the great Ptolemy of Alexandria. Between the twelfth and thirteenth centuries, many Tolomei's held positions of responsibility in the government of Siena. A Tolomei was ambassador of Alexander III. Pelacane was steward to the government in 1228 and in the same period Lotterengo carried out a delicate mission as Ambassador to Arezzo.
Partly due to well-chosen weddings with the heirs of other great Sienese families (Saracini, Piccolomini, Malavolti, Salimbeni) the family built up a conspicuous financial empire, based mainly on banking, foreign loans and tax collections for the papacy. But the Tolomei also invested their fortune in successful commercial activities, often visiting the great French fairs, and

especially the famous one of Champagne. There they purchased all kinds of goods: cloth and skins, spices and metals, alum and wax.
Due to its elevated economic position, that allowed the family to grant numerous loans even to the government of Siena, the Tolomei were more or less obliged to build a more prestigious residence that was constructed at the beginning of the thirteenth century on the site of previous and less noble buildings belonging to them. In Piazza Tolomei, much smaller than nowadays as the church of St Cristoforo had one more span, public ceremonies and popular assemblies were often held on the occasion of particular events and anniversaries. It must also be remembered that the heated debate in which, in September, 1260, it was decided to resist against the Florentines, was held in that church. The Tolomei participated in these important events as hospitable hosts. They were in fact owners of a number of buildings in the area, positioned according to the usual layout of a fortified residence.
As a sixteenth century tablet reminds us, the Tolomei had their palace constructed on these buildings following the architectural customs of the time.
The main façade and entrance to the palace opened onto Via dei Termini while only secondary and tradesmen's entrances gave onto the square. The

A. Palazzo a guisa di Fortilizio, della Nobil Conti Tolomei · E. Abitazione del Sig Pietro Comberti ·
B. Colonna con Lupa di metallo per sostenere l'Arma Tolo · F. Piccoliss.parte del Palazzo de Nob.SS.Palmieri ·
C. Piazza detta Tolomei ·   G. Piccole case attorno la Piazza ·
D. Palazzo Marescotti Tolomei ·   H. Strade che introducono nella Piazza Tolomei ·

construction of the building, however, continued hand in hand with historical and political events that at times stimulated the phases of growth but at others, sparked off tragic events that caused deep wounds to be inflicted on the building. The family was often the object of ferocious hatred and virulent popular demonstrations and on these occasions the palace, not only the place of shelter but also the symbol of power of the ancient family, was often attacked.
In 1267, this hatred resulted in the total, systematic destruction of the palace that even included a project of demolition entrusted to a diligent mason called Lotterio.
At around the end of the thirteenth century the building, probably rebuilt in its previous form, acquired the aspect that, for better or for worse, it has today, notwithstanding the fury of the centuries.
From the elegant mullioned windows, that served as an example to subsequent aristocratic residences, including Palazzo Pubblico, the Tolomei family continued for centuries to observe the flow of travellers, many of whom, probably, stopped to admire the beautiful cut stone palace. ●

● *This page:* An eighteenth century illustration of Piazza Tolomei, taken from the "guide" of the learned Giovanni Antonio Pecci. *Underneath:* A representative of the noble Tolomei family still takes part in the historical pageant of the Palio, together with the horsemen of the most important Sienese families.

IL CIRCOLO DEGLI UNITI:
A BALCONY OVERLOOKING THE PALIO

● *This page:* **Prospect of Casino dei Nobili facing Piazza del Campo.**

The Sienese aristocracy that gave life to the club of the "Signori Uniti del Casino" on 13th November, 1657, had completely changed since medieval times when it was excluded from the government of the city at the end of the thirteenth century upon the rise to power of the Nove. But the medieval heritage of the city with its rigorous class divisions was still strongly felt and, therefore, the various academies that had been founded in Renaissance times still heeded these distinctions. At the beginning of the sixteenth century, in fact, the Academies of the Rozzi and of the Intronati were already flourishing in Siena, both of which formed perfect examples of brotherhood dedicated to cultural enrichment and the organisation of celebrations and entertainment.

The members of the Rozzi were, however, almost all craftsmen while the Intronati mainly belonged to the bourgeoisie. The nobility was therefore almost obliged to found an exclusive organisation aimed mainly at intellectual exchanges and agreeable conversation and, as a result, sparked off a vast activity that anticipated by far the birth of the famous English clubs that only began to organise themselves in the eighteenth century. The Circolo degli Uniti of Siena can, therefore, rightly be considered the oldest brotherhood of its kind.

Their first headquarters was rented in Via di Città, next to Palazzo Patrizi, and must have met their full approval as, ten years later, they decided to purchase it, selling their furniture and silver to put together the necessary sum.

At that time, the statute limited the number of members to twenty-four, just like the ancient government of the Nove. People under twenty or over seventy and women were excluded.

The activity of the club immediately became very intense and included both events of a strictly cultural nature such as literary conversations and recitals of

poetic verse, and public celebrations, organised during carnival time and, above all, during the Palios with which the Uniti have always had strong links. In fact, both the Deputies of the Celebration and the Captains of the Contradas were almost always chosen from among the noble members of the club.

Many Palios were directly promoted by the Uniti, especially on the occasion of visits of illustrious guests for whom the Palio was both a source of entertainment and a good way of getting to know the city in its proudest moment.

After a period of scarce activity, caused above all by the ban imposed by the bigot, Cosimo III, the Uniti restarted their intense activity by organising an extraordinary Palio (2nd July 1717) in honour of the new governor Princess Beatrice Violante of Baviera, who, on her arrival, had received a clamorous welcome from the Sienese nobility. The celebration was magnificent and, as well as the race, a scenic apparatus of great effect was arranged. The Grand Duke was enthusiastic at the welcome received and the nobles took advantage of this situation to ask the Sovereign for Palazzo della Mercanzia, as their headquarters in Via di Città were by now inadequate to cope with the growing social requirements of the club.

A few days later, the Grand Duke granted the members what they had asked for and also authorised them to

carry out the rebuilding the palace. They were not permitted, however, to touch the splendid Renaissance loggia with the sculptures of Vecchietta and Federighi. Once the problems connected with the French dominion had been solved, after the Restoration, the Casino dei Nobili began its activity again and it was established that women, too, could frequent the social rooms as long as they were of noble descent, or married to noble strangers. Officers, too, were allowed to frequent the club (if they were not of noble birth, they were obliged to present themselves in uniform), as well as the professors

of the Studio Senese.

The Uniti still carry out activities principally aimed at the associative life of its members, even though the prestigious headquarters is revitalised in the days of the Palio as it offers the members of the Sienese nobility and their numerous guests a privileged position from which to watch the race. ●

St Catherine of Siena

The first painting depicting Catherine of Siena, a fresco by Andrea Vanni, realised for the church of San Domenico during the second half of the fourteenth century, seems to be, according to a strongly consolidated tradition, the only portrait of the Saint painted while she was still alive.

In this intensely gracious and moving painting with the beautifully sinuous lines of the veil and the habit, the intimate portrait of the Saint talking to a believer seems to sum up the character of this extraordinary person, whose fame, over the centuries, has spread throughout the whole of Europe.

Catherine was born in Fontebranda on 25th March, 1347, daughter of Jacopo Benincasa, a dyer, and Lapa Piagenti, a washerwoman. The second but last of twenty-four children, she entered, against the will of her family, the Mantellate of the third Dominican order of nuns when she was sixteen, immediately dedicating herself to the care of the poor and the sick. Her continual visions and the life dedicated to charity and human suffering roused in the Sienese population feelings of great admiration towards this courageous commoner from Fontebranda, who directly experienced the tormented political and religious events of the fifteenth century. She exchanged letters with the rulers and representatives of the ecclesiastical hierarchy

● *This page:* The oldest "portrait" of Catherine of Siena, realised by Andrea Vanni in the Church of San Domenico.
Facing page: A detail of the frescoes by Sebastiano Folli depicting episodes in the life of St Catherine, preserved in the Oratory of the Dying Shop in Fontebranda.

of all Europe; this important correspondence is contained in the famous *Epistolario* that comprises 382 letters, not written by her, but dictated to some of her disciples such as Stefano Maconi, Neri Pagliaresi, Barduccio Canigiani, Tommaso di Antonio da Siena, called il Caffarini, and the lawyer, Cristofano di Gano Guidini. Catherine died in Rome on 29th April, 1380, but, notwithstanding the great veneration in which she had been held during her life, it was not until 1461 that the Sienese Pope, Enea Silvio Piccolomini, Pio II canonised her.

The canonisation of Catherine was an event that shook the Christian world. In 1462, the "Societas Sancte Caterine" was founded; in the meantime, many pilgrims began to visit her birth place that was completely transformed by the people of Fontebranda in 1465, and immediately enriched with one of the greatest artistic achievements of the Sienese Renaissance, the polychrome wooden statue by Neroccio di Bartolomeo Landi. This oratory was not meant just to absolve its religious and symbolic functions, but also had to represent the complete synthesis of the cult of Catherine with the closely knit community of Fontebranda and the city itself.

The role that Catherine played in the public life of her time was very effective and she influenced many important politicals event: the crusades, the crisis of the Church, the papacy in Avignon, the Western Schism, the peace between Florence and the Holy See. The return of Gregory XI, a Frenchman, as were all his cardinals, to the Vatican after seventy years of exile in Avignon was perhaps the episode that best allows us to understand the power of persuasion that St Catherine possessed. In fact, she, together with a group of her disciples, among which her confessor and spiritual guide, Raimondo da Capua, after an adventurous journey that lasted two

weeks followed by a stay of four months, managed to bring the papacy back to Rome, *"its right place"*, as Catherine loved to define the seat of the successor of Peter.

The school of thought of Catherine places the dignity of mankind in pride of place, rational faith characterised by action and meditation. For Catherine, charity knows no limits and it is only by this means that man can reach God who created men so that they might love one another. A society is a union of individuals, a moral unity that has as its aim the very aim of the individuals that comprise it, therefore the common good is the primary aim of society and in this way justice is done. It's sufficient, however, just to read a few of her many letters to understand, even at a distance of centuries, the complexity and relevance even today of the ideas of Catherine that evoke the spirit of unity and solidarity among the peoples of the world. ●

● A beautiful representation of *St Catherine* concentrating on writing her famous *Epistolario,* by Rutilio Manetti (G. Pratesi Collection, Florence). Although it is known that the Saint was illiterate and dictated her letters to her most devoted collaborators, she was often represented by seventeenth century artists seated at her writing desk.

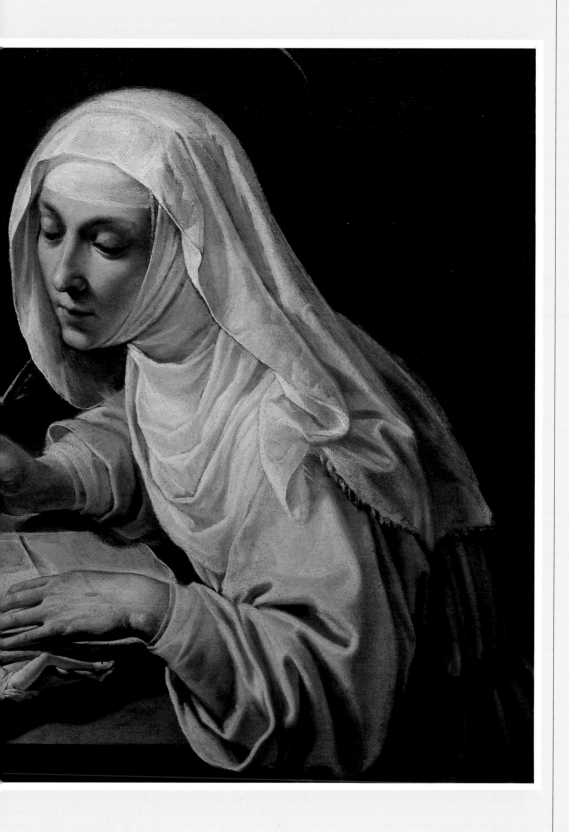

FONTEBRANDA

"Our city has always been the most delightful and refreshing in the whole of Tuscany and it boasts a most beautiful well. All the strangers who come here want to see Fonte Branda".

With this petition of 2nd February, 1397, a group of Sienese citizens asked the governors to repair the whole plain of Fontebranda, at the centre of which was situated the well that has always been recognised as the real hub around which the activity of the area revolves.

The exact derivation of the word "Branda" is unknown. Pecci, a Sienese scholar of the eighteenth century, held that it originated from the Brandi family, others believe it came from the French "Font evrand", others still think it comes from a certain Brandus, one-time owner of the place. We have access to a series of documents, the oldest of which is dated 1081, which talk of a *"Fossatum quod procedit a Fonte Branda"*. One document mentions the well together with that of Vetrice. These two wells, in fact, lay very near to one other in the same valley. They were situated between the actual plain of Fontebranda and the underlying zone, also at that time favoured by a conspicuous flow of water. An important document, referring to the work carried out in the entire area, establishes in the first ten years of the thirteenth century the beginning of the organisation of the plain as a productive area, closely connected with the centre of the city by means of important arteries such as Costa di Fontebranda and the actual Via Santa Caterina. Before 1246, new aqueducts, wooden breast-bands and troughs were built every year. This reorganisation included the repair of the main aqueduct and the location of new veins, works that caused great inconvenience to the public due to the various interruptions made to the water supply.

The importance of the well is also proved by the continuous maintenance work that was carried out on it. The hillside of San Domenico was often inspected to make sure that earth didn't fill the washing place or the watering place. We also know that from 1254 onwards the well was systematically emptied and thoroughly cleaned. We note, for example, that Jacopo di Sansone widened the mouth of a stone lion because the water that passed through this tight canal must have produced a layer of lime.

The *"Costituto"* of 1262 organically summarises all the regulations relating to the well and indicates the principal alterations carried out on the structure and the surrounding area. They included a new street behind the watering place, the repair of the road that leads from Vallepiatta to Fontebranda, the general repair of all the aqueducts, the raising of the bottom of the watering place and well,

A rare seventeenth century representation of the Plain of Fontebranda, conserved in the Circolo degli Uniti, that indicates the intense vitality of the area. *Following page:* Another detail of the well.

in Fontebranda that, at the end of the fifteenth century, they contributed towards the expense of increasing the water supply in the whole area. The cost was divided among the wool workers, the millers and the government. In the meantime, Fontebranda found itself inside the new city walls and the owners of the mills located outside the walls asked the government to channel the overflow from Piazza del Campo to Fontebranda as *"nobody uses it"* and, if this modification was carried out, *"eight mills could work that presently stand idle"*.

Up until a few years ago, the water from the well filled the basins and, overflowing into the underlying watering place (nowadays filled in and closed), finished up in the washing places, the so-called "fontini", the place of work of the women of the area.

The literary, political and religious connections and references to this area and the well are many and well-known, the most famous of all being written by Dante. ●

the locations of new veins, the construction of a pool for the wool workers, the repair of the vaults and the setting out of precise rules concerning safety and vigilance.

Moreover, the well supplied water to a large part of the city.

It was built by a certain Bellamino, as the inscription of 1193, still preserved in the rear wall of the central basin, informs us, while the vaults were constructed in 1246. The two side arches must have been added either at the end of the thirteenth or

at the beginning of the fourteenth century. The first basin was used to supply drinking water, the second, fed from the first by means of an overflow, was meant for domestic animals to drink from, while the third, still lower down, was used for washing. The waste waters were used for other purposes: to feed the water mills, the tanneries and the dye-works that continued their activity almost up to the present day.

The wool workers and the owners of the water mills of the area were so interested

VILLA RUBINI MANENTI

Situated between the old city walls and a long parapet that seperates it from Via Garibaldi, the splendid Villa Rubini Manenti is a discreet and pleasant place, built in the midst of a thick but cared for garden. It is a nineteenth century residence built in the middle of a city but conceived with rural criteria. The reason for its secluded position is definitel due to the nineteenth century custom adhered to by well-off Sienese families who possessed dignified extremely dignified residences, often bordering on the luxurious, but that always shunned unnecessary ostentation and tried to camouflage itself in the irregular conformation of the territory.

This is also a recurring characteristic of the Sienese, great lovers of beauty, who were ready to decorate even the most hidden corners of public places, but who also paid close attention to the uncompromising etiquette regarding the decoration and luxury of their private residences.

The peculiarity of this villa mainly lies in its park, a gentle slope composed of squares with box and laurel hedges, enclosed by orderly walls made of porous stone that, with the same regard to form as accurate nineteenth century handwriting, outline the shape of a perfect Italian garden.

Between the circular grove and the great greenhouse containing lemon trees, time appears to go backwards, the atmosphere becomes heavy

with memories that seem to chase one another between the shade of the holm-oaks and the fragrance of the myrtle.

Recently, the villa and garden were donated to the city council of SIena that transformed it into an old people's home. This place of peace, capable of evoking suggestions and memories like nowhere else, now caters for the noblest of causes, becoming finally that place of comfort to which it almost seemed predestined.

Following a correct policy of integration, the fresh garden

is used in Summer to hold open air performances to which the public is admitted while in the green house, exhibitions and other cultural events are held the whole year round so that villa Rubino doesn't become a luxurious ghetto but a place that is alive and throbbing, where old people come continuously into contact with the more active part of Sienese society. ●

● Villa Rubini Manenti in the midst of a park rich with fragrant essences.

THE NUN OF CAMPOREGIO

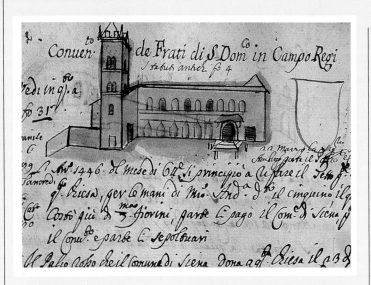

Conuen^to de Frati di S Dom^Co in Campo Regi

● The convent of San Domenico in Camporegio in an eighteenth century design by Girolamo Macchi.

The large number of ghosts that populate sultry summer evening stories can be explained by the centuries old history of the city, full of events that were often distressing, and disasters, both natural and induced by the violence of mankind, that have influenced the destiny of Siena, more so than in any other city.

Everything, every corner, even the most modest sign, boasts the glorious and complex past of Siena, an alternating chain of functions that is difficult to define with the privileged instruments of history, and obliges one to seek help in the illusions of legends and memories.

One of the most disturbing presences in the city is definitely the spirit of the poor little nun of Camporegio, a young girl, guilty of rebellion against the severe rules of her order to seek entertainment and love just like any other girl of her age.

Camporegio is now the headquarters of the society of the Contrada of the Drago, but the monastery of Paradiso, a community mainly reserved for the members of well-off families, once stood on this site.

For this reason, monastery life was fairly liberal and particularly comfortable, bordering on the opulent. It was not permitted, however, to exaggerate and the nuns who transgressed this rule were severely punished. One of them, pretty and full of life, following her incessant attempts to escape from the rigidity of the rules, was chained to her bed. Right at that moment, almost like the corny plot of a second-rate novel, a terrible fire broke out and the poor girl was found burnt to death by the many people who had tried to put out the flames.

There are those who swear that, even today, the spirit of the nun can be seen in the club rooms of the Contrada of the Drago, in search of justice for such an atrocious and undeserved fate.

A flag in a corner of the hall of the society is proof of her presence as it continuously moves very slightly even when the tiniest draught has been definitely eliminated and the smallest of holes has been covered. This flag must be, therefore, animated by a strange force, an inexhaustible tension, the gentle breath of a young life that ended too soon and for this reason not fully fulfilled. ●

THE GRATTACIELO: GASTRONOMY D'EPOQUE

The sign-board is pretentious and advertises an old and genuine wine shop-cum-inn that, according to modern commercial terminology, should be one of those artificially rustic shops that incessantly dispense gigantic sandwiches and greasy pasta and which are slowly replacing the relatively more expensive inns.

The Grattacielo, however, survives as a kind of reliquary of an extinct institution, suffocated by fast-food restaurants, but that in Siena, just as in a thousand other Italian cities, reached its peak between 1800 and 1900, when it often acted as an important cultural reference point for certain social classes.

The small inn called the Grattacielo, even though it is ignored by the young lions of Saturday night, remains a temple of good taste, refined by experience, and resistant to the onslaught of cholesterol. Above all, one drinks that wonderful, so-called, table wine, the right compromise between the mephitic fruits of large-scale industrial production, the terribly expensive "designer" wines, and the "reserves", more difficult to find than old stamps.

One can also taste the simplest dishes of Sienese gastronomy: Spartan seasonings, ground anchovies, quality salami. And on Friday, cod and chick peas to observe the vigil. In other words, the most suitable dishes to contrast the modern degeneration of "bite and run" meals.

Therefore, notwithstanding the tiny size of the place, the customers carry out a daily ritual of civil and serene resistance against the depersonalising fad of fast food and sandwiches, that does not allow, as we unfortunately know, even the smallest pause for reflection.

The values of friendship and pleasant conversation are still practised round the tables of the Grattacielo, in the presence of the most authentic and familiar tastes of our gastronomic tradition. This doesn't mean that the place is a club with its members chosen according to secret and exclusive rites. There are no barriers at all, in fact. The proprietor will scrutinise new arrivals suspiciously, but in a good-natured way, and if the customer demonstrates he is able to really appreciate the good things in life, a dusty bottle containing a robust, red potion, capable of melting even the most timid of men will appear, like magic, from under the counter.

There is one warning to be made: anyone more than 180 centimetres high should make sure they are served outside. They will so save their skulls from injury and will avoid regrettable situations both for themselves and for the people who surround them. Having said that, it doesn't seem necessary to explain why this delightful place is called the Grattacielo (Skyscraper). ●

● The inn of the Grattacielo under the Arco de' Pontani, last bulwark against the invasion of fast food.

Terzo
di San Martino

1 Loggia di Mercanzia
2 Church of St Christopher
3 Castellare degli Ugurgieri
   Prior Contrada of the Civetta
4 Università degli Studi
5 Palazzo Piccolomini - Museum of the
   Biccherne State Archives
6 Logge del Papa
7 University for Foreigners
8 Contrada of the Leocorno
9 Valley of Follonica
10 Palazzo De Vecchi
11 Palazzo Bruchi
12 Church of St George
13 Fountain of Pispini
14 Church of the Holy Spirit
15 Noble Contrada of the Nicchio
16 Porta Pispini
17 The wall fortified by Baldassarre Peruzzi
18 Church of St Raimondo al Refugio
19 Palazzo San Galgano
20 Church of St Mary of the Angles called
   "Il Santuccio"
21 Società di Esecutori di Pie Disposizioni
22 Museum of Bologna Buonsignori
23 Porta Romana
24 Contrada of Valdimontone
25 Oratorio of the Holy Trinity
26 Prato dei Servi
27 Basilica dei Servi
28 Church and Convent of San Girolamo
29 Palazzo Bianchi Bandinelli
30 Palazzo Vestri
31 Contrada della Torre
32 Sinagoga
33 Chiesa di San Martino
34 Arch-confraternity of the Misericordia

On leaving the shell-shaped Piazza del Campo by means of Vicolo di San Pietro, **Loggia di Mercanzia**, headquarters of the Circolo degli Uniti (see page 206), can be admired on the left. The elegant, Renaissance loggia was not touched at all during the rebuilding of the Mercanzia in the eighteenth century. During the second half of the fifteenth century, five statues depicting *San Savino, Sant'Ansano and San Vittore*

by Antonio Federighi and *St Peter and St Paul* by Vecchietta were placed in the niches on the pillars. Inside can be admired the beautiful stone benches by Urbano da Cortona and Federighi, while the vaults, somewhat modified in the nineteenth century, were frescoed at the end of the sixteenth century. Leaving the Croce del Travaglio, a part of the old Via Francigena that leads towards Via di Galgaria (now Via di Città), and going along Banchi di Sopra, full of prestigious palaces and modern shops, one can see to the right, Piazza Tolomei with its palace, and opposite, the **Church of St Christopher.** St Christopher is particularly dear to the

Sienese as it was the place of assembly of the Republican government before the Palazzo Pubblico was built. Here, in particular, the decision was taken by the Great Council to move against the Florentines at Montaperti.

The church contains an original, marvellous, Romanic cloister where legend has it that the "cursed" poet Cecco Angiolieri (see page 248) is buried, even if the tombstone refers to his son. It was greatly modified in the first years of the nineteenth century, after the tremendous earthquake of 1798, when a span of the nave was eliminated.

The church contains a beautiful pala by Girolamo del Pacchia, depicting the *Madonna with Child and Saints* and a

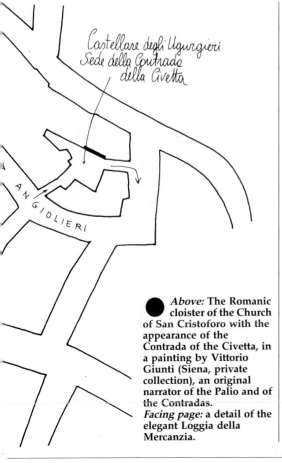

Castellare degli Ugurgieri
Sede della Contrada
della Civetta

● *Above:* The Romanic cloister of the Church of San Cristoforo with the appearance of the Contrada of the Civetta, in a painting by Vittorio Giunti (Siena, private collection), an original narrator of the Palio and of the Contradas.
Facing page: a detail of the elegant Loggia della Mercanzia.

polychrome, earthenware group by an artist close to Jacopo della Quercia. Still more relevant, however, is the table depicting *St George and the Dragon*, attributed to the Maestro dell'Osservanza.

On the right of the church, one enters Via Cecco Angiolieri, territory of the **Prior Contrada of the Civetta**; along this street, on the left, is the recently built oratory of the Civetta, and shortly after, again on the left, one enters, through a majestic closed lane, the suggestive Castellare of the ancient family of the Ugurgieri. This is one of the best preserved examples of a fortified residence, a singular urban element, organised both for defence and for total self-sufficiency, by the most important noble families, around which the medieval city developed.
Inside the Castellare is the Museum of the Civetta, recently reorganised, that displays, apart from the usual mementoes of the Contrada, a vast series of archaeological findings from the zone. This peaceful corner also contains the stall of the horse of the

Contrada, that, during the days of the Palio, houses the hopes of victory of the members of the Civetta.

Leaving the Castellare degli Ugurgieri along Via San Vigilio, one reaches Banchi di Sotto, a stretch of Via Francigena that, from the Croce del Travaglio, goes down towards Porta Romana. The street, like its neighbour, Banchi di Sopra, owes its name to the numerous stalls that Sienese merchants once kept on the sides of this important road.

Immediately after the cross-roads with Via Rinaldini are two of the most important Sienese monuments. On the left is the austere building of the old Jesuit college, where, in 1816, the **Università degli Studi** was transferred from its previous home in the rooms of the Sapienza. The latest reorganisation of the building was carried out by the purist Giuseppe Partini, extremely active in Siena during the second half of the nineteenth century. The courtyard

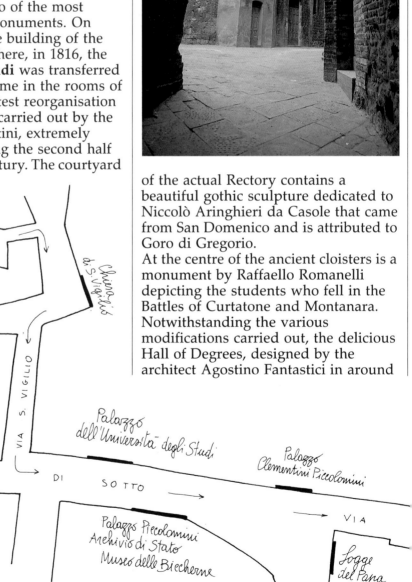

of the actual Rectory contains a beautiful gothic sculpture dedicated to Niccolò Aringhieri da Casole that came from San Domenico and is attributed to Goro di Gregorio.

At the centre of the ancient cloisters is a monument by Raffaello Romanelli depicting the students who fell in the Battles of Curtatone and Montanara. Notwithstanding the various modifications carried out, the delicious Hall of Degrees, designed by the architect Agostino Fantastici in around

This page: The particular "closed" structure of the Castellare degli Urgurgieri.
Facing page: The majestic prospect of Palazzo Piccolomini.

1820, still remains inside the university. Right opposite the University building is the massive Renaissance structure of **Palazzo Piccolomini.** The building was constructed in around 1470 from a design by the famous Florentine architect, Bernardo Gambarelli, called the Rossellino, who worked at Pienza for the Sienese Pope Pio II.

The façade of the palace displays the classical modules typical of the Florentine Renaissance with decorations in great blocks of cut stone. Inside the great building are now situated numerous administrative offices, among which the imposing **State Archives** and the **Museum of the Biccherne** (see page 244).

The archives contain, amongst other things, all the documents of the ancient Republic, many of which are richly decorated by the greatest Sienese artists. The documents tell the story of Siena and its territory from the eight century right up to modern times and, each year, are consulted by a large number of scholars and visitors from all over the world. The great palace, with the nearby **Logge del Papa**, is the most significant Renaissance monument in Siena and

introduces itself without any difficulty at all in the Gothic surroundings of the rest of the area, contributing towards realising one of the best laid out spaces, from an architectural point of view, in the city.

The three great travertine arches of the loggia were commissioned by the great humanist Pope Pio II to the Sienese architect and sculptor, Antonio Federighi, in around 1460.

Running alongside this Renaissance area is Via del Pantaneto which contains great palaces of various periods. The first building, on the left, belonged to a branch of the papal family: the Piccolomini and conserves, notwithstanding the recent modifications, a few significant hanging arches at the top and consistent traces of the original fresco decorations.

Further along Via del Pantaneto, still to the left, one can admire Via di Follonica that leads to Piazzetta Virgilio Grassi where the University for Foreigners is situated, together with the sober structure of the Church of San Giovannino, heart of the

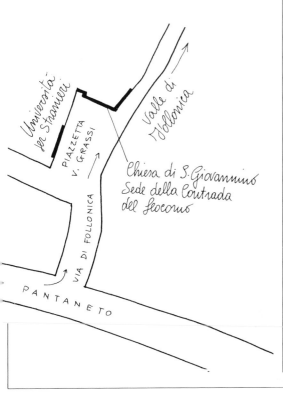

Contrada del Leocorno.

In the first half of the sixteenth century, Giovanni Battista Pelori restored it in the manner of Peruzzi with respect to the pre-existing medieval structure. The inside of the church contains a real and proper collection of sixteenth and seventeenth century Sienese art that includes important works by Rutilio and Domenico Manetti, Astolfo Petrazzi, Raffaello Vanni and Bernardino Mei. Also worthy of note is a beautiful fourteenth century table by Francesco di Vannuccio, depicting the *Madonna with Child.* The sacristy and other parts of the building of San Giovanni house the Museum of the Leocorno, rich in artistic objects and notable palios won by the Contrada, among which is the especially interesting "Victory Palio", painted by Aldo Piantini, in 1919, in Liberty style. The headquarters of the Contrada looks out onto the suggestive Valley of Follonica, one of the many green valleys to be found inside the city walls (see page 250), where one can admire, although in an extremely bad state of preservation, the well of Follonica that dates back to medieval times.

Back in Via del Pantaneto, on the right, is the majestic **Palazzo de Vecchi**, built by Paolo Posi (1771), that, together with the coeval Palazzo Sergardi, confirms the resumption of the use of late-Renaissance motives, even though they are expressed with

● *This page:* The façade of the church of San Giovannino in Pantaneto, oratory of the Contrada of the Leocorno. *Facing page:* A detail of the palio painted by Aldo Piantini (1919), on the occasion of the so-called "Victory Palio" (Museum of the Contrada of the Leocorno).

remarkable stylistic sobriety. Still on the right can be admired a beautiful sixteenth century palace built from blocks of cut stone and with the bust of Francesco I of Tuscany placed on the façade.

Almost opposite lies **Palazzo Bruchi** with its magnificent outlook onto the countryside while, right next to it, are the splendid columns of the beautiful eighteenth century **Church of St George.** The building, of medieval origins and dear to the Sienese for its links with the celebrated Battle of Montaperti, was internally restored and had its façade repaired between 1730 and 1738 as a result of a commission given by Cardinal Anton Felice Zondadari, to Pietro Cremoni,

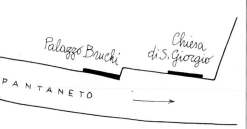

the detailed decorations of the ceiling and its elegant geometrical forms. The façade, of clear Roman inspiration, easily introduces itself into the surroundings thanks to its flowing and luminous shape, built according to well tried and tested formulae. Inside is a beautiful canvas by Francesco Vanni depicting the *Pietà*, the funeral monument to Archbishop Alessandro Zondadari, a *St George with Jesus* by Sebastiano Conca, and other works by Ventura Salimbeni and Raffaello Vanni.

A few yard further on, to the left, is Via dei Pispini, territory of the **Noble Contrada of the Nicchio**, which leads to the nearby Piazza Santo Spirito that contains the important Church of the Holy Spirit, of fourteenth century origins, rich in important works of art, and the Renaissance fountain of the Pispini, taken only recently to the centre of this square from the street that leads to the nearby Monastery of Santa Chiara, situated in the territory of this Contrada.

The Church and Convent of the Holy

from Lombardy, but who worked in Siena for many years.

The church is in the form of a Latin cross, divided by pillars and columns that form suggestive niches with the overlying arches. The refined plaster work inside generates an unusual monochromatic effect, dividing the space that is characterised by such a degree of luminosity that it highlights

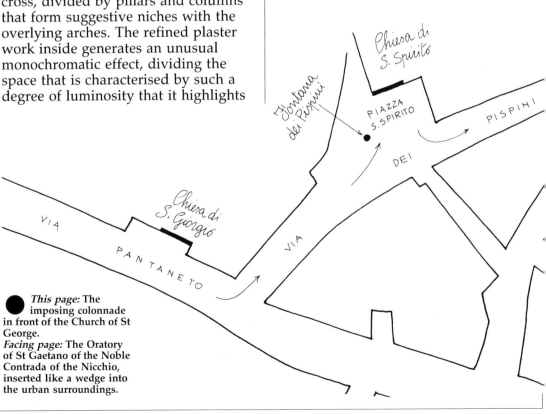

● *This page:* The imposing colonnade in front of the Church of St George.
Facing page: The Oratory of St Gaetano of the Noble Contrada of the Nicchio, inserted like a wedge into the urban surroundings.

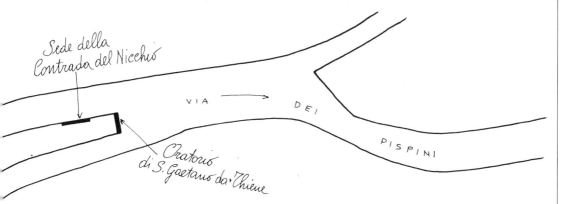

Spirit (the convent was converted into a prison in the last century), were built in the fourteenth century and belonged first to the Monks of Vallombrosa and then, during the fifteenth century, to the Dominicans. The church underwent substantial modifications at the beginning of the sixteenth century, so much so that the design is traditionally attributed to Cozzarelli and the portal to the great Baldassare Peruzzi.

The inside is richly furnished with works by the most important Sienese artists of the sixteenth and seventeenth centuries, including Giovanni Antonio Bazzi (il Sodoma), with his frescoes and canvases in the Chapel of the Spaniards (1530). Also to note in the third chapel are *The coronation of Mary* by Domenico Beccafumi, a sixteenth century earthenware *Crib* by Ambrogio della Robbia, a painting with a *Miracle of St Giacinto* by Francesco Vanni and two frescoes with stories of the Saint by Ventura Salimbeni (1610), a table depicting *The coronation of the Madonna* by Girolamo del Pacchia, a canvas by Astolfo Petrazzi with some *Adoring Saints* and a *Crucifix*, a late fourteenth century painting of the Sienese school.

Further down the street, on the right, is the Museum and the Victory Room of the Contrada of the Nicchio, next to the oratory of St Gaetano, built at the end of the seventeenth century by the members of the Contrada. This church is in a similar position to the previously mentioned oratory of the Madonna of the Rosary in Via San Marco, in that it inserts itself into the surroundings like a wedge, without distorting the area. On the contrary, it joins the colours of the material and bricks of the four ornamental columns of the façade to the splendid niche placed above the portal depicting the dominating heraldic emblem of the Contrada. The inside of the church is characterised by elegant, gilded plaster work, refined wood carvings and numerous frescoes depicting episodes in the life of St Gaetano by Giuseppe Nicola Nasini and his son Apollonio.

The recently restored museum displays many objects in gold, some costumes of the Contrada dating back to the last century, while, among the palios, can be admired the particularly significant one, painted by Valerio Adami in 1981, characterised by highly refined graphics and bright colours.

From the church of the Nicchio it's worthwhile continuing up to Porta Pispini. On the left, one can see the previously mentioned Convent of St Chiara, now completely transformed into a military building, and opposite, the façade of the oratory of St Stephen, the present day headquarters of the society of the Nicchio, "La Pania". Also on the left is a very important building that is now in the process of being completely restored: the former convent of the Nuns of Eternal Life. Inside the church, unfortunately closed to the public at present, is preserved, amongst others, a beautiful canvas depicting a *Miracle of St Giacinto* by Rustichino. Further along is **Porta Pispini**, built at the beginning of the fifteenth century. This gate is also known as "San Viene", recalling the episode of the arrival in Siena (1107) of the remains of the protector of the city, St Ansano, who

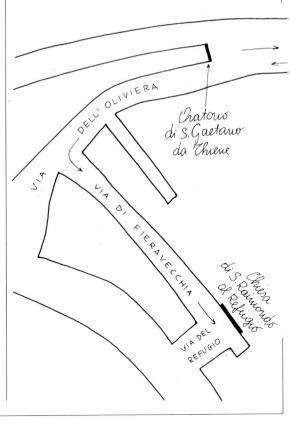

was martyred in the plain of Montaperti.

It is said the Saint's remains were received with the prayers of a great crowd of Sienese who continuously repeated "Il santo viene" (the Saint is coming), and this is the reason for the name given to the gate.

Porta Pispini was built at the same time as the last ring of city walls and Giovanni Antonio Bazzi, il Sodoma, in 1530, painted a great fresco depicting the *Nativity* on the inside, of which today, unfortunately, only a few fragments are conserved on a wall of the church of St Francis.

From the door on the left, one can see the powerful, semicircular structures of the fortress that Baldassarre Peruzzi designed to reinforce the city walls in the 1530's. It is a completely fortified brick structure, placed on three floors, and has been acclaimed by one and all as one of the most rational and significant examples of Italian military architecture.

Back in Via dei Pispini again, it's worthwhile returning to Via

dell'Oliviera and turning left into Via Fieravecchia to see the almost hidden **Church of St Raimondo al Refugio,** located right at the bottom of the street on the left.

This church was built by Pope Alexander VII (Fabio Chigi), during his reign (1655-1667), as the great papal stem, placed right in the middle of the

● *This page:* The façade of the church of St Raimondo al Refugio, built by Pope Alexander VII.
Facing page: Part of the imposing structure of the fortress of Baldassarre Peruzzi, erected to reinforce the defensive possibilities of Porta Pispini.

façade, testifies. The compositive articulation, the light and shade effect and the theatricality given to the front of the church by the architect Benedetto Giovanelli, all point to the influence of Gian Lorenzo Bernini, who worked for a long time for this Sienese pope. Inside the church are numerous works of art by the most important Sienese painters of the late sixteenth century: Francesco Vanni, Sebastiano Folli, Rutilio Manetti, Alessandro Casolani and Francesco Rustici.

At the beginning of the seventeenth century, the Convento del Refugio, that was later reserved to ladies of noble origins who wished to retire from the world, was built next to the church by Aurelio Chigi. At the end of the eighteenth century, the building was modified, incorporating other nearby constructions and, shortly after, was called "Conservatori Riuniti", a name that it still keeps today in its new function as an old ladies home.

● *This page:* The fifteenth century palace of St Galgano, built with great blocks of tufa. *Facing page:* A detail of the table by Niccolò di Ser Sozzo, depicting *The Madonna with Child and Saints,* conserved in the Museum of the Società di Esecutori di Pie Disposizioni.

Numerous paintings, ceramic objects, works in silver, furniture and furnishings, still decorate the vast rooms of the Refugio.

In Via Roma, on the right, is the recently restored **Palazzo San Galgano**, now used as a department of the faculty of literature of the university. This great, late fifteenth century building owes its form to the Florentine models used by Giuliano da Maiano, the architect of one of the most beautiful

Renaissance palaces (Spannocchi) in Siena. The two original floors in great tuff ashlars, later surmounted with a loggia, were built by the monks of the Abbey of St Galgano and the similarities between this building and the prestigious Sienese residence of the banker, Ambrogio Spannocchi, are so numerous and precise that they lead scholars to hold that they were both designed, if not built, by the same person.

Continuing towards Porta Romana, on the right, is a beautiful, recently restored, fifteenth century edicola by Giovanni di Stefano (1477) that bears the symbol of the monks of St Galgano. Shortly after, almost closing off Via Roma as if with a theatre backdrop, is the façade of the **Church of the Monastery of St Mary of the Angels known as the Santuccio.** The monastery has been totally modified and is nowadays almost completely occupied by the ''Giovanni Caselli'' Professional Institute, while the church, in its actual form, dates back to the middle of the sixteenth century with its brick façade that recalls the style of Peruzzo.

The Monastery is said to have been founded by the Abbess of the Augustinians, the blessed Santuccia, born in Gubbio in around 1320. Nowadays, this version has been replaced by the more credible theory that the origins of Santa Maria degli Angeli can be traced back to a group of nuns from the Sienese territory who were helped in their undertaking by a powerful local family called Santucci. The church has just one nave and contains some interesting frescoes by Ventura Salimbeni depicting *Stories of St Galgano.* The altars bear fine canvases, such as the *Madonna del Rosario,* realised by Alessandro Casolani and completed by Francesco Vanni in 1607. On the high altar is a beautiful canvas depicting the *Madonna with Child and Saints,* painted by more than one of the Sienese ''baroque'' artists (F. Vanni, V. Salimbeni, S. Folli), in around 1610. The last two buildings on the sides of

Via Roma belong to the **Società di Esecutori di Pie Disposizioni,** where the administrative offices of the ancient congregation and its two museums are situated.

One of the collections, still displayed according to its original nineteenth century lay out and containing works of great importance for the entire figurative Sienese culture, comes from the ancient Compagnia dei Disciplinati whose headquarters are in Santa Maria della Scala. Of particular interest are the two crucifixes by artists of the school of Duccio di Buoninsegna, a beautiful triptych by Niccolò di Ser Sozzo, depicting the *Madonna with Child and Saints* and an unusual Gothic reliquary painted on glass, attributed to Lippo Vanni. There are also four coffin heads painted by Cozzarelli, and other works by the imaginative Sodoma and the Flemish artist Van Rantwick. It is, in fact, an extremely representative collection of works of the Sienese school that proves the refined taste of the patrons of this important Sienese institution over the centuries.

The building opposite contains the Bologna Buonsignori collection, donated to the Society by the family, and recently rearranged, comprising archaeological findings, furniture, ceramic objects and paintings.

A gate, realised by the famous Sienese wrought iron manufacturers in the last century, leads to the large Psychiatric Hospital, built on the site of the ancient convent of San Niccolò. The building, now largely unused for health purposes, stands in the midst of a large park of old trees and looks out onto one of the most suggestive valleys inside the city walls.

At the end of the street is the monumental **Porta Romana**, the most imposing of all the gates of Siena. It was realised in around 1330 and enriched in the following century by an enormous fresco, depicting the *Coronation of the Virgin,* realised both by Taddeo di Bartolo, il Sassetta, who actually died of a disease caught during the execution of this work, and Sano di Pietro. The fresco, now reduced to a just a few fragments, was recently detached from the wall and collocated, like that of Porta Pispini, on a wall of the Church of St Francis.

This important entrance to the city, opening solemnly out onto the countryside, for centuries symbolised the territory of the Sienese Republic, so much so as to merit a precise citation by Ambrogio Lorenzetti in that idealistic, yet true, portrait of "Gothic" Siena, the *Effects of good government,* the fresco in Palazzo Pubblico.

Returning from Porta Romana to the Church of the Santuccio and turning left, after a few yards, on the same side, is the Museum of the **Contrada of Valdimontone**, contained inside the church of San Leonardo and in some

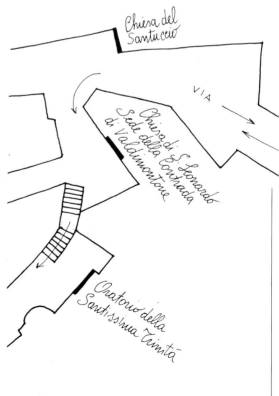

rooms behind it. These rooms were modified a number of times until their recent reconstruction as a museum which was carried out by one of the great interpreters of nineteenth century Italian architecture: Giovanni Michelucci.

The church belonged to the order of the Gerosolimitans right from the last ten years of the twelfth century, ownership then passed to the Knights of Malta that later gave it to for the first time to the inhabitants of this Contrada. After further changes of ownership and concessions, it finally returned to the Contrada in the first half of the last century. Apart from the usual objects regarding the life and territory of the Contrada and the palios conquered, St Leonardo also boasts numerous seventeenth century canvases by Dionisio Montorselli depicting *Rebecca, Moses extracting water from a stone, Judith, Manna,* other canvases representing

● *Above:* The imposing battlements of Porta Romana.
To right: Detail of the "romantic" steps that rise towards the basilica dei Servi.
Following page: A detail of the late-mannerist frescoes in the Oratory of the Holy Trinity.

biblical subjects, some frescoes by Vincenzo Dei of the first half of the nineteenth century, and a rich collection of silver and liturgical vestments.

A suggestive flight of brick steps leads to the **Oratory of the Holy Trinity**, the church used for the religious functions of the Contrada.

The Company of the Holy Trinity, of medieval origins, built its oratory at the end of the fourteenth century, but the building underwent a radical transformation in the last ten years of the sixteenth century, both as regards its structure and decorations. The inside was completely covered with plaster

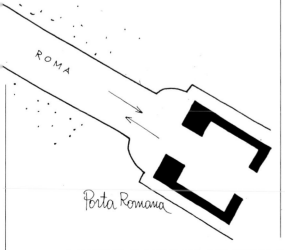

ROMA

Porta Romana

work and frescoes by some of the main interpreters of the "barroquesque" and late-mannerist styles.

Ventura Salimbeni, in fact, painted numerous scenes on the vaults and lunettes, while Alessandro Casolani painted a further two lunettes and a canvas for the high altar depicting the *Weeping under the Cross.*

Prospero Bresciani sculpted the great bronze *Crucifix,* while Lorenzo and Cristoforo Rustici were the authors of the beautiful plaster work on the vaults and the altar. The great fresco on the inside of the façade, depicting *The battle of Clodoveo,* is by Raffaello Vanni. In a chapel on the right can be admired a precious fifteenth century panel attributed to Sano di Pietro, depicting the *Madonna with Child.*

view of the walled city.

It's enough, in fact, to climb up the steps to the great **Basilica dei Servi** to have under ones eyes an extraordinary view of the medieval architecture of the city which allows one to easily perceive many distinctive features of the development of the complex history of Siena.

The great basilica was constructed by some monks from Montesenario who, in 1235, came to live in this part of the

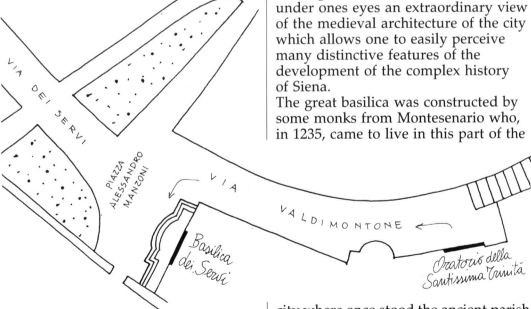

Above: A view of the Basilica dei Servi.
Following pages: A complete view of the inside of the basilica.

city where once stood the ancient parish of St Clemente, the name of which was later added to that of St Mary dei Servi (see page 252).

The construction of this church took a long time and was very complicated, so much so that work was terminated only in the first few years of the sixteenth century. It was finally consecrated in 1533 but, however, work continued on it in the following centuries; the medieval bell tower, in fact, was almost completely modified in around 1925 and the Renaissance façade has never been completed. The inside of the basilica is completely different, with its luminous and spacious naves divided by great pillars.

The enormous number of works of art conserved in the naves and chapels of the Servi constitutes a systematic narration of some of the highest moments of the Sienese figurative civilisation. Moreover, the second chapel leading off the right-hand side nave contains one of the most famous works of all medieval Italian art: *The Madonna with Child* by the Florentine, Coppo di Marcovaldo (1261), who, taken prisoner by the Sienese during the battle of Montaperti, was obliged to paint this celebrated canvas as a ransom.

In the following chapel is yet another portrait of Maria, a canvas by Rutilio Manetti depicting *The Nativity of the Virgin;* in the same nave one can admire a masterpiece by Matteo di Giovanni (1491), *The slaughter of the Innocents* with the lunette above representing the *Madonna with Child, angels and Saints.* Another table depicting the *Virgin and Child,* by Segna di Buonaventura, a painter of the school of Duccio di Buonisnegna, is hung over the door of the sacristy while a great *cross* painted in the right-hand transept is also referable to the school of Duccio.

The theme of the *Slaughter of the Innocents* recurs also in the frescoes of the first chapel in the apse. These are attributed to Pietro Lorenzetti and his collaborators and indicate great complexity of composition and remarkable psychological tension. On the high altar, instead, is placed a great Renaissance table depicting the *Coronation of the Madonna,* a work by the Sienese Bernardino Fungai. Pietro Lorenzetti also frescoed *The banquet of Herod and the Ascension of St John* in the last chapel on the left-hand side of the apse, while,

in the left-hand transept, one can admire a table, signed and dated by Giovanni di Paolo (1431), depicting *The Madonna of Mercy.* The table by Lippo Memmi (placed in the middle of a great seventeenth century canvas by Astolfo Petrazzi), depicting the *Madonna of the People,* is an authentic, fourteenth century, Sienese masterpiece. A beautiful, youthful work by Alessandro Casolani, depicting *The Adoration of the Shepherds,* is hung in the left-hand side nave, as are other admirable works attributed to Jacopo di Mino, Francesco Curradi, Dionisio Montorselli, Girolamo di Benvenuto and other important artists. Among these, a beautiful *Annunciation* with striking ''baroquesque'' colours stands out, painted in 1588 by Francesco Vanni and hung in the nearest chapel to the entrance.

In front of the basilica is the green Piazza Alessandro Manzoni, and from there, going down the whole of Via dei Servi, one reaches the **Convent of San Girolamo**, situated in a square on the left. The building was constructed halfway through the fourteenth century and, for many centuries, belonged to the order of the Jesuits. In the second half of the seventeenth century, the Congregation of the Vergini Abbandonate took

possession of the site, while today, the Nuns of the Carità di San Vincenzo de' Paoli live there.

Numerous works of art are also conserved in San Girolamo, both in the church and in the convent. In particular, there is a beautiful standard depicting *St Anna Metterza* by Giovanni di Lorenzo Cini (about 1530), the *Annunciation* by Rutilio Manetti, a canvas by Francesco Vanni representing *St Catherine drinking the blood of Christ,* a *cross* painted by an artist of the school of Duccio di Buoninsegna, and a table depicting the *Coronation of the Madonna* by Sano di Pietro.

Right in front of San Girolamo, in Ponte di Romana, is situated the ancient gate of St Maurizio, a name taken from the nearby church of Samoreci (St Maurizio), which, in this point, opened through the penultimate ring of city walls. St Maurizio is also the name of the nearby fourteenth century well, largely transformed in the sixteenth and the following centuries. Opposite,

● A detail of the *Slaughter of the Innocents,* a fifteenth century masterpiece by Matteo di Giovanni.

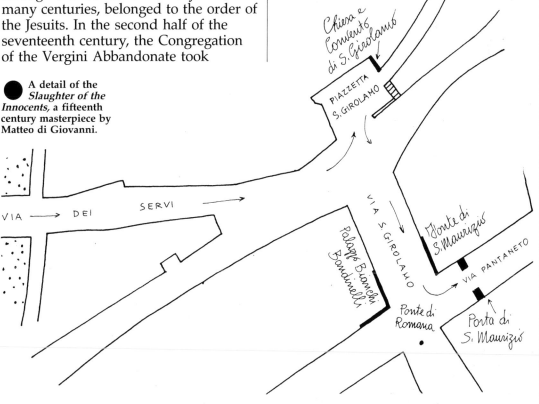

rises the great structure of **Palazzo Bianchi Bandinelli,** the most relevant architectural achievement in the city of the end of the eighteenth century (see page 246). Through the gate, on the left, is Via Cane e Gatto which leads to Via Salicotto. This is the main street of the **Contrada of the Torre** whose headquarters and oratory lie halfway down this long road that reaches as far as Piazza del Campo.

The whole of this area was object of a much discussed urban "restoration" in the 1930's, when, by means of a kind of "regothicisation", many houses were reconverted into palaces with forms suggestive of an improbable Middle Ages. Some were, fortunately, spared, like **Palazzo Vestri** on the left, which is still served by an original helicoidal ramp, realised in the first years of the last century. Also on the same side is the fountain of the Contrada, a recent work (1985) by Mauro Berrettini, realised almost completely in stone.

● *This page:* A detail of the ancient bell (1532), with the stem of the Contrada of the Torre, signed by Antonio da Siena and conserved in the museum of the Contrada.
Facing page: The suggestive Vicolo delle Scotte that connects the Synagogue with the Church of St Martino.

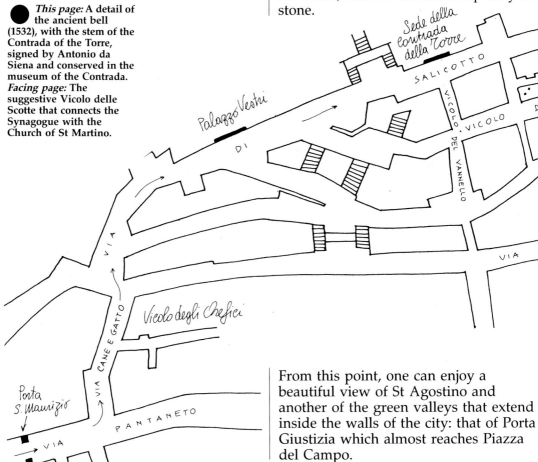

From this point, one can enjoy a beautiful view of St Agostino and another of the green valleys that extend inside the walls of the city: that of Porta Giustizia which almost reaches Piazza del Campo.

Next to the fountain are the headquarters and oratory of the Torre, built in about 1535 to commemorate the Battle of Camollia, won by the Sienese on 25th July, 1526, on St James' day, who, together with St Anna, is also the patron Saint of the Contrada. The church contains some recently restored seventeenth century frescoes by Dionisio Montorselli, two beautiful canvases by Rutilio Manetti depicting *The beheading of St James* (1605) and a *Crucifixion,* while the Museum displays an important collection of objects in silver and liturgical vestments, as well as a table depicting the *March to Calvary,* attributed to il Sodoma.

At the other end of the numerous lanes on the right of Via Salicotto, is the zone called the "Ghetto". In fact, the Jewish population lived in this part of the ward of the Torre right from Medieval times, even if the delimitation of the area only occurred in the second half of the sixteenth century, by order of Cosimo

of the Medici. Here also lies the **Synagogue,** built in the second half of the eighteenth century by the Florentine, Giuseppe del Rosso.

At the end of the lane, on the right of the Synagogue, is the side of the **Church of St Martino,** one of the oldest religious buildings in the city, modified many times before the construction of the façade at the beginning of the seventeenth century. St Martino, in fact, had always been without a seemly

prospect.

This suggestive double façade in travertine was realised to a design by Giovanni Fonatan with the projecting cornice joined to the tympanum by two large scrolls, while the inside, in its present day form, was realised by Giovanni Battista Pelori (in about 1540), an architect of the school of Baldassare Peruzzi.

St Martino also contains some works of art of great importance, such as the table depicting the *Nativity* by Domenico Beccafumi, a *Cirumcision* by Guido Reni, a canvas by Guercino depicting the *Martyrdom of St Bartholemew,* and, on the high altar, a beautiful ciborium of the mid seventeenth century, attributed to the Sienese sculptor, Giuseppe Mazzuoli. Also of interest is the table by Giovanni di Lorenzo Cini, placed on the contrafaçade of the church, depicting the *Madonna protecting the city,* while the battle of Camollia is raging. The work was painted in 1528.

At the foot of the steps is Via del Porrione where, before returning to Piazza del Campo, it's worthwhile visiting the **Oratory of the**

Arciconfraternita della Misericordia, situated a few yards further on, to the left. As well as many late fifteenth century lunettes by Sebastiano Folli, Rutilio Manetti, Alessandro Casolani, Pietro Sorri and Francesco Vanni, the church preserves two extraordinary wooden statues depicting the *Annunciation* by Marrina and the sixteenth century table on the high altar depicting the *Madonna enthroned and Saints* by Girolamo del Pacchia.

Via Porrione leads back into Piazza del Campo at the bend of St Martino. ●

● The elegant modelled tympanum of the church of St Martino.
Facing page: A detail of the painting of Giovanni di Lorenzo Cini, depicting *The Virgin protecting Siena during the Battle of Camollia,* conserved in the church of St Martino.

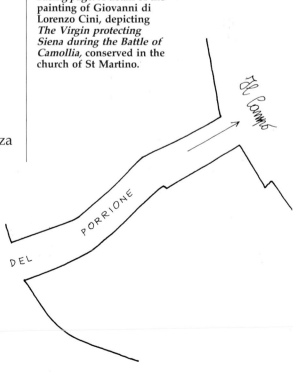

Le Biccherne:
THE BALANCE SHEET IN COLOUR

The adoration of beauty that has always inspired the people of Siena, even as regards their most everyday and modest activities, is significatively confirmed in a unique and suggestive collection of the Biccherne (state ledgers), now lovingly cared for in the very rich State Archives of Siena. Biccherna is a word of uncertain derivation. It was the name of the finance departmant of the Sienese state that drew its origins perhaps from the palace of "Blacherne", in Constantinople, where the imperial treasure was kept. A Sienese nobleman probably imported the word from the East, given that, at the end of the twelfth century, it was assigned to a city magistracy.

It was in 1257 that the Camerlengo and the Provveditori, the administrators of the finance department, began to commission painted wooden tablets to artists of the time to be used as covers for their ledgers. The first Biccherne generally depicted the stems and portraits of the holders of the magistracy during the execution of their duties. The paintings also showed the year of realisation.

At the beginning of the fourteenth century, during the government of the Nine, the tables began to describe more and more complex situations, often still retaining the representation of the Camerlengo, and were entrusted to the greatest Sienese painters, such as Ambrogio Lorenzetti. As

Two examples of Biccherne, the ancient covers of the city administration balance sheets.

time went by, they became increasingly more complex and articulated in their iconographic aspects, giving way to real and proper little masterpieces, works by artists of the standing of Giovanni di Paolo, il Maestro dell'Osservaza, Sano di Pietro, Lorenzo Vecchietta and Benvenuto di Giovanni.

The small paintings often depicted the most significant or dramatic events that had occurred in Siena during the year in question, such as the precious table attributed to Francesco di Giorgio Martini, of 1467, in which the earthquakes that had afflicted the city are recalled and the camps erected by the Sienese outside the walls to escape from the disaster are scrupulously described. The growing artistic

importance of the works began to present some problems with regard to a continuous and intense use of the registers of the accounts and deliberations, and this put their integrity into some doubt. For this reason, at the end of the fifteenth century, small paintings began to be realised that were separate from the books and hung on the walls of the department, still maintaining their usual characteristics.

Freeing the paintings from the bonds of the size of the registers led to the realisation of works of greater dimensions. In the seventeenth century the paintings had grown to a notable size.

Apart from their intrinsic and remarkable artistic value, the Biccherne constitute an authentic mine of visual news and information regarding Sienese affairs, on the urban evolution of the city, as well as constituting precise and inequivocable reference points regarding the activity of important painters of whom it would have been very difficult otherwise to recontruct their artistic development. For some years now, the city administration has rennewed this ancient usage, totally interrupted at the end of the seventeenth century, and its annual balance sheets are bound with a painted cover depicting the most important projects carried out during the year. ●

EVSCITA

QVESTA · E · LENTRATA · DELLVENERABILE · ANGNIOLO · DIPIET
RO · DIBALDO · CHVMARLENGO · ALTEMPO · DE · SAVI · HVOMINI · FILIP
PO · DIPIERVMIDI · BANTONIO · DABAGNIAIA · EPERO · DIBARTLOME
O · DICHARLO · ETO MASSO · D O R BANO · GIOVANNELI · ETO ASS
O DIMISERE GIORGIOTO MASSI · EANTONIO · DIGIOVANIPINI · EL
OTIODICHELO · DERONDIVA · EGIORGIO · DIFRANCIO · DACHA
RIGI · TLOMEI · E DOMENICO · DIVENTVRINO · VENTVRINI · MCCC 6 c

THE PALACE OF GIULIO BIANCHI BANDINELLI

● *This page:* A detail of the frescoes by Luigi Ademollo on the ceilings of Palazzo Bianchi Bandinelli.
Facing page: The courtyard of the palace

In a very short time - from 1802 to 1804 - Giulio Bianchi Bandinelli Paparoni finished building his new, imposing palace in VIa Roma on the remains of the ancient Spedaletto di Santa Maria Maddalena, and founded, like many others, on the old Via Francigena, by the powerful Piccolomini family.

Giulio Bianchi, too, like the Piccolomini, boasted a pope among his ancestors: that Alexander III, that fierce opponent of Federico Barbarossa and upholder of the struggle against the empire. His authority was therefore derived from this great forefather that, together with an uncommon political capacity, led him to occupy the most important public offices, both in Siena and the surrounding region, in the difficult years between the eighteenth and nineteenth centuries. He was, in fact, governor of Siena and Prefect of the Department of the Ombrone, both under the French domination and in the years

personalities, such as Ademollo, in his projects for the city.

The new family palace was, however, the most explicit example of his judicious and extremely civilised character, a lover of luxury not as a means to an end but as a way of creating a stupefying and fascinating image.

The palace grew like this, as the residence of a Renaissance merchant, full of the most luxurious commodities, graceded with a refined little theatre and a chapel, and cared for in every single detail according to an illuminated and knowledgeable overall project.

It is, not by chance, the first purely neoclassical building to be realised in Siena, where at that time, a late but not yet degenerated baroque influence reigned on one side, while on the other was still present a precocious Neogothic risk still impended, imposed by the conspicuous presence of monuments of the Republican era.

The cultural climate of Siena was definitely quite fervid and the eighteenth century, at first sight, sleepy and provincial, had registered vibrations under its skin that were definitely not mediocre, thanks also to the presence of Alfieri, Casanova and others in the exclusive city drawing rooms. Giulio Bianchi knew how to ennoble to the utmost these ferments, building, piece by piece, his residence, with its refined furniture and the "French"

following the Restoration and, as a result, participated in the most important undertakings of the city, giving life, in 1816 to that Academy of Fine Artsamongst others, that for the whole of the nineteenth century was to impose itself as a real and proper melting point for artists, admired both in Italy and abroad. Bianchi Bandinelli had a well-developed artistic sense and protected the most prominent city artists such as Dei and Fantastici not disdaining to use illustrious

garden, full of rare and fragrant essences.

In this splendid garden and in the still more magnificient reception rooms, an intense social activity took place at the beginning of the nineteenth century, with the organisation of balls, banquets and theatrical representations that, if they could be considered excessive in a period so marked with wars, gave an idea of the liberal mentality of an aristocrat who, both with the Jacobins and with the "reactionaries" never ceased to live "alla grande". ●

Cecco Angiolieri:
SCANDAL FOR AMUSEMENT

"If I were fire, I would burn the world..." thunders, in what are perhaps his most famous verses, Cecco Angiolieri, the "damned" ante-litteram poet, who set out to scandalise his contemporaries by exaggerating his feelings and poetising, as a consequence, in elaborate and exhibitionist terms. If Cecco, the greatest Sienese poet of all time, never reached the lyrical heights of the great Florentines of his time, this was due, with all probability, to the climate that existed in Siena in the second half of the thirteenth century, where excessive situations proliferated that caused Dante to ironically brand the Sienese as "vain and futile" people. In particular, the sovereign poet directed his arrows at the so-called "Brigata spendereccia", a group of youths from well-to-do families who wasted their fortunes on women, wine and a life of unrestrained luxury in general. And this episode seems taken at its face value from a sonnet by Angiolieri.

Cecco, therefore, anticipated that everyday realism, fed by popular humour, that was to be later exalted and developed by the works of Giovanni Boccaccio. His rhymes are not just the ravings of a singular character but they give an impression of the Siena of the Nove, optimist and bourgeois, well aware of its role and anxious to improve its economic state.

It is not yet the city of the great mystics, of the arduous dedication to the high civil and religious problems of Catherine Benincasa. Cecco, in the more than one hundred sonnets that he has left us, describes with his fervid imagination, the inns, the women of ill-fame and betting, in a blurred and indistinct picture, far from the simplicity and poverty preached by the orders of monks who, right at that moment, were building their glorious churches.

Perhaps his declared passion for the commoner, Becchina, of humble origins and not exactly spotless viture, surpassed the tightly literary sphere, to establish itself in a stormy and exhausting relationship. It's certain that his far from florid economic condition influenced for the whole of his life his preference for pleasure and dissipation and compelled his five sons to give up their scarce inheritances, burdened by heavy debts.

Other Sienese poets, such as Meo Tolomei and Folgore of San Gimignano, followed the path created by Cecco, but halted at much more modest results. ●

A TAME SHE-WOLF

It is quite easy in Siena to raise one's eyes and see oneself overloooked by the lean and nervous figure of a watchful wolf. It's sufficient just to observe the elegant and severe faade of the Palazzo Pubblico or the graceful shape of the Tower of the Mangia to avert the presence of the white marble wolves that hide their modest function of collection and draining rain water behind a menacing and solemn air. The Sienese chose the wolves as their emblem during an age in which, together with the discovery of classical texts, zealous investigations into the historical roots and the real identity of their ancestors were being intensly carried out all over the city. Anyone who was unable to trace an illustrious forebear, had to let fancy lend a hand. The Sienese did just this, recognising themselves as children of Rome and electing a she-wolf as their wet nurse, so identifying themselves with the history of Romulus and Remus and, similarly, of Senio and Aschio, sons of the less fortunate twin.
A proud wolf was born into the humanist era, while the tamest one, however, oversees the history of Siena and dominates the whole city with a powerful totemic presence.
It doesn't just limit its function to a solemn confirmation of the noble origins and the not less worthy destiny of the city, but also recites, with uncaring modesty, a civic role, marking out the city

wards, and delineating the places-cum-symbols of social living, the cardinal points of the "societas". The wolves thus watch over the entrance to Palazzo Pubblico and the ancient administrative boundaries: the three Terzi in which the city has been divided for centuries and that all three contributed to make more governable, with the unwavering knowledge of an unrestrainable unity.
The sculptures, both those

attributed to acclaimed authors such as Giovanni di Turino or to anonymous craftsmen, both laboriously smoothed in the clear marble of the Sienese Montagnola or enriched with gold plate and precious glazes, dominate the urban surroundings with equal solemnity and firmness.
The Sienese hold the wolves in absolute respect, the inhabitants of a Contrada even chose the animal as the emblem of their tiny ward, and the governors of the city were even induced, as Girolamo Gigli informs us in his precise eighteenth century diary, to keep a wolf in the Palazzo Pubblico, circulating freely among the offices of the magistrates and tranquilly devouring the remains of the parchments in the room where the famous and lost *Mappamondo* was painted by Ambrogio Lorenzetti. ●

● The she-wolf, symbol of the city of Siena, marks the most important points of the city.

THE CITY
COUNTRYSIDE

The apparently casual distribution of green areas inside the city walls has always been a reason for self-satisfaction for the Sienese even if these gentle valleys represent an inequivocable sign of the beginning of a slow by unstoppable crisis that later brought about the very end of the Republic.

The Sienese government, from the middle of the thirteenth century, began a building programme aimed at progressively enlarging the city by including small nearby villages inside the walls. Work on this new ring of walls continued for the whole of the thirteenth century. In the 1330's, work began on a new stretch that was to enclose the area in front of Val di Montone which is reached from Porta Giustizia.

Also at that time an ambitious project was approved that envisaged the construction of the whole ring of walls between Porta Ovile and Porta San Marco.

The project, that was laboriously concluded only in the first half of the fifteenth century, imagined, with excessive optimism, the possibility of creating new urban settlements in the southern part of the city, having been conceived in a moment of great prosperity and notable demographic expansion.

But the dramatic consequences of the epedemics of 1348 and 1363 and the real and proper collapse of the population and the ensuing crisis and famine that the city underwent, caused an immediate slackening in the speed of work, so much so that full rhythm was only reached many years later, for interpellant defensive reasons and no longer finalised to a far-sighted building programme.

From that time on, this suggestive "city countryside" lies peacefully alongside the powerful walls of the city, protected by the civic pride of the Sienese and object of continuous stupefied admiration from numerous foreign visitors, such as the American writer William Dean Howell who, in 1867, wrote:

"These gardens, or fields, of Siena occupy half the space that its walls enclose, and everywhere olive trees cover the boundaries of the old city with their soft leaves... a space that, long ago, overflowed with vitality and traffic. But five hundred years have passed since the plague reduced the one hundred thousand souls of Siena to fifteen thousand; one generation after another has passed its plough over the dead streets and the spade has seen to cancelling all traces of decadence, so much so that now no sign is left of that ancient opulence, but thorny thistles raise their heads and the tops of olive trees meet in the wind... the city is completely surrounded by these gardens shut inside the walls; they slope down from

every side of the elevated rocky bank on which the buildings take root - dominated by the Cathedral - covering the slopes with grass and leaves. ●

● The green valleys
embrace the city,
highlighting a far-sighted,
even though involuntary,
urban "project".

THE BASILICA DEI SERVI:
AN OBSERVATORY ON THE CITY

The Basilica dei Servi requires at least two visits, not so much for the time needed to appreciate the large quantity of works conserved in its naves and transept chapels, but rather for the particular atmosphere that is to be found there.

Every self-respecting Sienese citizen has, at least once in his life, looked out from Piazza dei Servi and proudly admired the refined profiles of the architecture of the city that, from Loggia dei Nove behind Palazzo Pubblico, reach, by means of the unceasing variety of the roofs of Malborghetto, the gigantic buttresses of the Church of St Agostino that stand guard over the green vegetable gardens in the beautiful valley where, in the fourteenth century, the hamlet of Santa Maria lay, protected by the solid city walls.

The hill on which the great basilica rose is a kind of privileged observatory on the city. In fact, the Serviti monks, who arrived in Siena from Monte Senario in the 1230's, immediately began to "deliberate" with the Sienese government, requesting, by means of numerous petitions, the necessary means to realise a great church that was later built, incorporating the ancient parish building of St Clemente.

Work proceeded very slowly, however, and the church thus remained an open building site for centuries. The fifteenth century façade was never finished, in fact, and the bell tower, built in the previous century, underwent continuous modifications,

of medieval Italian painting that, by the way, constitutes a reason for pride for the Sienese not only for its high stylistic quality, but, above all, for the story connected with its author, the Florentine, Coppo di Marcovaldo.

Coppo painted this celebrated *Madonna enthroned with Child*, commonly called "The Madonna of the Bordone" (right hand nave), in 1261, a few months after having been taken prisoner by the Sienese army on 4th September, 1260, during the Battle of Montaperti.

The artist who had fought with the Florentine army, realised this real and proper masterpiece, that still today is an object to be greatly admired, to buy his freedom. But the intense atmosphere of the Servi can be percieved above all on those magical Summer evenings when the sharp outlines of the basilica are sweetened by the passionate songs of the members of the Contrada of the Valdimontone or by the notes of some lonely musician lying on the steps of the sacristy of the church. It is in moments like this, from a quite and majestic observatory emerged in a transparent and reassuring obscurity from where one can view the lines of the city that inevitable flow towards the white travertine of the battlements of the Tower of the Mangia, that one understands the reason why Siena is justly considered "a category of the soul". ●

until the beginning of the twentieth century. The official consecration of the basilica, as can be read on a tablet, only took place in 1533. But, notwithstanding the unconformity of style and the heavy baroque and purist "restorations", the inside of the basilica is extremely fascinating with its three great naves and the gigantic pillars that mark out this typically Renaissance, suggestive, "open" space. Among the numerous works of art of every era conserved at the Servi is one of the most important paintings

● *This page: The Madonna del Bordone* by Coppo di Marcovaldo.
Facing page: The city lies gently in front of the Servi, identifying itself as a "category of the soul".

THE HISTORY OF THE GUIDES TO SIENA

by Ettore Pellegrini

Giovanni Antonio Pecci, a prolific and interesting writer of Sienese affairs, was the first to have the idea of publishing a snug pocket volume, "for the benefit of strangers" who meant to visit Siena to learn about the "most notable" aspects of each era. So was born, in 1752, a real and proper guide, with a modern conception as regards its structure and the way of presenting the material; with a text that, even though revealing the academic culture of the author, supplied much information, useful even for present day scholars of the art and history of this city.

At that time, Tuscany, and Siena in particular, was the centre of attention of many travellers, both Italian and foreign, who considered the visit to the region as the central point, also for obvious cultural implications, of their journey in Italy. Inevitably, the copies of the "Report" by Pecci were quickly snapped up and the author was forced to publish a second, corrected and enlarged edition of the guide, in which also appeared some suggestive copper-engraved views of the city, that enriched the book and helped sales so much that, in 1761, a new edition had to be made.

While the interest for the Sienese artistic tradition and the number of travellers that visited the city grew, another scholar called Giovacchino Faluschi, decided to amplify the work of his illustrious fellow citizen in a new "Brief report of the notable things of the city of Siena", published in 1784, that was not, however, particularly brief, representing, on the contrary, an important reference point for the study of Sienese artists and their masterpieces. This guide, too, was enriched by 12 copper-engraved tables from designs by Leonardo De Vegni and its much improved second edition was published in 1815.

A few years later, in 1822, a "Guide to the City of Siena for the lovers of Fine Arts" was printed with the type of the Publisher Mucci, as confirmation of the great interest aroused by the artistic and monumental beauties of the city. The work was published anonymously, but we know that the author was an attentive scholar of the history of Sienese art, Ettore Romagnoli, and was later reprinted for Marco Ferri, in 1832. Meanwhile, Romagnoli had started work on a more accurate and organic work, the "Historical and Artistic aspects of Siena and her suburbs", of which at least four appreciated editions were printed in 1836, 1840, 1852 and 1861; a work that, for the importance of the information, often never previously published, and for its clear and synthetic text, can be justly considered the first real guide to Siena.

By then, this kind of book had become enormously popular and was an irreplaceable travelling companion for the increasing number of foreigners anxious to visit Italy and its ancient cities. The volumes by Artaria, Treves and Karl Baedeker were printed in great numbers and it was found necessary to print many further editions in different languages so as to offer a general representation of the things to see in every part of the peninsular, irremediably compelling the authors to soul-destroying, short descriptions. But the things to see in Siena could not be liquidated in a few pages, and gave rise to publications that took up little space but that were, at the same time, very exhaustive in the descriptions and indications of the hotels, offices and shops that could be of use to the tourist. Together with Evaristo Micheli, who wrote for *"Siena and her Territory"* the illustration of the "religious and civic buildings" of the city, reprinted in 1863 and in 1883 in little monothematic volumes, and with Francesco Bandini Piccolomini, author, in 1882, of a guide supplied with a text both in Italian and French, we must mention Brigidi who edited a successful "New guide to Siena", destined to be reprinted various times between 1875 and 1902, and, in 1922, to even find a new editor willing to republish the text. Meanwhile, in 1905, an anonymous work was published, attributed, however, to the learned canon Vittorio Lusini, interesting for the attached bibliography and the large amount of information supplied - perhaps a little chaotically -, followed shortly afterwards by a little volume published by the Soc. ed. Fiorentina: "An artistic guide to Siena and S. Gimignano", enriched with the "Illustrated catalogue of the Academy of Fine Arts", which was reprinted many times by the publisher Enrico Torrini, and by the splendid work of Elio Manna, that was to surpass all the previous guides for abundance of information and organic treatment.

To cater for the demand from the numerous tourists who arrived from all over Europe, it was found necessary to publish texts in foreign languages; already in 1885, an English publisher had introduced the guide by Bevir, to which was added, in 1904, the beautiful book by Edmund Gardner "The Story of Siena and S. Gimignano", graciously illustrated by Helen James, in 1914, a succinct work by A. Lee Knight, and a more ponderous work written by Newell in 1926. But the most important of the guides to be written by a foreign author was, without doubt, that by William Heywood and Lucy Olcott, published in 1903 and entitled "Guide to Siena", for the peculiarity of its contents that, as well as having an artistic part, also included a vast historical essay and an accurate bibliography, resulting from the profound knowledge of the subject that the English author had matured during his long stays in the Tuscan city. The work of Heywood and Olcott had developed the by then consolidated editorial system of the guides into a more ample and enjoyable, in the case of Siena, historical-cum-literary scenography, also as an overall illustration of the traditions and cultural expressions of the city. The new style described had inspired Italian authors such as Giovanni Battista Prunai in "Siena: a fourteenth century city", Luigi Dami in "Siena and her works of art", or foreigners such as the Frenchmen, L. Gielly in "L'ame siennoise", C. Belin in "L'âme de Sienne et le Palio", the Englishman, E. Hutton in "Siena and southern Tuscany" and the German, L. Richter in "Siena".

This phenomenon, though somewhat putting to one side the other works more directly referable to the traditional guides, didn't, however, put production in crisis. From the 1920's until practically today, many writers of Sienese matters dedicated themselves to the compilation of guides to the city, such as L. Sbaragli, A. Rondini, R. Bianchi Bandinelli, E. Carli, A. Tailetti, A. Lusini, A. Cairola, P. Cesarini, just to mention the most appreciated authors. The little volumes, published in the usual pocket-size editions, are generally illustrated, supplied with maps and useful addresses; the texts are always written with the aim of directing the tourist in an easy visit of the city that cannot last more than a few days and end up with becoming descriptive exercises, compressed by synthesis and conditioned by repetitive schemes. However, every now and then, essays of a certain originality still appear, such as the "A new guide to old Siena" by Fernando Gianelli, written in vernacular rhyme, the "Guide to mystic Siena" by Idilio dell'Era, "Siena, a beautiful city" and "Siena by night", both delicious literary exercises by Giuliano Catoni and Roberto Barzanti, respectively, and "...a colour guide to the city" by John Kent, with nice graphic reconstructions of the streets of Siena.

In a very vast sphere, that stretches from a variety of books of photographs of a strictly figurative character to schematic brochures produced by tourist promotion associations, the more or less brief guides of Siena published in recent years are quite numerous and it is not possible to mention them all. We must, however, mention the agile and graceful work by Massimo Becattini that appeared in the collection of books published by "l'Espresso", the successful compendium published in "Museo Italia" with a captivating accompaniment of photographs, the precious research on the Sienese tabernacles by Alessandro Leoncini - unjustly obliged to wait for a publisher to understand its real value -, the very recent series of small guides published by Francesco Maria Ricci and edited by Giuliano Catoni and Alessandro Falassi to accompany the visitor around the "rooms" of the 17 Contradas. We must remember, above all, the precise and exhaustive work by Piero Torriti, rich in information and up-to-date references, as well as information that has been evaluated at the highest critical and exegetic levels, entitled "All about Siena, Contrada by Contrada"; a volume published in 1988, but already affirmed as one of the most accurate and successful descriptions of Siena as regards its artistic, historical and cultural aspects.

THE CITY GUIDES

1752 – G.A. PECCI, *Relazione delle cose più notabili della città di Siena*, Siena, 1752

1759 – G.A. PECCI, *Ristretto delle cose più notabili della città di Siena, ad uso de' forestieri*, Siena, 1759

1761 – G.A. PECCI, *Ristretto delle cose più notabili della città di Siena*, Siena, 1761

1784 – G. FALUSCHI, *Breve relazione delle cose notabili della città di Siena*, Siena, 1784

1815 – G. FALUSCHI, *Breve relazione delle cose notabili della città di Siena*, Siena, 1815

1822 – E. ROMAGNOLI, *Nuova guida della città di Siena per gli amatori delle Belle Arti*, Siena, 1822

1832 – E. ROMAGNOLI, *Guida della città di Siena per gli amatori delle Belle Arti*, Siena, 1832

1836 – E. ROMAGNOLI, *Cenni storico-artistici di Siena e de' suoi suburbii*, Siena, 1836

1840 – E. ROMAGNOLI, *Cenni storico-artistici di Siena e de' suoi suburbii*, Siena, 1840

1852 – E. ROMAGNOLI, *Cenni storico-artistici di Siena e suoi suburbii*, Siena, 1852

1861 – E. ROMAGNOLI, *Guida per la città di Siena e i suoi suburbii*, Siena, 1861

1862 – E.M.S. E. MICHELI, *Degli edifizi religiosi e civili in Siena e il suo territorio*, Siena, 1862

1863 – E. MICHELI, *Guida artistica della città e contorni di Siena*, Siena, 1863

1875 – E.A. BRIGIDI, *La nuova guida di Siena e dei suoi dintorni*, Siena, 1875 (successive ristampe anche con altri editori fino al 1922)

1882 – F. BANDINI PICCOLOMINI, *Siena, cenni di storia civile e guida italiana francese*, Siena, 1882

1883 – E. MICHELI, *Guida artistica della città e contorni di Siena*, Siena 1883

1885 – J.L. BEVIR, *Visitor's guide to Siena and S. Gimignano*, Londra (Stanford), 1885

1902 – G.B. PRUNAI, *Siena una città del Trecento*, Firenze (Lumachi), 1902

1903 – W. HEYWOOD, L. OLCOTT, *Guide to Siena, History and art*, Siena, 1903

1904 – E.G. GARDNER, *The story of Siena and S. Gimignano*, Londra (Dent), 1904

1905 – V. LUSINI, *Guida di Siena, e dei suoi dintorni*, Siena, 1905

1906 – *Siena*, Siena, 1906 (successive ristampe fino al 1915, edite a cura dell'Associazione Nazionale Movimento Forestieri)

1910 – E. MANNA, *Nuovissima guida di Siena*, Siena, 1910

E. HUTTON, *Siena and southern Tuscany*, Londra (Methuen), 1910

1913 – *Guida artistica di Siena e San Gimignano*, Siena, 1913

1914 – A.L. KNIGHT, *Siena the city of winghed thoughts*, Firenze (Seeber), 1914

1915 – L. RICHTER, *Siena*, Lipsia (Seeman), 1915

L. DAMI, *Siena e le sue opere d'arte*, Firenze, 1915 (edizione successiva 1921)

Siena e Provincia, Siena, 1915 (successive ristampe fino al 1920, edita a cura della Camera di Commercio e Industria)

1917 – *Guida di Siena, Monteoliveto, San Gimignano, San Quirico, Pienza,*

Montepulciano, Siena, 1917

1920 – *Guida storico-artistica di Siena,* Siena, 1920 ca.

L. GIELLY, *L'ame siennoise,* Parigi, 1920

1924 – W. HEYWOOD, L. OLCOTT, *Guide to Siena, history and art,* (IV edizione con note di F. Mason Perkins), Siena, 1924

1926 – H.A. NEWELL, *Siena and surroundings,* Siena, 1926

1929 – L. SBARAGLI, *Guida di Siena,* Siena, 1929

1931 – A. RONDINI, *Siena e la sua provincia,* Siena, 1931 (con successive edizioni)

1934 – C. BELIN, *Sienne la bien aimee et le "Palio",* Roma, 1934

R. BIANCHI BANDINELLI, *Siena,* Roma, 1934

1938 – *Guida turistica della città e dintorni,* Siena, 1938 (con successive edizioni)

1945 – E. CARLI, *Siena, guida turistica della città e dintorni,* Siena, 1945 (con successive edizioni)

1949 – A. TAILETTI, *Siena, guida artistica illustrata,* Siena, 1949 (con successive edizioni)

1950 – A.A.V.V., *Tutta Siena: guida turistica, artistica, industriale e commerciale,* Siena, 1950 ca.

I. DELL'ERA (M. CECCUZZI), *Guida di Siena mistica,* Siena, 1950

1954 – A. LUSINI, S. CHIERICHETTI, *Siena, guida artistica illustrata,* Siena, 1954 (con successive edizioni)

1958 – F. GIANNELLI, *Guida nova di Siena Vecchia,* Siena, s.d. (1958?)

1959 – A. CAIROLA, *Sena Vetus,* Siena, 1959

1961 – J. e M. FATTORUSSO, *Siena e San Gimignano,* Firenze, 1961 (con successive edizioni)

1962 – P. CESARINI, *Siena,* 1962 (con successive edizioni fino a quella del 1987)

F. BERTELOTTI, *Siena e la sua provincia,* Firenze, 1962

1969 – *Siena e San Gimignano* (guida fotografica), Siena, 1969

1970 – U. TOLOMEI, *Siena* (guida fotografica), Siena, 1970 (con successive edizioni)

1980 – M. BECATTINI, *Siena e la sua provincia,* (Guide dell'Espresso), Cuneo, 1980

1981 – R. BARZANTI, *Siena di notte,* Milano, 1981

1983 – R. VANTAGGI, *Siena e la sua provincia,* Siena, 1983

1985 – G. CATONI, *Siena un amore di città,* Milano, 1985

1987 – A.A.V.V., *Siena* (per Museo Italia), Milano, 1987

1988 – P. TORRITI, *Tutta Siena Contrada per Contrada,* Firenze, 1988

1989 – J. KENT, *Florence and Siena,* Londra (Viking), 1989

E. CARLI, *Siena e la sua provincia,* Bologna, 1989

1990 – S. ONOFRI, *Siena,* Roma, 1990

BIBLIOGRAPHY

The bibliography that follows has no pretence of being complete, given the number of works that, over the centuries, have been written about Siena, her story and art. However, it seems right to signal at least the principal texts, articles and studies that have been consulted during the writing of this book.

The decision not to use footnotes was made to help the reader, without obliging him to make the continuous and dutiful references that is the peculiarity of all guides, in other words, the most ample divulgation and the maximum syntheticy, also as regards completeness of treatment. The titles listed can, however, point the reader towards a more detailed study of the themes that have been treated in this book.

The bibliography also comprises the guides to the city, listed separately.

S. Tizio, *Historiarum Senensium*, Tomi I-X ms. della Biblioteca Comunale di Siena B.III 6-15. Copia del manoscritto conservato nella Biblioteca Apostolica Vaticana (sec. XVII).

O. Malavolti, *Historia de' fatti e guerre de' Sanesi, così esterne come civili seguite dall'origine della lor città, fino all'anno MDLV*, Venezia, 1599 (ristampa, Bologna, 1968)

G. Mancini, *Considerazioni sulla Pittura*, (1617-1621) ed. a cura di A. Marucchi - L. Salerno, Roma 1956-1957

F. Chigi, *Elenco delle pitture, sculture e architetture di Siena*, (1625-1626) ms. Chigiano I.I.11 della biblioteca Apostolica Vaticana; ed. a cura di P. Bacci, in "Bullettino Senese di Storia Patria", XLVI (1939), pp. 197-213, 297-337

G. Tommasi, *Historia di Siena*, Venezia, 1625 (ristampa, Bologna, 1973)

H. Nini Sernini, *Trattato delle famiglie nobili et huomini riguardevoli della città di Siena...*, (1637-1639), ms. B.IV.27 della Biblioteca Comunale di Siena (copia del 1724-25 di Giulio Donati)

I. Ugurgieri Azzolini, *Le Pompe Sanesi o' vero relazione delli huomini e donne illustri di Siena e suo Stato*, Pistoia, 1649

G. Macchi, *Origine dello Spedale di Santa Maria della Scala* (fine sec. XVII - inizio XVIII), ms. D. 113 dell'Archivio di Stato di Siena

G. Macchi, *Notizie di tutte le chiese che sono nella città di Siena* (1708-1733), mss. D. 107-12 dell'Archivio di Stato di Siena

A.M. Carapelli, *Notizie di tutte le chiese, e cose riguardevoli di Siena* (1720), ms. B. VII 10 della Biblioteca Comunale di Siena, II ed.

G. Gigli, *Diario Sanese*, Lucca, 1723 (II ed., Siena, 1854)

G.G. Carli, *Selva di notizie per la compilazione....*, ms. L.V.16. della Biblioteca Comunale di Siena

E. Sestigiani, *Ordini, Armi, Residenze e altre memorie di Famiglie nobili di Siena* (ultimo quarto del sec. XVIII), mss. A. 13-14 dell'Archivio di Stato di Siena

G. Della Valle, *Lettere Sanesi .... sopra le Belle Arti*, I, Venezia, 1782; II, Roma, 1785; III, Roma, 1786

G. Faluschi, *Chiese senesi* (circa 1821), mss. E.V. 13-19 della Biblioteca Comunale di Siena

E. Romagnoli, *Biografia cronologica de' Bellartisti senesi, dal Secolo XII a tutto il XVIII* (ante 1835), mss. L. II 1-13 della Biblioteca Comunale di Siena (ed. anastatica, Firenze, 1976)

A. Sozzini, *Diario delle cose avvenute in Siena dal 20 luglio 1550 al 28 giugno 1555*, Firenze, 1842 (riproduzione anastatica, Siena, 1987)

G. Milanesi, *Documenti per la Storia dell'Arte Senese*, Siena, 1854-56 (nuova edizione, Siena, 1969)

V. Buonsignori, *Storia della Repubblica di Siena*, Siena, 1856

F. Brogi, *Inventario generale degli oggetti d'arte della provincia di Siena (Siena intra moenia)* (1862-65), ms. presso l'Amministrazione Provinciale di Siena con copia dattiloscritta presso la Biblioteca della Soprintendenza ai Beni Artistici e Storici di Siena

V. Lusini, *Storia della Basilica di San Francesco in Siena*, Siena, 1894

F. Bandini Piccolomini, *La Madonna di Provenzano e le origini della sua chiesa*, Siena, 1895

L. Zdekauer, *La vita privata dei Senesi nel Dugento*, Siena, 1896 (ristampa anastatica, Bologna, 1964).

L. Zdekauer, *La vita pubblica dei senesi nel Dugento*, Siena, 1897 (ristampa anastatica, Bologna, 1967)

S. Borghesi, L. Banchi, *Nuovi documenti per la Storia dell'Arte Senese*, Siena, 1898

F. Bargagli Petrucci, *Le Fonti di Siena e i loro acquedotti*, Siena, Firenze, Roma, 1903 (ristampa anastatica, Siena, 1974)

A. Canestrelli, *L'architettura medioevale a Siena e nel suo antico territorio*, Siena, 1904

A.A.V.V., *Mostra dell'antica arte senese*, aprile-agosto 1904, catalogo generale illustrato, Siena, 1904

C. Ricci, *Il Palazzo di Siena e la Mostra d'antica arte senese*, Bergamo, 1904

V. Lusini, *La Basilica di S. Maria dei Servi in Siena*, Siena, 1908

V. Lusini, *Il Duomo di Siena*, Siena, 1911

G. Pignotti, *I pittori senesi della Fondazione Biringucci 1724-1915*, Siena, 1916

G. Chierici, *La casa senese al tempo di Dante*, in "Bullettino senese di Storia Patria", XXVIII (1921), pp. 343-380

V. Lusini, *Notizie storiche sulla topografia di Siena nel XIII secolo*, in "Bullettino Senese di Storia Patria", XXVIII (1921), pp. 239-280

V. Lusini, *Storia del Palazzo Chigi Saracini*, I, Siena, 1927

G. Chierici, *Luigi Vanvitelli e la Loggia della Mercanzia a Siena*, in "La Diana", VI (1931), pp. 60-63

C. Brandi, *La regia Pinacoteca di Siena*, Roma, 1933

F. Iacometti, *L'Accademia degli Intronati*, in "Bullettino Senese di Storia Patria", XLVIII (1941), pp. 189-198

P. Bacci, *Fonti e commenti per la Storia dell'Arte Senese*, Siena, 1944

E. Carli, *Il Museo dell'Opera e la Libreria Piccolomini di Siena*, Siena, 1946

C. Brandi, *Quattrocentisti senesi*, Milano, 1949

V. De Vecchi, *L'architettura gotica civile senese*, in "Bullettino Senese di Storia Patria", LVI (1949), pp. 3-52

G. Cecchini, *Il Circolo degli Uniti*, Siena, 1956

G. Cecchini, D. Neri, *Il Palio di Siena*, Milano, 1958

E. Carli, *Guida alla Pinacoteca di Siena*, Milano, s.d. (1958)

Archivio dell'Ospedale di S. Maria della Scala. Inventario, 2 voll. (Archivio di Stato di Siena). Ministero dell'Interno. Pubblicazioni degli Archivi di Stato, XXXVII - XXXVIII), a cura di G. Cantucci e U. Morandi, Roma, 1960-62

E. Sestan, *Siena avanti Monteaperti*, in "Bullettino Senese di Storia Patria", LXVIII (1961), pp. 28-74

R. Cantagalli, *La guerra di Siena*, Siena, 1962

Il Museo Civico di Siena, a cura di A. Cairola, Siena, 1962

A. Cairola, E. Carli, *Il Palazzo Pubblico di Siena*, Roma, 1963

U. Morandi, *Le Biccherne senesi. Le tavolette della Biccherna, della Gabella e di altre magistrature dell'antico Stato senese conservate presso l'Archivio di Stato di Siena*, Siena, 1964

G. Catoni, *Aspetti di cultura e di costume nella vita senese dell'ultimo secolo*, in "Annuario del Ginnasio-Liceo E.S. Piccolomini", Siena, 1965, pp. 35-84

M. Salmi, *Il Palazzo e la Collezione Chigi Saracini*, Milano, 1967

E. Carli, *I pittori senesi*, Milano, 1971

E. Guidoni, *Il Campo di Siena*, Roma, 1971

G. Prunai, G. Pampaloni, N. Bemporad, *Il Palazzo Tolomei a Siena*, Firenze, 1971

R. Barzanti, *Siena, una terra, una storia, una festa*, Siena, 1972

A.A.V.V., *Jacopo della Quercia nell'Arte del suo tempo*, catalogo della mostra di Siena, Firenze, 1975

A.A.V.V., *Jacopo della Quercia fra Gotico e Rinascimento*, Atti del convegno di studi (Siena, 1975), Firenze, 1977

D. Balestracci, G. Piccinni, *Siena nel Trecento, assetto urbano e strutture edilizie*, Firenze, 1977

P. Torriti, *La Pinacoteca Nazionale di Siena, i dipinti dal XII al XV secolo*, Genova, 1977

P. Torriti, *La Pinacoteca Nazionale di Siena, i dipinti dal XV al XVIII secolo*, Genova, 1978

Rutilio Manetti, catalogo della mostra di Siena, a cura di A. Bagnoli, Firenze, 1978

D. Balestracci, R. Barzanti, G. Piccinni, *Il Palio, una festa nella storia*, supplemento al n. 28 del "Nuovo Corriere Senese" del 22 giugno 1978, Siena, 1978

E. Carli, *Il Duomo di Siena*, Genova, 1979

Mostra di opere d'arte restaurate nelle province di Siena e Grosseto, I, catalogo della mostra di Siena, Genova, 1979

Siena le origini. Testimonianze e miti archeologici, a cura di M. Cristofani, catalogo della mostra di Siena, Firenze, 1979

A.A.V.V., *L'arte a Siena sotto i Medici*, catalogo della mostra di Siena, Roma, 1980

A.A.V.V., *I Medici e lo Stato Senese 1555/1609. Storia e territorio*, catalogo della mostra di Grosseto, Roma, 1980

E. CARLI, *Gli scultori senesi*, Milano, 1980

A. FALASSI, *La Santa dell'Oca*, Milano, 1980

F. CARDINI, *Santa Caterina da Siena nella vita del Trecento*, in "Bullettino Senese di Storia Patria", LXXXVIII (1981), pp. 7-20

E. CARLI, *La pittura senese del Trecento*, Venezia, 1981

C. DANTI, *Per l'arte neoclassica e romantica a Siena*, in "Bullettino Senese di Storia Patria" LXXXVIII (1981), pp. 115-168

I. MORETTI, R. STOPANI, *Romanico Senese*, Firenze, 1981

A. BAGNOLI, *Novità su Nicola Pisano scultore nel Duomo di Siena*, in "Prospettiva", n. 27, 1981

Mostra delle opere d'arte restaurate nelle provincie di Siena e Grosseto, II, 1981, catalogo della mostra di Siena, Genova, 1981

A.A.V.V., *Il Gotico a Siena*, catalogo della mostra di Siena, Firenze, 1982

A.A.V.V., *Rilievi di fabbriche attribuite a Baldassarre Peruzzi*, Siena, 1982

F. SRICCHIA SANTORO, *Ricerche senesi 2. Il Palazzo del Magnifico Pandolfo Petrucci*, in "Prospettiva", n. 29, 1982, pp. 24-31

G. CATONI, A. FALASSI, *Palio*, Milano, 1982

A.A.V.V., *Il giorno dei viventi. Tre poesie di Eugenio Montale*, Siena, 1983

Mostra delle opere d'arte restaurate nelle provincie di Siena e Grosseto, III, 1983, catalogo della mostra di Siena, Genova, 1983

L. BORTOLOTTI, *Siena*, Bari, 1983

P. TORRITI, *La casa di Santa Caterina e la Basilica di San Domenico a Siena*, Genova, 1983

G. BORGHINI, M. CORDARO, *Il Palazzo Pubblico di Siena, vicende costruttive e decorazione*, a cura di C. Brandi, Milano, 1983

A.A.V.V., *Piazza del Campo, evoluzione di una immagine, documenti, vicende, ricostruzioni*, catalogo della mostra di Siena, a cura di L. Franchina, Siena, 1983

M. L. LENZI, *La Milizia dei Comuni e la Battaglia di Monteaperti*, in "Quaderni della Biblioteca Comunale Ranuccio Bianchi Bandinelli" Castelnuovo Berardenga, n.1, Montepulciano, 1983

D. BALESTRACCI, *I Bottini, acquedotti medievali senesi*, catalogo della mostra di Siena, Siena, 1984

Le Biccherne. Tavole dipinte delle Magistrature senesi (secoli XIII-XVIII), Roma, 1984

G. PEPI, *Siena, Il Palio*, Milano, 1984

A.A.V.V., *Die Kirchen von Siena*, Vol. I, a cura di P.A. Riedel e M. Seidel, München, 1985

A.A.V.V., *Simone Martini e 'chompagni'*, catalogo della mostra di Siena, Firenze, 1985

D. GALLAVOTTI CAVALLERO, *Lo Spedale di Santa Maria della Scala in Siena. Vicenda di una committenza artistica*, Pisa, 1985

D. BALESTRACCI, G. PICCINNI, *L'ospedale e la città*, in *Lo Spedale di Santa Maria della Scala in Siena. Vicenda di una committenza artistica*, Pisa, 1985, pp. 21-39

G. RIGHI PARENTI, *Mangiare in Contrada*, Siena, 1985

E. TOTI, *Notizie per un repertorio dell'architettura barocca a Siena*, in "Storia Architettura", VIII, 1/2, Roma, 1985.

W. BOWSKY, *Un comune italiano nel Medioevo. Siena sotto il regime dei Nove 1287-1355*, Bologna, 1986

E. PELLEGRINI, *L'iconografia di Siena nelle opere a stampa, vedute generali della città dal XV al XIX secolo*, Siena, 1986

A. BRILLI, *Viaggiatori stranieri in terra di Siena*, Roma, 1986

A.A.V.V., *Paramenti e arredi sacri nelle Contrade di Siena*, catalogo della mostra di Siena, Siena, 1986

F. CARDINI, E. SALVINI, *Gli antefatti della battaglia di Montaperti*, in "Quaderni della Biblioteca Comunale Ranuccio Bianchi Bandinelli" Castelnuovo Berardenga, n. 6, Siena, 1986

A.A.V.V. *Sassetta e i pittori toscani tra XIII e XV secolo*, catalogo della mostra di Siena, a cura di L. Bellosi e A. Angelini, Siena, 1986

G. CATONI, *Il Monte dei Paschi di Siena nei due secoli della deputazione amministratrice (1786-1986)*, Siena, 1986

A.A.V.V., *Palio e Contrade tra Ottocento e Novecento*, catalogo della mostra di Siena, a cura di M. Civai e E. Toti, Siena, 1987

E. PELLEGRINI, *Palazzi e Vie di Siena nelle opere a stampa dal XVI al XX secolo*, Siena, 1987

A.A.V.V., *Banchieri e mercanti di Siena*, Siena, 1987

A.A.V.V., *Bernardino Mei e la pittura barocca a Siena*, catalogo della mostra di Siena, a cura di F. Bisogni e M. Ciampolini, Firenze, 1987

C. BRANDI, *Aria di Siena, i luoghi, gli artisti, i progetti*, a cura di R. Barzanti, Roma, 1987

P. TORRITI, *Il "Pellegrinaio" nello Spedale di Santa Maria della Scala a Siena*, Genova, 1987

A.A.V.V., *La sede storica del Monte dei Paschi di Siena. Vicende costruttive e opere d'arte*, a cura di L. Gurrieri, L. Bellosi, G. Briganti, P. Torriti, Siena, 1988

A.A.V.V., *Siena tra Purismo e Liberty*, catalogo della mostra di Siena, Roma, 1988

M. BILIORSI, *Al di là di Siena*, Firenze, 1988

G. RIGHI PARENTI, *Il buon mangiare, ovvero la cucina genuina d'altri tempi*, Siena, 1988

P. TORRITI, *Tutta Siena, contrada per contrada*, Firenze, 1988

A.A.V.V., *Da Sodoma a Marco Pino, pittori a Siena nella prima metà del Cinquecento*, catalogo della mostra di Siena, a cura di F. Sricchia Santoro, Firenze, 1988

T. BURCKHARDT, *Siena città della Vergine*, a cura di M. Magrini, Milano, 1988 (Titolo originale: *Siena, Stadt der Iungfrau*, Alten, 1958)

A. MIDDELDORF KOSEGARTEN, *Scultori senesi nel "Duomo Vecchio. Studi per la scultura a Siena (1250-1330)*, Siena, 1988 (Titolo originale: *Sienesische Bildhauer am Duomo Vecchio. Studien zur Skulptur in Siena 1250-1330*, München, Bruckmann, 1984)

La Pittura senese del Rinascimento, edizione italiana del catalogo della mostra di New York (1988), a cura di K. Christiansen. C.B. Strehlke. L. Kanter, Siena, 1989

M. ASCHERI, *Siena nel Quattrocento, una riconsiderazione*, in *La Pittura senese del Rinascimento*, edizione italiana del catalogo della Mostra di New York (1988), a cura di K. Cristiansen, C.B. Strehlke, L. Kanter, Siena, 1989

La scultura. Bozzetti in terracotta, piccoli marmi e altre sculture dal XIV al XX secolo, catalogo della mostra di Siena, a cura di G. Gentilini, C. Sisi, Firenze, 1989

G. PICCINNI, L. VIGNI, *Modelli di assistenza ospedaliera tra Medioevo ed Età Moderna. Quotidianità, amministrazione, conflitti nell'ospedale di Santa Maria della Scala di Siena*, in *La società del bisogno, povertà e assistenza nella Toscana Medievale*, a cura di G. Pinto, pp. 131-174, Firenze, 1989

M. CIVAI, E. TOTI, *Il rinnuovo del corteo storico del Palio di Siena (1876-1879)*, Siena, 1989

J. HOOK, *Siena. Una città e la sua storia*, Siena, 1989

E. CARLI, *Il Museo dell'Opera del Duomo di Siena*, Sinalunga, 1989

A.A.V.V., *Il Palazzo della Provincia a Siena*, a cura di F. Bisogni, Roma, 1990

A.A.V.V., *Domenico Beccafumi e l'arte del suo tempo*, catalogo della mostra di Siena, Milano, 1990

A.M. GUIDUCCI, *San Michele...*, in *Domenico Beccafumi e l'Arte del suo tempo*, catalogo della mostra di Siena, pp. 168-170, Milano, 1990

I Teatri storici della Toscana, censimento documentario e architettonico, Siena e provincia, I, a cura di E. Garbero Zorzi e L. Zangheri, Roma, 1990

A.A.V.V., *Cambellotti illustratore, da "Le Mille e una notte" a "Il Palio di Siena"*, a cura di M. Quesada, catalogo della mostra di Siena, Roma, 1991

A.A.V.V., *Prima di Leonardo. Cultura delle macchine a Siena nel Rinascimento*, catalogo della mostra di Siena, a cura di P. Galluzzi, Milano, 1991

M. BUSSAGLI, *Arte e Magia a Siena*, Bologna, 1991

A. FALASSI, G. CATONI, *Le Contrade di Siena*, 17 Voll. della serie "Le Guide al Gran Tour" di F.M.R., Milano, 1991.

A.A.V.V. *La caduta della repubblica senese*, a cura di E. Pellegrini, Siena, 1991

M. CIVAI, E. TOTI, *Vicende di uno spedale millenario: il Santa Maria della Scala*, in *L'assistenza pubblica nella Siena di fine '800*, catalogo della mostra di Siena, Milano, 1991

A. FIORINI, *Siena. Immagini, testimonianze e miti nei toponimi della città*, Siena, 1991

Santa Maria della Scala. Archeologia e edilizia sulla piazza dello Spedale, a cura di E. Boldrini e R. Parenti, Firenze, 1991

A.A.V.V., *Il Palio visto dagli altri*, a cura di M. Civai e E. Toti, catalogo della mostra di Siena, Siena 1991.

A.A.V.V., *Agostino Fantastici. Architetto senese 1782 - 1845*, a cura di C. Cresti, catalogo della mostra di Siena, Torino 1992.

A.A.V.V., *Pallium, Evoluzione del drappellone dalle origini ad oggi*, a cura di Luca Betti, 5 voll., Siena 1992.

A.A.V.V., *Francesco di Giorgio e il Rinascimento a Siena*, a cura di L. Bellosi, catalogo della mostra di Siena, Milano, 1993.

G. Catoni, A. Leoncini, *Cacce e tatuaggi. Nuovi ragguagli sulle contrade di Siena*, Siena 1993.

M. A. Ceppari Ridolfi, P. Turrini, *Il mulino delle vanità. Lusso e cerimonie nella Siena Medievale*, Siena 1993.

W. Heywood, *Nostra Donna d'Agosto e il Palio di Siena*, a cura di A. Falassi, Siena 1993.

A.A.V.V., *La cultura artistica a Siena nell'Ottocento*, a cura di C. Sisi e E. Spalletti, Siena 1994.

A.A.V.V., *Santa Maria della Scala. Dall'Ospedale al Museo*, Siena 1995.

A.A.V.V., *Lo scaffale della pubblicità. Manifesti liberty della collezione Bargagli Petrucci nella biblioteca comunale di Siena*, catalogo della mostra di Siena, Siena 1995.

A.A.V.V., *Storia di Siena. Dalle origini alla fine della repubblica*, a cura di R. Barzanti, G. Catoni, M. De Gregorio, Siena 1995.

A.A.V.V., *Siena tra Storia e Mito nella cultura anglosassone*, atti del Convegno di Studi, Siena 1996.

A.A.V.V., *L'oro di Siena. Il tesoro di Santa Maria della Scala*, a cura di L. Bellosi, Milano 1996.

A.A.V.V., *La scienza illuminata. Paolo Mascagni nel nel suo tempo (1755 - 1815)*, catalogo della mostra di Siena, Siena 1996.

E. Carli, *Arte senese e arte pisana*, Torino 1996.

A.A.V.V., *Storia di Siena. Dal Granducato all'Unità*, a cura di R. Barzanti, G. Catoni, M. De Gregorio, Siena 1996.

P. Turrini, *"Per honore et utile de la città di Siena". Il Comune e l'edilizia nel Quattrocento*, Siena 1997.

GLOSSARY

Balzana - araldic term indicating Siena's coat of arms, which is a field divided horizontally by two black and white stripes. Girolamo Gigli, an XVIII century Sienese scholar, gives us an account of how the Roman consol Flaminius, sent from Rome to mediate a peace between the two communities of Castelmontorio and Castelsenio, induced them to get together and form a city. A sacrifice was to be held to celebrate the event. During the ceremony, a prodigy took place: the smoke rising up from Apollo's altar was candid, while the smoke from Minerva's altar was as black as ink. The two streaks of smoke met up in the air forming a black and white cloud. This was taken as a sign that the two colours should be used in the coat of arms of the new city.

Bandierino - iron flag on top of a pole, indicating the start and the arrival of the horse race in piazza del Campo.

Barbaresco - the *contradaiolo* in charge of looking after the horse (*barbero*) during the days of the Palio.

Barbero - name given to the horses taking part to the Palio. The term seems to originate from the region of "Barberia", corresponding to the geographical area of Algeria, Morocco, Tunisia and Tripoli, where horses of the "berber" race are still bred in the present day.

Batterie di selezione - series of trials held in order to select a group of ten horses out of all those that are taken to the piazza four days before the Palio.

Battesimo contradaiolo - the christening in the contrada. The rite is slightly different from the religious one. Every contrada has its own fountain, where the *priore,* on the *festa titolare,* christens all the young *contradaioli* born in that year. The rite is extended to all those who wish to confirm in such a solemn way their belonging to the contrada.

Benedizione del cavallo - in the early afternoon of the day of the Palio, every contrada taking part to the race bring their horse to the contrada church, where the priest gives it a solemn blessing.

Biccherna - One of the oldest institutions of the comune di Siena, the finance department. The term now indicates the wooden covers of the balance sheets, splendidly decorated by the finest Sienese artists. The name *biccherna* seems to derive from the term *blacherne,* which the Sienese merchants might have borrowed from Costantinoples, a city they used to visit on their business journeys, where the palace in which the imperial treasure was kept bore that name. The actual painted ledgers are nowadays on display in the Archivio di Stato, which has its seat in the Palazzo Piccolomini.

Bottini - an underground system of canals and tunnels built in tuff and bricks, through which spring waters from the countryside were conveyed into town. The *bottini* - first mentioned in a document of 1226 - get in some points wide and high enough to stand in them, and they are still open to the public by appointment. This water system was highly sophisticated, and it needed skilled men to survey it: one of the directors of the *bottini* office was the famous Renaissance architect and engineer Francesco di Giorgio Martini.

Braccialetti - street lamps with several arms, painted in the colours of the contradas, used to decorateand light the streets during festivities.

Brenna - slang word for a bad horse.

Bulgano - the ancient mint of the Sienese Republic.

Caccia dei tori - an ancient game organised in piazza del Campo, in which wild game and bulls were set free and hunted by the citizens. The contradas as territorial units made their first appearance in the occasion of one of these feasts.

Camarlengo - administrative charge in the Sienese Republic.

Canape - thick hemp rope, used to determine the limits of the start of the Palio race.

Capitano - the highest charge of the contrada during the Palio.

Carriera - the Palio race.

Carroccio - a reproduction of the Florentine war cart captured by the Sienese in the battle of Montaperti (1260). The *carroccio* parades, carrying the *drappellone,* during the *corteo storico*.

Casa del cavallo *(the house of the horse)* familiar name for the horse's stable.

Cencio - slang word for the *drappellone*. In current Italian, it means "rag".

Chiarine - Sienese silver-made wind instrument reminding in its shape an elongated, thin trumpet.

Chiasso - narrow alley or side street. The term originates from the latin *classis*, meaning 'suburb', subsequently defining the empty space in between buildings belonging to private citizens.

Colonnini - the thick and short travertine columns delimitating the nine sections of the shell-shaped piazza del Campo.

Contradaiolo - a person belonging to the people of a contrada.

Correttore - old-fashioned term used by some of the contradas to indicate their parish priest.

Costa - term indicating a road going uphill, generally stressing the steepness of the hill.

Diana - legendary underground river quoted by Dante Alighieri (Purgatorio:XIII) when he meets the Sienese Sapia (...Tu li vedrai fra quella gente vana/che spera in Talamone, e perderagli/più che speranza ch'a cercar la Diana...).

Drappellone - the painted silk cloth which represents the only prize for the winner of the Palio race.

'Duomo nuovo' - the ambitious project to enlarge the cathedral on which the Sienese embarked before being stopped by the epidemic of the plague of 1348. The present church would be used as the transept of the new construction, which the Sienese wanted to become the largest temple of Christianity. The remains of the unfinished building are still visible in the piazza Jacopo della Quercia.

Elmora - a medieval game, consisting in mimicking a fight with wooden weapons and wicker shields.

Entrone - Sienese term for the yard of the Palazzo Pubblico.

Facciatone - the remains of the façade of the *duomo nuovo*. From the top of the *facciatone,* which is open to the public with access from the Museo dell'Opera del Duomo, one can enjoy a wonderful sight of the Sienese countryside.

Festa titolare - the celebrations for the contrada's patron saint, which can last for just a day up to a week.

Fisiocritico - member of the Sienese "Accademia delle Scienze" (Academy of Sciences), also called "of the

Fisiocritici", founded by Pirro Maria Gabbrielli. The name, of Greek origin, "in the Tuscan language means judges of nature, to prove that the aim of our Academy is to investigate and analyse the secrets of nature, and, almost in the guise of judges, reject what is false in natural sciences, to better comprehend that which is true..." (*Costituzioni*, chapter IV).

Gavinone - large opening, in the shape of a shell, set in the middle of the straight side of the piazza, into which the rain waters flow down.

Gettatello - name given to the children entrusted to the charity of the Hospital of Santa Maria della Scala.

Grancia - fortified farm belonging to the Hospital of Santa Maria della Scala, used by the latter to provide food supplies for the hospital and to host the pilgrims on their way to Rome.

'Intronato' - member of the Sienese "Accademia degli Intronati", founded in the XVI century as the natural continuation of the "Accademia Grande", founded the humanist pope Enea Silvio Piccolomini (Pius II). The six fundamental rules of the Accademia, drawn from some maxims expressed by the Sienese scholar Bernardino Bellanti, are: *Deum colere, studere, gaudere, neminem laedere, nemini credere, de mundo non curare* (honour thy God, study, enjoy, hurt no one, believe no one, take no heed of the world).

Limosina - alms, charity.

Lupa senese - the legendary she-wolf that bred the twin sons of Remo, Senio and Aschio, who founded Siena after having escaped from the rage of their uncle, Romolo.

Magistrato delle Contrade - Magistracy of the contradas, an institutional body founded in 1894 to co-ordinate all the activities and the issues concerning the common interests of all the contradas.

Mangia or Mangiaguadagni - Giovanni di Duccio o Giovanni Ducci, a.k.a. *Mangia* (Eater) or *Mangiaguadagni* (Earnings-eater), was the bell-ringer of the Tower. In the second half of the thirteenth century, an automaton chiming every hour on a new clock took Giovanni's place. The robot was called Mangia, to honour the memory of the former bell-ringer.

Mangino (or **tenente**) - the *capitano*'s right hand during the Palio.

Masgalano - prize - normally a plate or sculpture made of silver - assigned to the contrada that is judged to have best paraded in both the July and August Palios. The name originates from the Spanish *más galán*, the most elegant.

Massa - term indicating the landed property of the Comune di Siena outside the city walls, the roads and streets of which were not identified by any names. Documents dating back to 1871 certify the existence of the autonomous *Comune delle Masse di Siena* (including all the suburbs, i.e. *le Masse*), an administrative body that was later to be absorbed by the Comune di Siena.

Mezzana - a *cotto* brick three times less thick than a standard brick.

Moggia - ancient unit of weight for cereals.

Mortaretto (or **mortaletto**) - a device signalling with an explosion the entrance of the horses into the piazza, the false start and the arrival, both on the occasion of the Palio race and during the *prove*.

Mossa - the start of the races (*palio* and *prove*).

Mossiere - the umpire for the start.

Nervo (or **nerbo**) - whip used by the riders only during the Palio race.

Offerta del cero - a religious ceremony of ancient origins, celebrated on August 14th, during which the contradas and the

Comune di Siena offer votive candles to the Virgin.

Palco - make-shift wooden structure on which the seats to watch the Palio from are placed along the ring.

Palio (*pallium*) - see *drappellone*.

Palio alla lunga - the race that used to be held along the city streets, crossing it from gate to gate.

Palio alla tonda - the palio run on the piazza del Campo ring (i.e., 'going round').

Pan pepato - apparently invented by a nun, sister Leta, who was the first to mix together honey, dried fruit, almonds, spices and masses of ginger, for medical purposes. It was thought to have excellent effects on the ailing and wounded. It was also used during the 1555 siege to cure the injured men.

Piaggia - originated from the Latin *plaga*, the term is used to indicate the declining area of a valley or a sloping down street.

Piazza - short for piazza del Campo. The 'piazza' with no further specifications is, for the Sienese, strictly piazza del Campo.

Pigiama - the outfit worn by the riders during the *prove* and the Palio race.

Priore - the highest charge in the contrada during peace time (see *capitano*).

Prove - the six races that take place in the Campo in the three days before the Palio race. Their purpose is for the riders to get familiar with their mount, and for the new horses to practise the peculiar race-track.

Prova generale - the *prova* held on the night before the Palio.

Provaccia - the last of the *prove*, run on the morning of the Palio, in which the riders never push their horse too far, in order to spare it for the big event of the evening.

Pugna - ancient Sienese game, quite similar to the *elmora,* in which the opposite teams mimicked a bare-handed fight .

Ragatii - the joung jockeys (*boys*) called to show the horses' qualities and capabilities during the race.

"Rozzo" (lit. 'uncouth')- member of the Sienese *Accademia dei Rozzi*.
"The Rozzi confraternity was founded in 1531 and chose as its symbol a cork-oak with four interlacing branches, symbolizing the four seasons of the year and the *motto*: He who with us dwells, gains what he loses.
By which they meant that those who belonged to the Academy were named *Rozzi* (uncouth men) but on the contrary by their joining the Academy they would leave behind all trace of roughness and ignorance." (Fiorini)

Scosso - the horse whose rider has fallen off during the race. A *scosso* horse can still win the Palio, if it is still wearing the *spennacchiera* on top of its head.

Segnatura - ceremony taking place on the morning of the Palio, in which the riders officially state the contrada they are going to run for, and viceversa. From that moment on, the name of the rider cannot be substituted.

Signori del Brio - ancient institutional body, in charge of the organization and supervision of any celebration in town.

Sovatto - ancient elaborated whip, used before the present *nervo di bue*.

Spennacchiera - a special element of the horse's harness, worn around its head, reproducing the colours of the contrada. Should the horse lose it, it could not claim to have won the Palio.

Studio Senese - original name of the University of Siena.

Sunto - nickname given by the Sienese to the bell of the *Mangia* tower, originally named Maria Assunta.

Tratta - four days before the Palio, the ten chosen horses (see *batteria*) are assigned to the contradas running that Palio by drawing lots. Chances of getting a good horse therefore mainly depend on luck.

Trombetti - the musicians who play the *chiarina*.

Tufo - a thick compressed mix of turf and clay used for covering the track of the race.

'Unito' - member of the Sienese "Circolo degli Uniti" (Circle of Noblemen).

Verrocchio - the device actioned by the *mossiere* to drop the *canape* and give the start.

Vicolo - see *chiasso*. Originated from the Latin *vicus*, meaning small village or suburb.

Zucchino - light helmet wore by the jokeys exclusively in the Palio race .

INDEX OF NAMES AND PLACES

INDEX OF ILLUSTRATIONS

FINITO DI STAMPARE DA ALSABA, SIENA
NEL MESE DI MAGGIO 1997